Civil War Comes Home
Williamsburg, Virginia

Jake McKenzie

AuthorHouse™
1663 Liberty Drive
Bloomington, IN 47403
www.authorhouse.com
Phone: 1-800-839-8640

© *2012 Jake McKenzie Enterprises, LLC. All rights reserved.*

No part of this book may be reproduced, stored in a retrieval system, or transmitted by any means without the written permission of the author.

Published by AuthorHouse 7/19/12

ISBN: 978-1-4772-0484-9 (sc)
ISBN: 978-1-4772-2890-6 (e)

Library of Congress Control Number: 2012911414

Any people depicted in stock imagery provided by Thinkstock are models, and such images are being used for illustrative purposes only. Certain stock imagery © *Thinkstock.*

This book is printed on acid-free paper.

Because of the dynamic nature of the Internet, any web addresses or links contained in this book may have changed since publication and may no longer be valid. The views expressed in this work are solely those of the author and do not necessarily reflect the views of the publisher, and the publisher hereby disclaims any responsibility for them.

Table of Contents

Foreword	ix
Acknowledgements	xiii
Major Characters	xv

<u>Chapters:</u>	<u>Setting:</u>	
One: April 1861		
War Threat Made Real	*Washington, D.C. and the entire South.*	1
Two: May, 1861.		
General Butler's contrabands	*Fort Monroe, VA*	5
Military Disposition,	*Lower Peninsula, VA*	23
Colonel James Magruder, Commanding	*Yorktown, VA*	42
College of William & Mary closes!	*Williamsburg, VA*	45
Three: June 1861		
First Fight: The Battle of Big Bethel	*Big Bethel, VA*	66
Four: October, 1861.		
Summoned to Command	*Washington, D.C.*	89

Five: December, 1861 - January 1862

    Frozen in Place   *Washington & Manassas, VA*   96

Six: March, 1862

    Spring Thaw…   *Manassas & Virginia's Peninsula*   103

Seven: April, 1862

    Stride of a Giant – Preparations for War   *Virginia's Peninsula*   108

Eight: May, 1862.

    Withdrawal, Pursuit, & The Battle Is Joined   *Yorktown to Williamsburg, VA*   173

Nine: June – July, 1862

    Long Journey: *Danville to Williamsburg, VA*   196

Ten: August, 1862

    Wedding Bells   *Williamsburg, VA*   240

Eleven: Until April 1865 and Beyond

    Life under occupation.   *Williamsburg, VA*   259

Postscript   268

References   279

Educators note   283

Dedicated to America's military men and women, still sacrificing to preserve freedom.

Foreword

Like John Jakes' North & South, "the purpose is to entertain. Still, I wanted an accurate reflection of the period…a fair presentation of the prevailing attitudes and tensions…(and)…I have tried to make the book historically correct, though there have been minor alterations… in a few places."

This is narrated nonfiction; characters, places, and major events are real. Where the historical record allows, specific quotes they are incorporated, but most dialogue is fiction. Such speech, motivations, and character interactions are the author's interpretation providing a plausible though fictional account for the purpose of storytelling. Neither motivation nor slander is intended or implied towards any person or cause.

A decade before, a soldier stationed at Fort Monroe penned home, describing life on the Peninsula, "…a veritable Garden of Eden, with numerous fine homes and beautifully cultivated lands.…" His opinion was shared by George Ben West, who similarly recorded, "No one could desire to live in a more favored place with its mild climate, its delightful and health giving sea breezes, its accessibility both by land and water… settled by a happy and contented company of prosperous farmers, with comfortable homes, loving families, well tilled and fertile lands, and loyal slaves, everything to make them free from care."

In contrast, spring 1861, a year before armed conflict arrives on the Peninsula, was a time of vexing uncertainty. No one knew what the very next day, let alone the future held. Economic hardship, deep political divide, and vicious political rancor ruled the day.

These are the stories of; runaway slaves who risked death to obtain freedom while brothers followed masters into war, students and professors who suddenly become soldiers, some eager others reluctant, a few would become heroes, but far more, casualties, politicians who would be generals, and generals who venture into politics -neither transformation successful and often resulting in tragic loss and wasted opportunity, and the stories of determined women opening hearts and homes to countless wounded.

As Virginia military men resign Federal commissions to join the Confederacy, Union forces quickly reinforce Fort Monroe. Tensions rise as the two still amateur armies eye each other warily from winter quarters; occupying themselves with training, equipping, and preparations. With the coming spring thaw, President Lincoln's patience is severely tested, before the Union's massive Peninsula campaign finally begins assembling what will become the then, largest force in U.S. history. Meanwhile, Confederates, fully cognizant of the strategic importance of the Peninsula, labor to build extensive defense works. With the navigable York and James Rivers on the flanks, the Peninsula is the direct land route to Richmond. There was only one road, and it passes through Williamsburg.

The Civil War history of the Peninsula is as equally rich as that of its Colonial era. The same earthworks where colonists won independence were again occupied and expanded by the Rebels during the Peninsula campaign. Action at nearby Big Bethel, involving some twelve hundred Confederates and three times as many Yankees, was the opening engagement of the Civil War. The Battle of Williamsburg, May 5, 1862 involved much larger numbers of troops under famed Confederate Generals; Joseph E. Johnston, James Longstreet, A. P. Hill, George Pickett, J.E.B. Stuart and Jubal Early, and Union Generals: Fightin' Joe Hooker, Philip Kearny, and Winfield Scott Hancock. Thousands locked in mortal combat during a pitiless rain within earshot of Williamsburg's remaining residents. Although the battle receives but passing consideration in many texts, had that day ended differently, the Civil War could well have been brought to an early end.

The death toll, 3,843 was more than double Williamsburg's entire population. The wounded soon filled every public space; business, church, school and many private homes. Residents suddenly found themselves in a battle zone, then trying to survive in its occupied aftermath. Every aspect of life from what was available to eat, to the toys children played with, was affected.

Yet, despite hardship and deprivation, life went on; though nothing was 'normal' with the western edge of the campus of the College of William & Mary a kind of no man's land between Union and Confederate territories.

Civil War Comes Home

Although freedom from foreign tyranny had been secured in nearby Yorktown four score years earlier, freedom for all Americans would not be won until the national catharsis of the Civil War, and not fully realized until many years later. Setting the stage for the Civil War in Williamsburg is the decision that runaway slaves were contrabands of war, an important step towards ending slavery, made at nearby Ft. Monroe, now a national historic monument.

* * *

Acknowledgements

The author is deeply indebted to the exhaustive scholarly work of many on the Civil War on the Peninsula, notably, but not limited to, Earl C. Hastings, Jr. and David Hastings, Carol Kettenburg Dubbs, Carson O. Hudson, Jr. Sean Heuvel and John V. Quarstein. Without the excellent work of many, the present contribution would not have been possible.

Thanks also to several patient readers of early drafts including but not limited Sean Heuvel, Christopher Newport University, Carson O. Hudson, Jr. Colonial Williamsburg Foundation, John Quarstein, Teri Toepke, and Michael Cobb, Hampton History Museum. Ms Bethany Austin, Hampton History Museum, Ann Drury Wellford, Museum of the Confederacy, Marianne Martin, John D. Rockefeller, Jr. Library, David Johnson, Casemate Museum, Fort Monroe, Jamison Davis, Virginia Historical Society, and Susan Riggs, Special Collections Research Center, Earl Swem Library, College of William & Mary kindly assisted with illustrations. Special thanks to Julia Shaffner for a fresh edit. The insightful comments of all improved the work, while any errors remain the author's responsibility.

Photographs and illustrations are courtesy of: Library of Congress, National Archives, Colonial Williamsburg Foundation, Earl Swem Library, College of William & Mary, Museum of the Confederacy, Virginia Historical Society, Hampton History Museum, Daily Press, Virginia Gazette, and Casemate Museum, Fort Monroe, Va.

Major Characters

Confederate States of America

President Jefferson Davis

General Robert E. Lee

General Joseph E. Johnston

Major General John Bankhead Magruder

Colonel Benjamin Ewell, President, College of William & Mary

Major William H. Payne, 4th Virginia Cavalry and wife, Mary

Captain Octavius Cook, Williamsburg lawyer, and Commanding Officer Williamsburg Junior Guard

Captain John Willis Lea, 5th North Carolina Infantry

Private Thomas J. Barlow, former student College of William & Mary

Reverend Thomas M. Ambler, Rector, Burton Parish Church

Mrs. Letitia Tyler Semple, daughter of former President John Tyler

Miss Margaret Durfey, a young woman growing up in Williamsburg

Mr. William W. Vest, proprietor of Williamsburg's general store

Miss Victoria King, a young woman growing up in Williamsburg

1st Lieutenant Decimus et. Ultimus Barziza, Company C, 4th Texas Infantry, former W&M student

Mr. William Peachy, lawyer & his wife, Mary

W.B. Nelson, slave to Captain Cook

Til, a slave cook[1]

Sleepy Jake, Til's husband

Isom, an old slave

Yellow Jim, slave and member of the Legal League

Unnamed slave to Thomas Barlow, student

James Townsend, runaway slave of Colonel Mallory and first contraband

Sheppard Mallory, runaway slave of Colonel Mallory and first contraband

Frank Baker, runaway slave of Colonel Mallory and first contraband

UNITED STATES OF AMERICA,

President Abraham Lincoln

General George Brinton McClellan

Major General Benjamin Butler

Colonel Hawkins, 9th New York

Colonel Phelps, 1st Vermont

Colonel David Campbell, 5th Pennsylvania Cavalry, first **Military Governor** of Williamsburg

Lieutenant Colonel Justin Dimick, Commanding Officer, **Fort Monroe**

Captain George Armstrong Custer

First Lieutenant W.W. Disoway, acting Provost Marshall

---

1 Although cast as a slave for the purpose of this story, Til and her husband Jake were free, operating the ever popular, Frog Pond Tavern, where Til's cooking was reportedly legendary.

Private Robert Boody, Medal of Honor recipient

Private William Boyle

1

April 1861

War Threat Made Real

Called to the White House the afternoon of the 20th to escort President Lincoln to an evening function, Lieutenant Colonel James B. Magruder confides he, "very much regretted secession, but felt compelled to fight with those among whom I was born and bred, my relations, and friends, all of who believe they are right."

Taken aback, President Lincoln carefully considered what this decorated hero of the Mexican War had said. *I fear there may be additional resignations of others placing heritage and home above Union*, Lincoln worried.

Later that day, Magruder resigned his commission, proclaiming with bravado, "I have just crossed the Long Bridge, which is guarded by my old battery. Give me 5,000 men and if I don't take Washington, you may take not only my sword, but my life!"

Lincoln's concerns were valid for, like Magruder, Robert E. Lee also resigned that very day, noting, "I cannot raise my hand against my birthplace, my home, my children."[2] Soon, others in leadership positions would join the ranks of defectors including fellow West Point graduate, Benjamin Ewell, President of the College of William & Mary.

Figure 1. Major General John B. Magruder. Courtesy of the Museum of the Confederacy, Richmond, VA.

---

2 http://thomaslegion.net/roberteleesresignationletter.html

Figure 2. General Robert E. Lee. Courtesy of the Library of Congress, Washington, D.C.

Union losses that fateful day were not limited to the resignations however, as they evacuated and torched Gosport Navy Yard in Portsmouth, scuttling and burning nearly a dozen warships still moored. The inferno signaled the arrival of the Civil War in Tidewater.

Earlier that day, cheers went up from skeleton force manning the ramparts of Fort Monroe, when the steamer transporting the 4th Massachusetts Volunteers docked at 6:00 a.m. at Old Point Comfort, Hampton. Their sister unit, 3rd Massachusetts, sailed all night at full steam, finally embarking at noon, weapons loaded against an anticipated attack. In a matter of days, Fort Monroe was transformed from an undermanned back-water outpost, to the largest Federal fortification in the South. Even with arrival of thirteen hundred Massachusetts Volunteers, the fortress was still at only half strength, two thousand six hundred twenty five being called for in war plans. The massive stone bastion, designed by military engineer Robert E. Lee, held just forty-one guns though had emplacements for ten times that many.[3] U.S. Army Chief of Staff General Winfield Scott, himself a Virginian, knew the strategic importance of the fort, ordering it reinforced as quickly as possible in the face of the Confederate attack on Fort Sumter the week before.

Fort Monroe's commanding officer, Lieutenant Colonel Justin Dimick, hadn't waited for Scott's orders, however for the threat was real. Dimick, a decorated veteran of Mexican and Seminole wars, immediately grasped the danger, not from the sea, the traditional direction of attack, but landward. Dimick ordered the laborious task of turning the seaward aimed guns around, and moving the many tons of supplies stored outside to within the Fort's moated walls. No sooner than this was accomplished, all but one of the entrances, the southwest gate, were sealed. Dimick's measures and the arrival of reinforcements placed Fort Monroe on a wartime footing.

With these changes, Fort Monroe's turned from protector against foreign attack by sea, to an occupying Federal force deep in Rebel territory. Palpable fear of invasion spread rapidly -first through nearby Hampton, then immediately up the Peninsula to Williamsburg and Richmond.

***

---

3 Quarstein, J.V. The Civil War on the Virginia Peninsula, Arcadia Publishing, pg. 12.

MAY, 1861.
GENERAL BUTLER'S CONTRABANDS

Fort Monroe, Virginia.

The three escaped slaves, James Townsend, Sheppard Mallory, and Frank Baker could have been swept out to sea but they were fortunate, and their luck would hold.

With spring crops planted weeks prior and nothing ready for harvest, their enterprising master, Colonel Charles K. Mallory, Commander, 115th Virginia Militia, hired his slaves out -to his own Confederate Army. While they toiled all day constructing defensive batteries at Sewell's Point, across Hampton Roads from Ft. Monroe, Colonel Mallory collected $11.00 per month for each slave hired out.

Being overworked and underfed, these three finally decided they'd had enough and began to secretly plan their escape. But there was far more to their motives than finding greener pastures and the trio spent many an evening whispering about what their chance for freedom could mean, not only for themselves, but in a broader context. Their planning took considerable time for it was necessarily limited to nights when the overseer was away. Otherwise they lived in fear, besides being dog-tired from the day's labors. Eventually, they came to understand that Washington politicians, including President Lincoln, much as they respected him, were in no particular hurry to free the slaves. They'd bide their time, one compromise after another, trying to do everything or anything, year after year, to avoid having to face the intractable question: can the nation continue to abide slavery?

James, who'd developed a good sense of politics, both local and national, summed it up. "Yes Suh, if we leave it up to the white man, we be slavin' many a year, probably the rest of our lives. But, if we take measures to 'force' the issue or at least move it forward, by showing strength in numbers, what can they do? They ain't enough Marsa's in all da' South to whip all da' slaves at once. Once this is started, ain't no way Old Uncle Abe or the rest of them politicians gonna come out against freedom. I tell you they will have no choice but to declare for our side. Yes Sir, I say it's time we play the hand we're dealt. We got to make our move; otherwise you can forget about freedom. Hell, our grandchildren still be slavin' if we don't act."

After many such quite conversations, usually while lying exhausted on the dirt floor of their slave quarters, the trio; James Townsend, Sheppard Mallory, and Frank Baker finally reached a mutual decision to take the opportunity to seek their freedom. "Yes Suh," James boasted, "We gonna beat the abolitionists at their own game. They talk about freedom but we still doin' the slavin' but no more."

"Yes, we got to force the issue. Make headlines, North and South," Sheppard agreed.

Barely able to contain their apprehension, the trio bided time 'til all was right. Tides, moon and weather were favorable and their overseer was otherwise occupied, probably having his way with one of the young woman slaves, as had become his nightly practice. They slipped away, making for nearby shore, quickly untying and launching a small skiff. They knew full well that either act attempting escape or stealing, was punishable by a whipping that would bring even the stoutest to within an inch of life.

Taking turns rowing steadily, the three managed to cross the swirling currents of the huge natural harbor of Hampton Roads, proceeding northward across its mouth towards Ft. Monroe. Having spent many an hour fishing these waters for their master, they had learned the treacherous tides. They'd timed their escape perfectly; no wind to speak of and seas flat calm, the gentle swells reflecting a new moon in a clear balmy sky.

"Lord, Almighty, He done leadin' us da' way," Sheppard said softly. They spoke infrequently and when they did, whispered, for they knew sound traveled over water. They kept as quiet as possible, oars muffled with rags.

"Thank you sweet Jesus," and "Amen," came James' and Frank's replies, the latter not missing a strong, full stroke of the oars. Though they'd already been pulling for what seemed like several hours at least, their hard work all day every day for their entire life prepared them.

"Yes Suh' with the Good Lord Almighty guiding us, we's gonna make it, Yes Suh."

Taking turns rowing to exhaustion, strong tides first carried them easterly, close by dangerous shoals and rocks near Fort Wool. Then slack tide gradually turned to flood tide as the night wore on, and the current helped the weary men as they made a final exhausted pull, now westerly back towards Engineer wharf on Fort Monroe's south shore.

"Shush, quit rowing," James cautioned, the three peering through the mist rising off warm waters into the cool predawn, sensing they were finally close but unable to make out the shore.

"Halt, who goes there?" An alert sentry challenged.

"Please Suh, don't shoot. It's only us fishermen," James replied.

"Advance and be recognized," came the stern reply, the guard suspicious in the darkness and the thick bank that obscured vision, rifle at the ready.

"Please Suh, just us slaves. We got no gun. We mean no trouble, Suh. We done made our escape, the good Lord willin' and we seek our freedom, Suh," Sheppard entreated.

"What you saying boy?" the tired guard understanding neither dialect nor what was happening.

"Yes Suh, facts is, we was hired out," James explained, "working over to Sewell's Point. All day, we digs and digs, hauling dirt and rocks, under the guns of Confederate guards, building up their defenses against ya'lls. They like to starve a man too, not feedin' us anything after they worked us like dogs. Nothing hardly to eat day-after-day, now days be getting longer, and every day we works more, with no end to it."

"A fore long, we'd be diggin' our own graves, Suh," Frank added. "So one day, Sheppard here says, we should be building yonder defenses for freedom," pointing to Ft. Monroe, "and not Marsa Mallory's against it. And that Suh is when we made our plans to escape."

"You sure boy, I never heard tell anyone rowing across these waters," the skeptical guard replied, "least of all three slaves."

"Go ahead tie up. I'll call for the sergeant of the guard to see what to do."

"Yes Suh, thank you Suh. We be right here. My Suh, this is a mighty fine wharf you gots here," Sheppard added.

Sending word for the sergeant of the guard, the sentry hoped he'd done the right thing. Soldiering was still quite new as he'd only joined up a short time ago for a ninety day enlistment and had precious little training –mostly marching back and forth and the manual of arms, good for a parade but of little practical use at the moment.

"All right who are you? Identify yourselves!"

"Why yes Suh, I be James Townsend, and this here's Sheppard Mallory, and in the stern is Frank Baker," James replied to the sergeant's question. The sentry quickly summarized the slave's story for his sergeant who was likewise not exactly sure what to do in this situation. His brow furrowed, one could sense the wheels turning under his matted filthy hair for nothing quite like this had come up before. Usually, sentries mostly kept an eye for masts of approaching ships, lest a Confederate vessel dare to enter Hampton Roads. Instead, now they had a skiff bobbing like a cork, containing three slaves desperate to hold the small boat to the wharf's pilings against strong tides sweeping the rocks.

"Please Suh, can we come ashore? We be rowing most the night," Sheppard continued, "And Suh, we not feelin' none too good."

"Very well, step lively and don't try anything," the sergeant allowed, placing his hand firmly on his weapon just in case.

Stowing the oars and lashing their vessel fore and aft, the three clambered to the wooden ladder, climbing onto the wharf, taking care not to slip on treads slick with algae and fouled with marine life. *It would not do to drown within arm's reach of freedom*, James thought. The private helped them up, understanding the difficulty as he'd negotiated the same slippery steps when helping tie up the steamers calling regularly at the wharf.

All three were soon stretching their wobbly sea legs on the dock, tired and somewhat dehydrated from the night of heavy rowing.

"Privates, git out here," the sergeant of the guard shouted, calling for the supernumerary guards who at the time were engrossed in a never-ending card game.

While waiting momentarily for them to report, the sergeant explained to the private posted there, "we dare not leave the wharf unguarded any more than either of us can march these three off by himself, lest we be out manned, even if the slaves are unarmed. " Momentarily, two privates ran up on the double.

"Yes Sergeant."

"Come on, we're taking the runaways to the brig," the sergeant ordered.

He and the two additional guards soon left with the prisoners, leaving the sentry to return to the loneliness of his post.

What's happenin' now? Where they takin' us? Sheppard, James, and Frank each wondered, but were afraid to ask. *Where they headed? Least wise, we on dry land*, they noted, after their harrowing night on the sea.

Passing through the sally port entering the massively thick stone walls of Ft. Monroe, "Lock 'em up," the sergeant of the guard called to the jailer, a large greasy man, teeth mottled and stained from many years of chewin' tobacco. The slaves looking at each other in disbelief, simultaneously wondering, w*hat we done got ourselves into?*

"Well now, what we got here, three trouble makers?" the jailer gruffly asked, spitting vile tobacco saliva at their feet.

"Well, I don't rightly know what they are" said the sergeant. "Claims to be runaways, and to done rowed all the way accrost from Sewell's Point."

"How you reckon three ignorant slaves done navigated accrost all that way?" the jailer replied sarcastically. It was his custom to belittle anyone, and everyone, prisoner and fellow soldiers.

"How the hell do I know?" The sergeant replied, annoyed. "There's a skiff tied up down to the wharf, who it belongs to and how these three came by it, I have no idea."

Seeing the bars on the door and one small hole in the brick cell wall that overlooked the water-filled moat, James, Frank, and Sheppard glanced at each other, terror in their eyes and hearts. Each was too afraid to raise a question, for they had learned long ago and the hard way, never, ever question the white man, no matter what.

"Put 'em in here for now," the sergeant instructed.

"What they done, anyway," the jailer questioned, "besides causing' a disturbance and making up some lying' story about navigating' accrost?" He was accustomed to knowing the reason for each prisoner's incarceration, if for no other reason than to taunt with tales of the gallows.

"Like I said, I don't know if they done anything, 'cept show up here as runaways, but I'll be damned if I know what to do with' em. Sure as Hell can't leave them running free all over Ft. Monroe in the middle of the night, can I? We'll let the Lieutenant figure out what he wants done with 'em in the morning," the sergeant continued.

Prodded by the jailer, James, Frank and Sheppard shuffled along, having no choice, but to enter the dark, damp cell.

"Please Suh, we ain't done nuthin' Suh. Why you gots to be puttin' us in 'dis here jail," Sheppard finally mustered the courage to ask.

"Shut up," the jailer snarled, jabbing him painfully in the ribs again with the end of his lead-filled oak night stick.

"The Lieutenant will decide what to do with y'all when he gets here. I sure ain't waking him just to come down and see a couple of runaways showing up in the middle of the night," the jailer snarled.

"Give 'em some water," the sergeant instructed, now that the three were behind bars. Though they posed no threat, the sergeant knew to never relax one's guard around any prisoner.

Momentarily, one of the privates returned carrying the old wooden bucket, water sloshing onto the grimy floor. He grabbed a tin cup for the three to share.

James drank first – wincing at the foul taste. The wells on Ft. Monroe were not deep and tapped brackish waters of a salt lense situated below the nearby marshes on this point of land jutting into the Chesapeake Bay. Despite the strong smell of rotten eggs, the thirsty men drank for they were dehydrated. Thirst was the only thing satisfied, however, as they remained hungry and were quite fearful about this turn of events. Each began to wonder, *what we done got ourselves into?*

Their unkempt jailer stood nearby, eyeing them threateningly, still playing with a length of rope, fashioning it into a hangman's noose.

Reading the fear on the inmate's faces and the jailer's evil intent, the sergeant turned to address them before leaving. "This is just temporary, 'til the Lieutenant gets here in the morning and tells us what he wants done. Just get some rest."

But James, Frank, and Sheppard took little comfort the remainder of the long night.

"Put that damn thing away," the sergeant ordered the jailer, still flaunting the hangman's noose.

The jailer complied for the moment, but with a hideous smirk at the imprisoned freedom-seekers.

The remaining wee hours passed slowly for the three, discussing in muted whispers their fate. Though none of the three could hazard a guess at what awaited them, they surely hadn't figured on incarceration. Though they had cause for worry, Sheppard kept counseling, 'remain calm,' 'don't do nothin' to provoke 'em,' and as he had from the outset, repeatedly advised, "we got to bide our time and play this hand we been dealt."

When dawn finally broke, the Lieutenant was soon spotted making his morning rounds, verifying that some semblance of good order and discipline had indeed again been preserved through the night.

"Sir, there is one more thing," the sergeant of the guard advised, "There's three escaped slaves in the brig. They rowed up to the wharf in the middle of the night and we weren't sure what to do with 'em so we held them temporary. Their skiff's tied up at Engineer wharf."

"What? Why wasn't I informed of this?" the Lieutenant snapped.

"Beggin' your pardon Sir," the sergeant replied.

"Well, move the skiff from the wharf, we got a steamer due in later this morning, can't have it in the way. If you can't hoist it, have some men row her 'round the point and run her ashore on the beach. Mind you now, find someone who knows boats so they don't upset and drown in the surf," the Lieutenant instructed. "And when you get back, we'll pay a visit to the jail. I got to get to staff call." They headed in opposite directions, the sergeant back out the sally port to the wharf, the Lieutenant to post headquarters.

"Attention!" the officers jumping to their feet, rigid attention as Lieutenant Colonel Justin Dimick entered.

"As you were," he barked, signaling his assembled staff to retake customary seats.

Immediately, the commander started around the table hearing brief reports on any developments since they'd last met. The intelligence officer gave a somewhat cursory accounting of the disposition of enemy forces, followed by the Quartermaster who went on far too long about delayed shipments of first one item, then another. Next came the sick call report by the Surgeon, "Sir, as of today, May 24th, there are six men on bed rest from severe diarrhea and dehydration, twelve more with somewhat milder gastroenteritis, two with minor wound infections and one man on light duty due to bad sunburn. But I am pleased to report no contagious diseases at this time."

"Thank you doc, let's hope it stays that way."

"Yes, Sir, but it'll take more than hope what with all the new personnel reporting in." The Surgeon explained, "Some of 'em is more than likely carrying something and will infect their tent mates once all are crowded together." Dimick nodded and went on.

"Next." Finally, it was the Lieutenant's turn as the adjutant called, "Provost Marshall." Clearing his throat to calm his nerves for he was the junior officer, the Lieutenant responded, "Yes Sir, all quiet among the men, but one new item Sir. There's three runaway slaves arrived last night, came in by boat reportedly from Sewell's Point, temporarily held in the brig, Sir, pending disposition."

"Very well," Lieutenant Colonel Dimick replied, surprised at this development. *Why wasn't I informed of this development earlier*, he wondered. *No officer worth his salt would be caught uninformed these days.*

"Lieutenant, make the slaves available to the intelligence staff. I want them questioned thoroughly to see what information they might provide, especially anything on the progress of enemy gun emplacements -if they really did come over from Sewell's Point. Then, make arrangements 'til their master comes for 'em. I expect he'll be along shortly to fetch 'em, once he realizes they're missing," Lieutenant Colonel Dimick instructed.

"Yes, Sir," the Lieutenant replied, gladly retaking his seat.

"Sir, if you don't mind, I'll examine the prisoners as well?" the Surgeon offered, but before receiving the commander's answer, continued, "Sir, I need to ensure these three from last night are not carrying something infectious. It would never do to have runaways bring disease in and then have it spread amongst the troops."[4]

"Of course, Doctor. Let me know if you find anything," Lieutenant Colonel Dimick replied, sharing his surgeon's concerns. "And while you're examining the prisoners, I mean slaves, Doc, see if they've been beaten lately. I don't want their master coming here charging us with abusing them when he's been whipping 'em," Lieutenant Colonel Dimick instructed.

"Yes, Sir, of course, Sir," the Surgeon responded, hoping he'd find neither wounds nor scars of past whippings. He found it abominable. *I try to heal people and others whip them*, he shuddered.

With morning staff call complete, each officer turned to his respective responsibilities, Lieutenant Colonel Dimick departing to call upon the new Commanding General, Major General Benjamin Butler, heading the recently created Department of Virginia. Lieutenant Colonel Dimick was prepared to explain to his new boss the progress they'd made on reinforcing the fort and where problems still remained, such as obtaining sufficient artillery. In so doing, he'd learn if General Butler had any special concerns or instructions since arrival on the 18th.

Though tasked specifically by General Winfield Scott to reinforce Ft. Monroe, Butler had no prior military experience, being one of the Union's many politically-appointed Generals. Despite knowing little about the

---

4 Although the germ theory of disease remained unknown at the time, some military surgeons had come to understand an association between overcrowding, especially new recruits, and communicable disease outbreak.

military, he now held a very senior rank. It was a classic case of who he knew for his Generalship was based on shrewd maneuvering, politics, and an earlier incident that some said preserved Maryland in the Union, despite the hotbeds of secession in Baltimore and the southern part of the state.

An astute criminal lawyer and Democratic politician, Butler made a name for himself by seizing control of a 1,000 man Massachusetts militia unit from its commanding officer, then tricking secessionist mobs running amok vandalizing Baltimore and lynching blacks, by taking the commandeered troops out of town by rail. While the Free State secessionists celebrated their easy victory in supposedly chasing the Yanks out of town, Butler ordered telegraph lines cut, reversed the train, and with his commandeered troops regained control of Baltimore. As it was told, he'd thus retained the Free State in the Union, and protected nearby Washington from angry mobs. While Butler was quick to tout his role as hero and savior of Baltimore and Union, General Scott could not stomach all of the 'pro-Butler' press coverage this generated. Scott was not looking forward to answering either reporters or politicians about how and why Butler managed to quell a mob situation while the bona fide Union officers in command had been unable to do so. Although Butler's unilateral action in commandeering Federal troops ultimately proved successful, the facts he'd acted without approval or even any coordination, and that Butler harbored his own political agenda did not sit well with Scott. Concerned the droopy-eyed, forty-three year old Butler would continue to grow his power base in Washington, Scott figured to prevent such an outcome by reassigning Butler to what he assumed would be mundane duties - overseeing the build-up of troops at Fort Monroe. After all, troop shipments to that bastion of Union strength would be controlled by Washington and all that Butler, as senior officer on the receiving end, would be responsible for was maintaining good order and discipline, and signing requisition forms. General Scott confidently assumed Butler could not cause much trouble at an isolated post. He also knew competent career officers like Dimick would oversee day-to-day operations, while Butler's duties would be largely ceremonial. Most of all, Butler would be far from Washington politics and access to the press.

Figure 3. Major General Benjamin Butler. Courtesy of the Library of Congress, Washington, D.C.

However, General Scott would soon regret giving Butler any authority whatsoever as the man seemed to have a propensity for stirring up political issues. He continued taking unilateral actions, uncoordinated with anyone, seemingly whenever or wherever opportunity arose.

Still relishing the success of his Baltimore 'command,' Butler was enjoying his new found notoriety, and used this to manipulate behind the scenes to ensure his political status continued to rise. The last thing Butler wanted was to be transferred from Washington, but with his recent appointment as Major General, he knew enough, or at least had the good sense to not immediately counter, at least not publically, Scott's selection for him for duty at Fort Monroe. He was shrewd enough to figure out that should he protest in the least, Scott would not hesitate to claim he was simply offering Butler 'reward' for a job well-done in Baltimore.

Civil War Comes Home

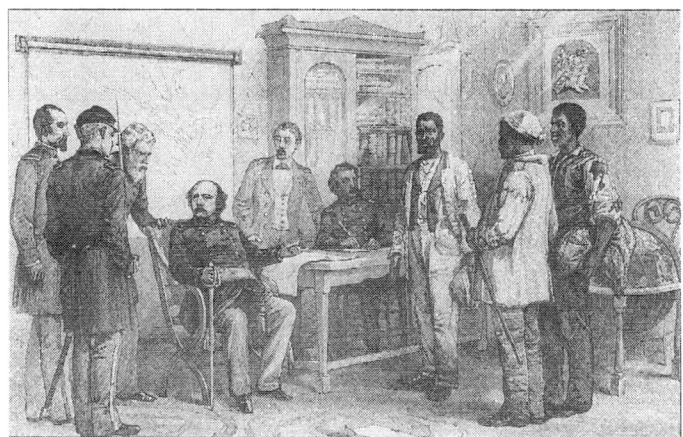

Figure 4. Major General Benjamin Butler and escaped slaves of Colonel Mallory of Hampton, James Townsend, Sheppard Mallory, and Frank Baker, declared by Major General Benjamin Butler as 'contraband of war,' at Fort Monroe, VA. Courtesy of the Casemate Museum, Fort Monroe, VA.

But with aspirations of a larger national role, Butler was secretly furious at being moved out of Washington to be sent to some outpost in south eastern Virginia. He imagined opportunities to get his name in the papers would be dismal at best but he also sensed that somehow Scott had managed to maneuver him into a position from which he could not easily extricate himself, at least not without political damage. Butler set his anxious mind to figuring out how to somehow replicate his Baltimore successes in Virginia.

General Butler knew from his reading of law and history, that Virginia had flirted decades earlier with ending slavery, and a measure to do so had barely missed becoming state law. He also knew that Virginia, then among the richest of the states and domicile for one fifth of the nations populous, was a grievous loss to the Union. Virginia, despite a delayed and narrow vote for secession was essential to whatever the fledgling Confederacy would be able to accomplish. *As Virginia went so went the nation,* he recalled -still a prevailing view at the time. Butler knew he could not reverse the Commonwealth's reluctant decision for secession, but if he could find a way to somehow limit Virginia's role, he figured his political stock would again soar. Fancying himself one day holding national office, *if I could just pull this off,* Butler speculated longingly.

Settling his button-popping girth comfortably into his new command, General Benjamin Butler, astutely decided to give his subordinates, who were all well-experienced in every aspect of the military and war-fighting, a relatively free hand to do their jobs. Whether this wise decision was due to his recognition of his own limited knowledge of such matters, or his indifference to anything but politics, was not entirely clear. Perhaps it was some of both.

As regards knowledge of the military, Lieutenant Colonel Dimick was the perfect counterpoint to General Butler's lack of experience. Dimick had already served a distinguished four decades in uniform, having been brevetted for gallantry in both the Seminole and Mexican Wars.

While military preparations were actively reinforcing Fort Monroe, keeping Dimick and staff busy as bees to the hive, General Butler's focus remained elsewhere —chiefly, the law and trying to remain involved in the nation's tumultuous politics. Consistent with his well developed opinion of himself, Butler came to view his assignment as the senior Union General Officer posted to Confederate territory in a new light. *This could be quite advantageous*, Butler daydreamed. At the same time, however, Butler also felt himself at considerable disadvantage, having left the lively Washington scene for the relative obscurity of a moated fort on land's end at the mouth of the Chesapeake. These perceived limiting factors only fueled Butler's political aspirations further and he vowed his position as Commanding General would be a springboard for his triumphant return to Washington. *Somehow I will make this work, and sooner rather than later,* Butler kept reminding himself.

"Good morning General," Lieutenant Colonel Dimick remarked, entering Butler's spacious office, bright sun pouring in tall windows, ajar slightly to allow the ever-present blue cloud of cigar smoke to dissipate.

"Yes, good day, Colonel," General Butler replied, "I trust all is well? Anything to report?" Lieutenant Colonel Dimick could not help but notice the General was already deeply involved in reading the Washington newspapers brought in by overnight steamer. Though the news they contained was by now several days old, it was the latest available.

"Actually, General, there has been one new 'development,' shall we say, a bit out of the ordinary," Lieutenant Colonel Dimick announced, hoping to draw the General's attention from the newspapers. "Seems three runaway slaves stole a skiff and rowed across," pointing out the window at the waters of Hampton Roads. "They're in the brig now, and the surgeon is examining them. I expect we'll be hearing from their master as soon as he finds out they're missing. Most likely, we'll be the first place he comes looking. As you see in the press, motioning towards the newspapers the

General was still reading, "Northern papers have been full of coverage about how the Union must put an end to slavery. That bit of news if one dare call it 'news' at all Sir, has been widely circulating here in the upper South. How far that idea has penetrated the Deep South, I couldn't really say, but if it has, I expect it would stir up rebel war sentiments considerably. I'm just wondering Sir, do you think these three runaways might have acted on such news. Or, is the timing of their escape coincidental?" Lieutenant Colonel Dimick speculated.

General Butler finally put down the newspaper giving his subordinate his undivided attention, "Colonel, I expect you may well have something there. It has been my experience after many years of trial and politics, there's really very little that is, 'just coincidence.' Did you say the three slaves escaped, came here seeking freedom, and now we got 'em locked up?"

"Yes Sir, that's correct. Came ashore in the middle of the night and the sergeant of the guard thought it best to hold them for safe keeping until they could be returned to their rightful owner," Lieutenant Colonel Dimick explained.

"I am well aware of the provisions of the Fugitive Slave Act, Sir," Butler snapped. "I was just wondering Colonel, how you suppose it would look if the headlines of these newspapers read, "Slaves seeking freedom, jailed at Ft. Monroe!"

Taken aback momentarily, Lieutenant Colonel Dimick paused before replying, "Well Sir, I don't know. I guess that would not look so good actually. But I leave politics to you Sir"

"You're damn right it wouldn't do, Colonel!" General Butler exclaimed. "We've got all these abolitionists, half the North hollering, 'free the slaves,' and the issue gets hotly debated back and forth in what's left of the Congress, in hotel lobbies and saloons across Washington all day and half the night. I'm from Boston and I know the abolitionist's fervor! Now, these three take the initiative and make good their escape to freedom, only to be jailed by the U.S. military and after we lock 'em up, we're supposed to return them to their masters for more whippings and chains? I don't think that is something I want to try explain to the Commander-in-Chief, the abolitionists, or the press," General Butler posited. *Let me think about this,* Butler mulled, *this could work to advantage somehow. I've got to think through this scenario.*

Lieutenant Colonel Dimick was trying to formulate a reply but found himself momentarily speechless, the General's position so foreign to anything previously imagined, let alone discussed.

"Wait, Colonel," the General continued, standing, hands behind his back staring off into the distance of the Chesapeake Bay, "this may just be the event that turns the tide. This spark could blow the whole powder keg on the slave issue," Butler continued, more excited the more he thought through ramifications, *not the least of which was propelling him onto the national political scene.* Meanwhile Lieutenant Colonel Dimick hadn't exactly followed where the master politician was going with this.

"Don't you see my good man" General Butler went on, "ending slavery would become the new cause for prosecuting this damn war. Otherwise, the North might as well just let the South go; secede if that's what they are so damned determined to do, and be done with it. Then, we're not shedding our sons' blood and nation's treasure to maintain an imperfect union, and one that abides slavery. The war is not just about preserving the nation, mankind's 'last best hope,' as President Lincoln likes to call it. There is that cause, of course, but that is too abstract to generate real support and get people out for rallies in the streets. This war is going to be much more. It has got to be both, 'Preserve the Union,' and 'free the slaves.' Lincoln may not see that yet, or he may resist it, or claim the time is not right politically. But if freeing the slaves were made the cause, then finally, this could rally everyone. It would bring the United States together, acting as one nation, rather than a collection of member states," General Butler explained.

"Or, rip it apart forming two separate nations, abutting but forever divided," Lieutenant Colonel Dimick countered. General Butler, however, was no longer even listening.

"Why we've often heard," General Butler continued, "pronouncements like, 'these United States' are going to do this or that, but when this war is won, it will become, THE United States." General Butler clearly grasped the long strategic view.

"Uh, I see Sir. I hadn't thought of it that way," Lieutenant Colonel Dimick reflected, then continued trying to explain, "I just got first word of the runaways at the post staff meeting a short time ago," trying to distance himself from the decision to jail the trio. *Apparently, holding them was not the correct response, at least according to the politics of General Butler, though I do not for a minute, fault the sergeant of the guard,* Lieutenant Colonel Dimick thought. *Butler's the new commanding general, Union Department of Virginia*, Dimick reflected, *I'll stick to soldierin' and leave damn politics to him.*

As Lieutenant Colonel Dimick was turning to leave, Butler stopped him.

"Colonel, we can make this work to our advantage." *Especially mine*, Butler thought. *If this plays out with the three runaways I'll be right back in the Washington headlines*, Butler relished. "Send for the three," Butler demanded.

"Bring the prisoners, err, slaves to headquarters," Lieutenant Colonel Dimick ordered.

"Yes Sir, right away," as a messenger was dispatched on the double to the brig.

Momentarily, Sheppard, James, and Frank heard the commotion outside their cramped cell and the rattling of the jailer's large ring of keys.

"Now listen," Sheppard quickly counseled, "let me do the talkin'. We gots to play our hand best ways we know." Frank and James readily agreed, only too glad to have their friend do the negotiating for whatever was about to happen.

"Well boys, looks like I'll deal with y'all later," the filthy jailer snarled, still swinging a length of rope fashioned into hangman's noose, "that is, if there's anything left of y'all when the big boss general gets through with your sorry asses. I hear he can lay on a whippin' that'd do your Master proud. He ordered lashin' of soldiers don't you know? Works 'em over right good."

Sheppard glanced at his mates, but dared not speak. He tried to reassure Frank and James to pay no heed to this scoundrel jailer, though he saw genuine fear in their eyes.

Once out of the brig, they marched as prisoners across post. As their guards exhibited no signs of roughness, the three took some comfort in the fresh morning air, but were by no means assured of what their fate now held.

"Sir, per your orders, the slaves are in the entrance way outside," the sergeant of the guard reported to Lieutenant Colonel Dimick.

"Very well, have them stand by. I will inform General Butler, they are ready for his questioning."

"General, the three escaped slaves are downstairs."

"Very well, send them up. I will see them in my office. You will join me and instruct the guards to stand at the ready."

"Yes Sir."

Presently the trio was marched in and instructed to present themselves to General Butler.

"State your names," the General pronounced sternly.

"Suh, my name is Sheppard Mallory, and this here is Frank and James.

We done escaped last night, seeking our freedom and took refuge here, Suh."

"So I heard. Now tell me man, where were you and what were you doing before your escape?" General Butler inquired.

"Suh, we's slaves of Colonel Mallory of Hampton. Only he hired us and a bunch more out to work for the army," Sheppard explained.

"What kind of work did they have you doing, Sheppard?"

"Suh, well we usually plants and tends crops and livestock and such, but now we's hired out to the army and we mostly digs," Sheppard explained.

"Digging? What have they got you digging?"

"Suh, mostly defense works, accrost the way. We dig trenches and pile up the dirt into earth works. Into some we place stones and logs too, as barricades and some places got roofs overhead, then we cover with dirt. Always more dirt piled on.

"And they work us seven days a week," James interjected, drawing a stern glare from Sheppard reminding him to keep quiet.

"Suh, if I may explain," Sheppard offered, and seeing the General nod, went on, explaining that on the Mallory estate they were usually granted at least part of the Sabbath as a day of rest, or at least a few hours in which they could attend church and tend to their affairs. "Since we was sent across the water to work, the army works us seven days a week. We start at sunrise and work 'til the day light ends, and this is everyday includin' the Sabbath, and regardless of heat or weather."

"And they don't hardly feed us," James added, drawing another stare from Sheppard for him to be quite.

"And how much are you paid for these long days of hard work?" General Butler asked.

"Suh, we's slaves. There is no pay. No matter what we do, or how long we work, we's never paid, Suh."

"I see," General Butler replied, glancing at Lieutenant Colonel Dimick, and then thinking for a moment asked, "and why did you come here to Fort Monroe?"

"Suh, why to be free, Suh. This army labor is killin' us and many more all accrost the South, Suh and it ain't right by Lord God Almighty, Suh making us work for the army to keep us slaves," Sheppard replied.

General Butler let the slave's words sink in. He realized Sheppard had hit upon an important point, that it was unchristian for the military to use forced slave labor to maintain the institution of slavery. From what

Butler understood of the abolitionist movement and national politics, he was quite certain that argument could be made and it would carry the day, both in Washington and in streets, shops, schools and homes throughout the North.

Finally after a long pause General Butler scanned the room, slowly rose from his chair, and addressed a question, not to the slaves, but to Lieutenant Colonel Dimick.

"Colonel, from the testimony of these slaves, did we not just hear first-hand how the Rebels are using slaves to defend against us, and no doubt at some point, prepare for an attack upon us?"

"Yes Sir, that is correct Sir," Dimick replied, then adding,"and we have heard similar reports in the past but this is the first time we heard it directly from slaves."

"Yes, as I have also been led to understand," Butler replied, then continuing, "Then as these slaves are being used against us in time of war, the same as weapons, provisions, or other military materiel is employed against us, I declare them to be contrabands of war," General Butler pronounced.

"Sir," Lieutenant Colonel Dimick questioned, "in the past, contraband referred to goods and supplies captured from the enemy, not people."

"Yes, I am well aware, but does not slave labor, as we have just heard, employed in the construction and strengthening of defensive works constitute military action against us," Butler posited.

"Well, yes I guess it could be so construed, Sir," Dimick agreed.

"Indeed, and I hereby declare these and all runaway slaves as contraband of war. They are to be housed here and will not be returned to the enemy where they would only again be employed against us." Looking at James, he continued, "and they will be paid for their employment, and of course, fed."

"Contrabands, you are now free to work for us, *and the freedom of your fellow slaves everywhere,* Butler declared.

"Thank you Suh," Sheppard replied, remaining calm but inwardly overjoyed at this outcome for it was beyond their wildest dream, freedom and Federal protection.

"Lieutenant Colonel Dimick, take charge of the contrabands and see that they are fed, given a place to live, and useful work," Butler directed.

"Yes Sir," Dimick replied, knowing he'd be executing the General's orders for a lot more than these three. *When word of General Butler's contraband decision, effectively freeing escaped slaves and providing then protection, gets out, we are going to see a flood of former slaves.*

Mouthing prayers of thanks for their deliverance, James Townsend, Sheppard Mallory, and Frank Baker had similar thoughts.

***

Military Disposition,

Lower Peninsula

"And Lieutenant Colonel Dimick as soon as you've got the contrabands situated, tell me Sir, how good is our intelligence on the enemy," General Butler asked.

"Yes Sir, right away. The Provost Marshall will see to the contrabands, Sir. As for intelligence, well Sir, actually, our situation is not that good and needs to be a whole lot better. We've lately gotten some reports from the newsboy, Charles Phillips,"[5] Lieutenant Colonel Dimick offered, wondering, *what does the General have in mind now?*

"A newsboy," General Butler interrupted.[6]

"Why yes Sir, though he is but 14 years of age, he served as a courier for information gathered by his father, John, and the lad has a good understanding of the kind of information needed. So I am told," Dimick quickly added. "His cover is selling newspapers all over the town and encampments which gives him free access to come and go without suspicion."

"Well, I may not have much military experience as you know Colonel, but I never heard of relying on a civilian boy for critical information," the General replied. "This is not as I had expected. I want a reconnaissance

---

5 Newsboy Charles Phillips successfully collected information critical to the Union, personally delivering intelligence gathered to General U.S. Grant before his arrest January, 1865 and imprisonment for the remainder of the war.

6 (Markle, Donald E., 1994, Spies and Spymasters of the Civil War, Hippocrene Books, New York)

mission mounted. Send units out and see what the Confederates are up to. Right here in Hampton, see what they do when we probe their lines. Not a full engagement, mind you," General Butler explained, "just reconnaissance."

Within the short span since arriving, General Butler assessed quite correctly that better information on the disposition of enemy forces was needed. While Lieutenant Colonel Dimick had lacked the manpower to undertake reconnaissance, the steady stream of arriving troops solved that problem. Fort Monroe's strength would soon number in excess of sixty-seven hundred. To assimilate such rapid growth, only about fourteen hundred actually remained garrisoned at Fort Monroe, while the balance were reassigned elsewhere, notably Camp Hamilton nearby, and a camp named in honor of the General. Camp Butler occupied strategic ground, the high bluffs of Newport News overlooking the James, thus giving Yankee gunners control over river traffic, critical in defense of Union flanks, or to attacking the Confederate flanks or rear.

"Very well General, I will see to it," Dimick replied, thinking, *he doesn't even understand what a reconnaissance mission is.*

As the Union leaders tried to figure out what their Southern counterparts were up and vice versa, local citizens were interacting regularly with both sides. As Fort Monroe became heavily reinforced and troops were relocated to newly built camps, the spread of increasing Union forces into Hampton and Newport News drastically changed the lives of residents like George Benjamin West, who recorded the following in his reflections,

"On Monday March 27th...soon after breakfast, several boats were seen loaded with troops going up the river and being so near the land, it was apparent they intended to land at the wharves. One wharf, fathers, was at the foot of now Eighteenth Street, and the other...was at the upper side of Pier 5...

I was the only male at the house, father being out in the field attending to his hands. Mr. Marrow, whose wife and child were here, had gone to the Casey farm, a part of which he cultivated, and brother was at his own place, the Burk farm. One can imagine the great excitement produced by the sight of the troops. War seemed to have come in the midst of perfect peace. I went at once in search of father, who was so large and fat and so troubled by rheumatism that he could not walk, but had to attend his farming riding in a carry-all.

Before I reached the bridge that crossed the Newport News creek, I

met James Henry Tabb in a hurry to carry his sister home. He continued to the house and fortunately returned then crossed the bridge with her before it was picketed by the Yankees. I could not find father, so I returned home. Soon brother came up on horseback, being a member of the cavalry. He had to report and, concluding he would of no great advantage to use and fearing arrest as a (Confederate) soldier, he forged the creek at its mouth, thinking the soldiers had reached the bridge.

In a short time father came to the house. And Mr. Marrow, who was a member of the Wythe Rifles, and who had been persuaded by father on Friday to move his furniture from Hampton to Mr. Lewis Davis' near New Market, and bring his family to us, came to get his uniform and rifle. He had walked from the Casey farm and since all our horses were in the fields at work and the Yankees were by this time all in sight, we did not think he could escape, so he concluded to stay and leave at night.

Very soon after a squad of marines came to the house and advise father to go and ask protection of the commanding officer, who turned out to be General Phelps. They said many of the soldiers were the roughs and jailbirds of Boston and would steal and destroy everything unless it was guarded. We took their advice, and father and I went over and found the general laying off the entrenchment, afterwards built.

General Phelps was the colonel of the 1st Vermont (Regiment), but on account of his West Point training had been made brigadier general, though the Massachusetts colonel was his senior in point of service.

There were three regiments landed: the 7th New York, all Germans, was stationed next to our house, all on our land; the 1st Vermont, and the Massachusetts, next to Captain Wilbern's.

We found the General in the center of the camp, and as soon as the request was made and the house pointed out, he turned to a corporal and said, "Take three men and go with Mr. West and guard his property and do as he tells you." They returned with us, and up to this time only the Marines had been to the house. Our yard enclosed all the outhouses, barns, stables, and all, and the fence was made of horizontal plank. A partition fence separated the barn from the house yard. I wished the corporal to place the guard on the outside of the fence, and thus they could keep anyone from the rear of the houses, but he was a timid fellow and as the guards would not be in sight of each other this way, he placed them inside of the fence, and their beats were in front of the houses instead of the rear.

The Negroes in the fields had, on the landing, gone to their quarters and left the horses and mules in the field. The quarters were near the bridge (over Newport News creek), and Mr. Tom Skinner, our overseer, lived in the house nearby. Our cook, Aunt Lucy, and her family lived in the kitchen in the yard, but her two boys, who were in the field, went to the quarters and we did not seem them again.

As the soldiers were now walking around, Mr. Marrow and I asked the corporal to go out in the fields with us while we caught the horses. We feared we might be shot by some of the soldiers, who might think we were trying to escape. The corporal evidently thought this a ruse on our part to get away, and was very careful to keep us at a distance and always in his front. We after while caught all the horses and put them in the stables.

In the excitement of the morning, the family, fearing to have the rifle and the uniform belonging to Mr. Marrow in the house should the house be searched, had gotten Aunt Lucy to put them under the smokehouse, which was on low pillars, with the rear exposed to anyone who should look under. When we began to realize this and that Aunty Lucy or her daughter might tell some soldiers, it became a question how to get them out unobserved by anyone on guard, for we were sure that if found they (the Federal soldiers) would accuse Mr. Marrow as the owner, for the uniform was too small for me, and of course, we believed he would be at once imprisoned.

We had dinner cooked for the guard, and as all the other soldiers had gone to camp to dinner, we invited them (the guardsmen) to go to the front porch to eat. We also got all the Negroes out of sight, and then I took the bundle and rifle and carried them to the barn and hide them in a large pile of oats. In the afternoon we feared that the oats might be taken to feed any horse that they might have, and as things became quiet and we did not fear so much that the house would be searched, we concluded it was better to have them in the house. We had no difficulty in getting the guard to their supper on the porch, and I brought them (the uniform and rifle) back to the house. I do not know where they were kept, but they were sewed up in a bed when we moved away and thus saved.

We were all anxious during our stay for fear that Mr. Marrow would be arrested. The Negroes informed the soldiers that he was a volunteer and several times he was accused by them, but whether or not Phelps knew it we never knew. Marrow kept as much as possible from all intercourse with the guards or any other soldiers. This had been a very exciting and fatiguing day to us all, yet we feared to go to bed, but what

Civil War Comes Home

sleep we got was lying down in our clothes while the other watched. We early put out all the lights in the house and watch from the windows the campfires and the guard in the yard. Some of us were going from one window to another all night long; whether so ordered or not, the guard kept their beat around the house instead of the premises; I think they feared that Marrow and I might escape. The long dismal night passed, but we dreaded the day; we did not know what it would bring but we feared every imaginable thing.

The guards of the Vermonters proved to be efficient and reliable and considerate. They were most country lads and felt for our situation. They allowed no soldiers in the yard, but numbers of them came to the fence. In order to conciliate the guard, we furnished them with food, but they were very suspicious, and I usually had to eat some of it to show that is was not poisoned. They would say, "We have plenty to eat and do not need anything," but after I would eat some, they seemed to enjoy it. Father did not go over to the camp on business again, but when we wished any information or favors I would write a letter in father's name and take one of the guards as a protection, and have the interview with the general. I am glad to record that I was always received by him as well as his adjutant with the utmost courtesy and consideration, and the requests were always granted in a kind and cordial manner. They seemed to realize the embarrassing and unfortunate position in which the family was placed and did all they could to help us and make our stay as pleasant as possible."[7]

"We were very grateful that we were treated so much better than we expected or feared. I think it was all due to the fact that General Phelps was a gentleman and felt sorry for us in the position in where we were placed. Though there were many rumors about the Yankees marchin up the country, we did not believe them and therefore lay down this Thursday night with less nervous strain and a greater feeling of security than we had since Sunday night.

The carts were left loaded and drawn up close to the house, with a hound dog tied to one of them for a guard.

We went to very early to sleep as we all were entirely worn out. I lay out on the porch near the carts and was awakened by the dog's furious attack on someone, and as I arose someone struck the porch with his

---

[7] West, George Benjamin, edited by Parke Rouse, Jr. 1977, When the Yankees Came, Civil War and Reconstruction on the Virginia Peninsula, Dietz Press, Richmond, VA. Pgs. 45-49.

sword, and I though the Yankees has us again. Mr. Ivy and Mr. Pompey Marrow had come over to see us and the dog had broken loose and had been so ferocious that Ivy had drawn his sword to protect himself and had struck the porch instead of the dog. It was quite early in the night. We learned that our outer pickets were then at Persimmons Ponds bridge, a few miles above, so father decided we would go up to Mr. Walls' just inside the outer pickets.

After breakfast we started and met [Colonel, later General [John Bankhead] Magruder [CSA] near the picket, with some cavalry, reconnoitering. He stopped and enquired as to the number and position of the Yankees –whether they had thrown up entrenchments-and intimating that he would attack them. He seemed to feel very sorry for father and told him to go to Yorktown, and he would furnish us quarters and would supply all our wants as long as he had anything to eat himself. We have always felt very kindly to him for his kindness and offer, and in fact, he was kind to all of the refugees and did all in his power to help them. We found Mr. Walls' family had gone to Williamsburg, and he being at home alone, he put his house and everything else he had to our service. We remained there until Monday.

What a week this has been! I was completely broken down, and all of us were more than half sick. My sickness and the reports about Magruder's going to attack Newport News caused me to give up all idea of going back for the furniture and Negroes.

Father found out that a great many of the refugees were living in Williamsburg and concluded we should go up there and believed the war would be of short duration. We started Monday morning, but in the afternoon a thunderstorm appeared, and were overtaken by Mr. Richard Lee near his home, Lee Hall, so we stopped there, as Mr. Lee was very pressing in his invitation. The storm proved to be a very severe one, and we remained all night. We rented a house in Williamsburg with Uncle Robert Davis and lived in camp style, sleeping on the floors and having very few comforts and no conveniences. With the exception of a few families, the people of Williamsburg seemed to think we were intruders, and they would have to support us. They showed very little sympathy for our condition."[8]

Meanwhile back at Fort Monroe,
"Yes General Butler, very well Sir, I'll set up the reconnaissance mission as you wish," Lieutenant Colonel Dimick replied.

---
8 op. cit. pgs. 62-65.

"Today, Colonel," General Butler said firmly.

"What? Sir, do you mean send 'em out today without preparation? General these missions take a few days to organize, even small units going for a short time. I hope you can appreciate Sir there are myriad details to be worked out. Just getting mules hitched to the wagons can take the better part of the day, Sir," Lieutenant Colonel Dimick explained, but General Butler wasn't hearing any of it. He didn't want a litany of excuses, even if what his subordinate spoke was the practical truth.

General Butler continued, "Well, just march on foot then, it's not that far. I can see a steeple and the chimneys of Hampton from the gun emplacements. Today, Colonel," reiterating his order that had taken the post commander by surprise.

"Colonel," General Butler went on to explain, "Washington sent me down here to reinforce the fort and ensure a strong Federal presence in the South. Ft. Monroe is key. If not already, it is fast becoming the most secure Union area in the entire South, thanks to your good work. But, we'll not save the union or accomplish our mission if we remain walled up inside. No, Colonel, the battle must be won outside these walls, throughout the South and especially in Virginia and we don't even know the enemy's strength or position. I expect we best turn to, Colonel and gather some basic information about these rebels," General Butler concluded.

"Yes Sir," was all Lieutenant Colonel Dimick could offer. Not in his wildest dreams had he expected a political general to, within days of arrival, order runaway slaves freed and now a movement against the enemy –even if it was supposed to be a probing action for reconnaissance.

"Now, Colonel, which unit in your judgment is best suited, and prepared for this –to test the enemy lines?"

Lieutenant Colonel Dimick replied, "Sir, some of the units are not even here yet. Others only partially arrived, strung out from all the way back to New York. And, none of them is ready for a mission, even next week, let alone today. If you're going to do this immediately Sir, I'll take the 3rd and 4th Massachusetts myself. These garrison troops been here a while and we've managed to get them pretty well-equipped. For the most part, they remain healthy," Dimick explained. "Besides, General the 3rd and 4th Massachusetts are 90 day enlistees and their time is almost up. We might as well get something out of them before they go home."

"Very well, take the 3rd and 4th Massachusetts then," Butler readily agreed for as a Bostonian, he was already preparing to dispatch reports of 'heroic action' to all the hometown press. One way or another he was determined to remain in the national news.

"Yes General" Lieutenant Colonel Dimick dutifully replied.

After several hours of hurried preparations, the units were ready and would soon be out the gate, marching west towards Hampton. Lieutenant Colonel Dimick sat mounted near the sally port observing, and rendered his crisp salute as the national colors passed. *I sure as hell hope all goes well*, he thought. Inexplicably, General Butler did not bother to see them off, instead watching passively from his office, as the long blue line twisted from the gate, like a snake slithering from its hole.

Let's just see what they uncover, Butler thought, returning to his desk and what seemed like a never ending pile of supply requisitions. He had to complete them in time for dispatch with the overnight steamer from Alexandria expected later that morning. The reinforcement of Fort Monroe, Butler's primary mission, succeeded or failed based, of all things, on paperwork, - completion of logistics forms; requisitions, purchase contracts, delivery orders. If necessary, the steamer's return could be held up pending completion of such documents, but that would only delay things and there was a short window between the changing tides when she could launch.

As the march into Hampton was just a little over a mile, it was not long before the formation entered town. Children and dogs ran out to see the commotion as if it was a 4th of July parade. Womenfolk dropped their sewing, baking, or whatever task was at hand to run out, then invariably and immediately, call after their young 'uns 'Get on this porch right now!' or 'Get inside the house this instant,' when they saw the hated Yankees. Men likewise dropped their work as word quickly passed, 'the Yanks are coming.' Some, unloading fishing boats stopped, the overnight catch from the gill nets half on the wharf and half still in the hulls. Incessant hammering of blacksmiths and wheelwrights gone strangely quieted. Whatever they'd been doing ceased as most grabbed whatever weapon was at hand, coming on the run.

The arriving Yankees brought the coastal town's population rushing into the streets. Militia and home guard units quickly formed up, at least partially, but their weapons consisted mostly of antique breech-loading fowling pieces and even a few pitch forks and axes. Shocked to see the enemy entering Hampton at will, citizen reaction ranged from praying for deliverance, to cursing and taunting the invaders, to outright disbelief.

Civil War Comes Home

Immediately, Lieutenant Colonel Dimick was accosted by none other than Colonel Charles Mallory, Commanding officer, 115th Virginia Militia.

"Sir, what is the meaning of this invasion?" Colonel Mallory challenged, his men lining up behind him.

"Invasion," Dimick countered, "My good Sir, how do you consider this an invasion? We are the Army of these United States, not some foreign power. We are merely exercising the troops this fine day. Indeed, had we intended to 'invade' as you term it, there would be firing and taking any who resisted as prisoners, wouldn't you imagine?"

"I'll not pretend to understand what perverse logic you hold Sir! I invite you to leave now, in order that we may get along with polling," Colonel Mallory countered.

"Polling? I had not realized it was Election Day. What office are citizens voting to fill?" Lieutenant Colonel Dimick inquired for he had no idea to what election Colonel Mallory was referring.

"I guess you Yanks ain't heard much news while invading from up north," Colonel Mallory replied. "Today, we freedom – loving Virginians of Hampton, and I dare say throughout the Old Dominion, are exercising our right to vote to endorse the Confederate Congress' resolution to secede from the Union, Sir." This brought shouts of support, and several 'Amen's' from the crowd.

Lieutenant Colonel Dimick, recalling General Butler's specific instructions to not engage, saw the growing crowd and sensed increasing agitation. Nevertheless, he was not one to back down and simply walk away. After all, the very fabric of the Union was at stake and he felt he must act.

Standing tall in his stirrups, calling out in his loudest voice Lieutenant Colonel Dimick advised, "Attention everyone. The polls are closed. There'll be no voting today."

The crowd instantly went silent, but only momentarily. What had this Yank just said? No voting? The muttering increased to a crescendo as Colonel Mallory spoke on their behalf.

"How dare you Sir, We are simply exercising the right, and duty of every American to vote as established under the Constitution."

"Sir, how dare you mention the Constitution while speaking of secession," Dimick challenged. "No Sir, not here, not today" Dimick declared, signaling his sergeants to seize the ballot boxes.

A roar of angry protest went up from the crowd, prompting the order for 3rd and 4th Massachusetts, "Fix bayonets."

Colonel Mallory was taken by surprise. Although he was personally prepared to fight, he knew only a fraction of his Virginia Militia had assembled, most still being on distant farms or at their places of employment, for the Yanks' appearance was completely unexpected. Mallory also saw the majority of the crowd were woman and children, and addressed Lieutenant Colonel Dimick, again loud enough for all to hear.

"Sir, stand down. You see before you God-fearing women and children, a handful of peaceful boys and a few old men. I'll not allow you to shed their precious blood needlessly here today in your foolishness," Colonel Mallory declared, even those furthest to the back of the crowd heard his logic clearly.

Lieutenant Colonel Dimick seeing his opponent was correct about the crowd's composition and again remembering General Butler's explicit instructions not to engage, and recalling the result when British troops had fired on civilians in Boston Square so many years ago, ordered his men, "Port arms!"

For the moment, tensions eased, but the crisis was not over.

"Very well, Colonel," Lieutenant Colonel Dimick responded, "I see you mean no threat, and nor do we. We'll just close the polling, take the ballots and depart."

Again, loud shouts went up, "No! Get out Yankees!" The crowd seethed forward despite being outgunned.

Colonel Mallory raised his pistol, firing into the air, "Quiet! Everyone stop! I'll not allow these invaders to murder any citizen this election day. Let them take the ballot box if that's what they came for. We will vote again as our forefathers here in Virginia ordained!"

Lieutenant Colonel Dimick seeing his soldiers who'd grabbed the ballot boxes returning to ranks, ordered, "Attention. About face." followed quickly by "Forward march!" The officers trotted their horses to the opposite end of the long formation. After an abbreviated tense visit, the Yankees were headed out of town. No casualties to report and seized property limited to a couple of mostly empty ballot boxes, and a current assessment of the 115th Virginia militia and its leader.

Seeing hated Yankees turning tail and departing, raucous cheers went up from the crowd, "Huzzah!" "Huzzah!" Colonel Mallory was congratulated roundly for 'standing down those damn blue-bellies.' But he was just glad bloodshed had been avoided, and resolved then and there to have a better system for alerting and assembling his militia. He was chagrined the Yanks had the audacity to march in to town at will and he had no capability to counter their move. He vowed they'd never be caught off guard again. *That would have to wait, however,* he thought, *we still got a vote to take.*

"Ladies and gentlemen, you see what these fool Yankees are about, coming in to our town and telling us we cannot exercise our rights as Americans to vote," Mallory loudly proclaimed, fueling the crowd's wrath now that the immediate danger had passed.

"Are we gonna let them get away with this?"

"Hell no!" came the resounding reply, unanimous far as anyone could tell.

"Then God-willing, let's get on with the vote!" Mallory proclaimed as cheers again went up!

Notwithstanding the shortcomings of the 115th Militia, Colonel Mallory was satisfied with the outcome. Both mob attack and the possibility of mass fatalities had been averted. In the crowd's opinion, Mallory emerged as hero of the day, having stood down the invaders, sending the hated blue bellies from beloved Hampton without so much as a shot being fired.

A large white oak basket, the kind used to bring eggs to market, was quickly procured, serving as the new ballot box. While overseeing the polling Colonel Mallory received congratulatory handshakes from the many citizens standing in line. Contemplating the scene he wondered, *in attempting to prevent a vote, have the fool Yankees unknowingly ensured a strong turnout and swung any fence sitters towards secession? It would serve 'em right.*

Headed in the opposite direction back to Fort Monroe, their 'show-the-flag' and reconnaissance mission complete, Lieutenant Colonel Dimick went straight to the commanding general's office. Returning Dimick's crisp salute with a dismissive wave, General Butler shuffled the logistics forms still covering his desk. The growing troop strength under his command, now well over six thousand, required an endless stream of supplies just for daily subsistence. Butler was busily signing and dating each, *May 23rd 1861*, while Dimick began describing the day's events in Hampton. They were soon interrupted.

"Begging your pardon, Sir," the adjutant said, opening one half of the double doors slowly.

"Yes, what is it?" Butler asked, still thinking about the polling place incident Lieutenant Colonel Dimick had just described.

"Begging your pardon General but there is a Major Cary here to see you Sir," the adjutant replied.

"Damn it, man can't you see I'm busy? Who is Major Cary anyway?"

"Sir, my apologies, the requesting officer is Confederate Major John Baytop Cary, Sir. He is here under a white flag of truce, demanding to speak to none other than the Commanding General. He is apparently seeking the return of three escaped slaves, under the Fugitive Slave law as I understand it, Sir."

"Damn. Why didn't you say so man?" Butler demanded. "Glory be, a real live Confederate right here inside our Fort." Butler remarked to Dimick. "Very well, send him in."

The double doors flew open with a crash as Major Cary strode in, resplendent in dress uniform, halting just short of the General's desk, rendering the military courtesy of a crisp salute to a General officer, even if he was the enemy.

Though Lieutenant Colonel Dimick returned the salute, General Butler barely raised his arm.

Disgustingly typical for a blue devil, thought the proud Confederate Major.

"My compliments, General Butler," Major Cary announced, still at attention before General Butler slouching in his over-sized chair.

"And likewise to you too Major, and what in God's name brings you here?" Butler asked. Though he was pretty sure he full well knew the reason for the Confederate officer's presence, Butler was interested in hearing what the Major had to say. He enjoyed a sharp cross examination, in or out of court. Meanwhile, Lieutenant Colonel Dimick anticipating Major Cary's request, signaled the adjutant, whispering, "Quick man, send word to the mess tent or wherever they are, to bring the prisoners, err, slaves, I mean contrabands, here on the double. Have them stand-by downstairs, and make sure the guards keep a close eye on 'em. The General will want the good Major Cary to get a good look at his runaways. "

The adjutant nodded, departing to accomplish this latest task.

"Why General, I would have thought your staff would have informed you, Sir" Major Cary opened sarcastically, giving Lieutenant Colonel Dimick an icy stare before continuing.

"Sir, I demand, under the Fugitive Slave law, prompt release of three runaway slaves said to be here, returning them to their lawful owner and master, along with the skiff they stole," Major Cary boldly claimed.

"You needn't trouble yourself about how you think my staff keeps me informed Major Cary," Butler mocked. "Major, are these slaves yours?"

"No Sir, the runaways are the property of Colonel Charles K. Mallory, my commanding officer, 115th Virginia Militia, Sir." At this Lieutenant Colonel Dimick perked up having just returned from confronting Colonel Mallory in Hampton. "Colonel Mallory dispatched me to pick up his slaves. He's a prominent lawyer and quite busy today overseeing other matters vital to the Old Dominion, Sir."

"So I've heard Major," Butler replied, granting an all-knowing smile towards Dimick. "And what, may I ask is Colonel Mallory up to today, Major?"

"Well Sir, I am not privy to all of the Colonel's actions let alone his thoughts, but I would imagine Sir, he is quite concerned about the welfare of his missing slaves," Major Cary explained.

"I see," Butler replied, raising his bushy eyebrows then slowly elevating his massive body to standing, deliberately protracting his response in order to elicit the best 'courtroom' drama. After a fashion, he had Major Cary and the Confederacy on trial. The General took his time; making certain the Major and everyone present were listening attentively. "Major, you may inform Colonel Mallory that his request for return of property is denied."

Major Cary was dumbfounded, and initially did not know how to respond. Struggling to formulate a reply, he managed, "Sir, I understand if the skiff the slaves stole is confiscated, though I can hardly imagine one small skiff is going to mean a damn thing for the Union Navy, but I reiterate Sir, under Fugitive Slave law, which has heretofore always and everywhere been enforced without delay as law of the land, and on behalf of their rightful owner, Colonel Charles K. Mallory, I demand return of his property, three escaped slaves; James Townsend, Sheppard Mallory, and Frank Baker." Major Cary firmly concluded, "I seek nothing more than the return of property to its rightful owner, Sir."

"Precisely," was all that General Butler calmly replied.

"Sir, what do you mean?" Major Cary asked, looking puzzled, as did Lieutenant Colonel Dimick.

"Return of slaves is no longer possible," Butler stated unequivocally. "Because, as you just explained, Major, they are PROPERTY and under the rules of war, property which is used by an enemy combatant may be seized and held as contraband of war," Butler explained, matter-of-factly. "By your own explanation, the Confederacy uses such 'property' as these and all slaves, against us. Thus, it is logical and proper to conclude said 'property' is hereby seized as contraband. Why these very contrabands were working on your gun batteries to be used against this very office were they not?" Butler added, obviously relishing the skewering of a Confederate officer as cleanly as had he run him through with saber.

"Sir, I do protest!" a shocked Major Cary exclaimed. "Always, in the past, we sought and obtained prompt return of runaways, and they were handed over to their rightful owner. Why Sir would you summarily reverse long-standing legal practice and custom?" Although Cary knew he'd not change Butler's mind, he felt compelled to ask, for no other reason than his honor.

"Because Major," Butler countered, Lieutenant Colonel Dimick also anxious to hear his argument, "As you state, in the past such returns have been made, despite their inhuman nature and an affront to the laws of God, because it was the law of the land at that time, however disagreeable or unjust. However, with the Confederate Congress resolving to dissolve Virginia's and the rest of the South's membership in these United States, then the legal protections deriving there from, as well as any customs, traditions or precedents of the past, no longer apply. Quite simply Sir, as you state yourself, slaves are property, and property is seized as contraband.

Just then the sergeant of the guard and several soldiers arrived with the three former slaves.

"Begging your pardon, Sirs," the adjutant again interrupted.

"Yes, what is it," Butler replied.

"Sir, the slaves, or rather the contrabands are here Sir, awaiting instructions regarding their disposition."

Ignoring the adjutant for the moment, "I believe this matter is closed," General Butler pronounced, "good day, Major Cary, my regards to Colonel Mallory. Would you care to bid these three, adieu," Butler mocked.

Major Cary stormed out, riding boots stomping heavily down the stairs. He wanted to dispute Butler's policy but thought better of it. Had he caught anyone's eye, his look would have said more than any words, his seething rage cutting through the mocking Yankees. Striding quickly to his horse, he mounted and rode briskly out the sally port, crossing the bridge over the water-filled moat, back through Union lines, then his own, wondering all the while, *how had it come to this? How was he going to explain what had just transpired to Colonel Mallory? If slaves can now supposedly be seized as 'contraband of war,' how will we manage planting and harvest —the Southern way of life?*

Meanwhile, back inside Ft. Monroe's massive walls, the discussion continued in the Commanding General's office, Lieutenant Colonel Dimick commenting, "Sir, I do believe you have stirred a hornets' nest on declaring runaway slaves contraband of war."

"Indeed, Colonel and with good intent, I dare say, we've not heard the last on this one, not only from the likes of Major Cary and Colonel Mallory seeking return of 'property,' but General Scott, Lincoln, and the rest of that Washington crowd as well."

"Yes Sir, and what do we do we now do with these three, Sir?" the adjutant inquired.

"You heard the General, Major," Lieutenant Colonel Dimick pronounced, taking the initiative, "they are henceforth contrabands of war. They are free and we put 'em to work."

At hearing the word, 'free' the three escapees were ecstatic, dancing a jig, exclaiming, "I's contraband," over and over, grinning ear-to-ear, jubilant in their long-awaited triumph.

"Yes, take 'em down to join the hired labor, find out what skills they got," Lieutenant Colonel Dimick instructed. "If nothing else, they'll draw pick and shovel and get to diggin' only this time for us. "

"First though, I expect these fellas are hungry," the adjutant told the sergeant. Before the three could answer, the adjutant continued, "Take 'em down to the mess tent and get 'em some breakfast. After what they been through last night and this mornin' I doubt anyone could expect much work out of contrabands with empty stomachs, no more than soldiers."

Beside themselves at the sudden turn of events, the three former slaves were elated. Not only had their dangerous escape across Hampton Roads been successful, but they'd just gained their freedom their ancestors dreamed of for generations. Now it was even better than they could have imagined, the Army was going to feed 'em, protect, and employ them, just like that.

The ecstatic trio greeted everyone they encountered on the way to the mess tent, only just beginning to fathom what freedom felt like, noticing for the first time in their lives, no one held a gun or whip over them.

"Glory be" Sheppard said, no longer whispering. Looking around he realized the soldiers walking alongside were not guarding them, just accompanying -a feeling he'd never experienced.

"You know James," Sheppard said, "we gots to spread the word to the rest of our folks. You know, tell all the brothers they can stop being slaves, starved and whipped, and come here to be contrabands just like us. Work for pay, and they feed us and protects at Fort Monroe. Thank you Sweet Jesus!"

Figure 5. Refugees. Original drawing by Edwin Forbes. Courtesy of the Virginia Historical Society, Richmond, VA.

Figure 6. Coming into the lines. Original drawing by Edwin Forbes. Courtesy of the Virginia Historical Society, Richmond, VA.

Civil War Comes Home

Figure 7. Contraband working party, vicinity of Fort Monroe, Va. Courtesy of the Library of Congress, Washington, D.C.

Figure 8. Contrabands construct fortifications. Courtesy of the National Archives, Washington, D.C.

Hampton

Major Cary rode up hard. "Sir, Sir, I have news!"

"Very well, but in a moment," Colonel Mallory replied.

"Yes, Sir, I rode here quick as I could, Sir," Major Cary explained, dismounting, trying to catch his breath.

"Very well, what is it? Did you find my three runaways?"

"Sir, uh, yes Sir, I found 'em all right."

"Did you drop them off at my place? Where are they?"

"No Sir, I didn't get 'em. That new Union General, Butler refused and is seizing them as contrabands of war."

"What? How dare he keep my slaves! They are to be returned to me, their rightful owner under the Fugitive Slave law, just like always."

"Of course Sir, and I explained that to the Yanks, General Butler included, believe me Sir in most vehement terms, but they claim it's new policy, that slaves are property and captured property can be held in time of war as contraband. They were impossible to reason with Sir, and would hear nothing of my argument for their lawful return," Major Cary explained.

"Damn," Mallory exclaimed. "That politician is going to be the ruin of us all. A perfect example of why Virginia is forced to leave the Union!" Colonel Mallory then paused for a moment. His first inclination was to announce the Yankee theft of his three runaway slaves to the townsfolk remaining at the polls. He knew they'd surely have keen interest, but then thought better of it. *If I were to announce now the Yanks are keeping runaways, who knows what our citizens might do? Probably try to march in protest to the fort or something that would end up getting folks killed.*

"Very well Major, we will speak of this later" Colonel Mallory instructed, not certain what his course of action would be, or even if he had any options. While they deliberated, word of General Butler's contraband decision was already spreading like wildfire throughout the Fort, and beyond its walls. Within days, the news made it north to Washington as well as Boston and throughout the South. Soon it was on front pages everywhere, lauded by the abolitionist press who made Butler their new hero, while the Southern press vilified him as the worst of interfering northern politicians.

On news of this chance for freedom, many slaves would seek to escape at their first opportunity. Their masters and overseers, anticipating this, increased surveillance, further restricted movement, and heightened punishment. Nevertheless, every slave could not be chained or watched day and night. Soon eight more runaways followed the initial trio, and within a few short weeks nearly a thousand settled in the protective shadow of Fort Monroe. The fortress took on an almost mythical role as the 'magnet of freedom,' a bastion of compassion and security in what otherwise remained slave territory in a time of war. Before long, freedom-seeking escapees numbered approximately thirteen thousand five hundred. The Union Army fed them all and employed hundreds as day laborers –a new humanitarian mission unlike anything previously undertaken. The new arrivals built shanties in what became known as "Slabtown," -a name derived from the scrap slabs of bark and wood left-over when round pine logs were sawn into square lumber. The slabs of waste wood were gathered by the newly freed to construct their first homes, prized no matter how crude.

No one in Washington yet had any inkling of events unfolding at Fort Monroe, yet Butler's declaration would force President Lincoln's timetable on the critical issue of slavery, thus changing the very cause for the war.

***

COLONEL JAMES MAGRUDER, COMMANDING
CALLED TO PERFORM

At the same time in nearby Yorktown,

"Assume command of the troops and military operations on the line to Hampton," General Robert E. Lee, then Commander of the Provisional Army of Virginia, wrote Colonel James Bankhead Magruder, May 21, 1861. Adding, "take measure of the safety of the batteries at Jamestown Island and York River and urge forward the construction of the defense between College and Queen Creeks in advance of Williamsburg."

Colonel Magruder, a fifty-one year old West Point graduate now led all Confederate forces between the York and James Rivers, known as the Department of the Peninsula. Affectionately known as, 'Prince John,' for his theatrical flourishes and affected elegance, Magruder was no transplanted politician like his adversary Butler. A favored son of the Old Dominion, Magruder was awarded a gold sword for conspicuous gallantry in Mexico where he was brevetted to the rank of Lieutenant Colonel. Since these youthful adventures, however, his fortunes had taken a turn. As a result of heavy drinking in a peacetime Army, his military career seemed destined for little more than the elaborate show drills for which he displayed an untiring fondness. But, in war time, battle-experienced leaders were hard to come by and within days of Lee's orders, Magruder disembarked from the steamer, *Logan,* at Yorktown, assumed command May 24, 1861, quickly discharging his considerable new responsibilities.

Civil War Comes Home

"We will conduct a reconnaissance ride first thing tomorrow morning," Magruder announced in his first staff meeting. "I mean to reconnoiter the landscape thoroughly in order to design defensive works. Gentlemen we shall leave not so much as a foot path unguarded. Nothing is to be left to chance for the safety of Richmond and very life of the Confederacy depend on it." For once he was not over-stating the importance.

Despite a propensity for showmanship and libation, not necessarily in that order, the boastful Magruder possessed a sharp military mind and had repeatedly proven himself in battle. Commanding an artillery battery in Mexico, he developed a good sense for placing artillery to best advantage. Although he understood the use of natural barriers, he also harbored self-doubt as to his skills as a military engineer. The happy result was he understood both the importance of defensive works and the necessity to rely on those better trained in their design and construction. He recalled West Point classmate, Benjamin Ewell, now President of the College of William & Mary, was nearby in Williamsburg. *Perhaps Ewell will help,* Magruder hoped. The arduous work awaiting was a matter of life or death for his men for he soon learned he commanded fewer than twenty-five hundred troops but assessed he needed at least eight thousand more to have a creditable chance to counter the growing Union forces a short distance east.

Magruder's urgent missives to General Lee for additional manpower were eventually answered. First came the 1st North Carolina Volunteers under the capable leadership of Colonel Daniel Harvey Hill and his deputy Lieutenant Colonel Charles C. Lee, both fellow West Point graduates. Arriving with eleven hundred men on the 25th they occupied entrenchments outside Yorktown remaining from the Revolutionary War. An accompanying war correspondent penned in his *Carolina Western Democrat,* "We now occupy the point of danger between the enemy and Richmond. This is not playing solider now, it is stern reality."[9]

Close behind Hill's Tarheels was Lieutenant John Bell Hood, who, in the midst of an alert for a threatened attack, was immediately given command of several batteries wheeled into position. The attack never materialized and sitting on his still unpacked suitcase, thirty-one year old Lieutenant Hood recorded in his diary he'd spent the, "greater

---

9 Britton, Rick. "To War! Big Bethel: The Civil War's First Battle." Command Magazine, 53: 34-43.

portion of the night, gazing intently every few minutes in the direction of Fortress Monroe, in the expectation of beholding the enemy. Such was my first night of service in the Confederate Army."[10] Lt. Hood, future commander of the Army of Tennessee, would spend many such nights, trying to anticipate enemy plans. Lt. Hood was not the only one trying to anticipate what to do.

***

---

10 op. cit.

College of William & Mary closes!

Williamsburg, Virginia

The town occupies a flat plain, deeply dissected by ravines and marshes, 12 miles west of Yorktown. Some two miles east of town, College Creek runs inland from the James River to the south, while Queens Creek flows northeasterly to the York. Together the streams narrow the width of the Peninsula to just 4 miles –a natural funnel for transportation and key terrain feature impacting military movements.

Residents number fewer than two thousand, the majority female; more than a third are slaves.[11] Like the South at large, the population is young, a third under the age of eighteen. It is also largely native born, less than one per cent foreign. Society is highly stratified with wealth and power concentrated in the hands of just seven per cent of the populous who own all the land. The remaining; indentured servants, a handful of apprentices, and many slaves, toil from before sunrise to nearly nightfall every day. Food, shelter, well-made clothes and shoes were not necessarily assured for many of Williamsburg's working class and slaves. In town, most slaves are house servants, and are usually somewhat better off than the field hands and laborers living on surrounding farms, but no one has an easy life by any means.

After working all week, and depending on the master's mood and custom, slaves were granted Sunday afternoons off. While this allowed

---
11 Hudson, pg. 14.

socializing, everyone remained ever mindful of a strict 9 p.m. curfew by which slaves must have returned to their masters. Any slave violating curfew was subject to being whipped, and their master fined the then considerable sum of one dollar.

By 1860 the town bore little resemblance to the hustle and bustle of its Revolutionary past.[12] No longer the colonial capitol, it had fallen on hard times, buildings in disrepair, cattle, chickens and other animals wandering freely in the streets. Describing it as a 'sleepy place' was accurate if not generous.

What today is Duke of Gloucester was then Main Street. Richmond Road was Stage Road; Jamestown Road was Mill Road, while today's York Street was then Woodpecker St. Differences were far more than in name, for these were merely narrow paths winding through woods and fields, turning widely to avoid creeks and wetlands. Save for occasional filling of low areas with oyster shells or wood planks, maintenance was nonexistent. Depending on recent weather, roads were either choked with dust and full of many dried ruts which made for bone-jarring rides, or quagmires in which wagons sunk to axles and animals were hopelessly stuck. The latter was the case when an unseasonable cold front brought unrelenting, 'pitiless rain'[13] as the battle of Williamsburg unfolded.

The town's principal activities were limited to the College of William & Mary and the lunatic asylum. The former was much smaller, while the asylum, much larger.These endeavors gave rise to popular derision of residents as either 'lazy or crazy.'

There was no railroad, telegraph, bank, nor public school, though nine private schools operated.[14] Although the College of William and Mary had undertaken the education of Native Americans early in the colonial days, there was no school for slaves, two hundred years later and it was illegal to teach a slave to read or write.

The newspaper, the Weekly Gazette and Eastern Virginia Advertiser, was published by E.H. Lively in his mother's house. But with low literacy, news often passed by word of mouth, sometimes, surprisingly quickly depending on urgency, but often separately among free and slave.

Thus far, town life had been comparatively little affected by calamitous national events. Everyone knew there was war, but the daily impact was usually limited to trying to obtain the latest news about those hot heads

---

12 op. cit, pgs. 13-17.
13 Hastings and Hastings,
14 Hudson, pgs. 13-17.

in far away South Carolina or politicians in Richmond and Washington, none of whom were necessarily held in much regard. Typically, the latest word was already days or weeks old.

Deliberation by Virginia's secession convention began in Richmond in February, 1861, delegates voting a clear 2-1 majority to remain in the Union. As arguments wore on however, secessionist's eventually prevailed and after the attack on Fort Sumter, Virginia's ordnance for secession passed and Federals moved quickly to reinforce Fort Monroe. Locals viewed this as an overt threat.

The tenth of the following month, by unanimous faculty vote…

"Whereas—Civil war is imminent, and the state of Virginia is threatened with an armed invasion, and whereas the exposed position of this section of the state requires that every citizen should be free to enlist in its defense, and whereas a large majority of the students have already left college, and those who still remain-most of whom propose to leave-are unable, from the excited state of the public mind, to pursue their collegiate duties with profit -Therefore-Resolved –that the exercises of the College should be suspended during the remainder of the present session."[15]

The College of William & Mary closed and remained shuttered for the duration of the war.

Campus sentiments echoed those of town, and because of the vulnerability and imminent threat, it became every citizen's duty to defend against what was viewed as foreign invasion. Within weeks the secession flag flew from the offices of the *Weekly Gazette*, and in short order, 90% of the college's student body and the faculty joined the Confederacy. Volunteers ranged from student Thomas J. Barlow, to an initially reluctant Benjamin S. Ewell, President of the College. The former enlisted as private, the latter, a West Point graduate, was commissioned, and would lead several vital military initiatives while closing the College.

Arriving at the College in 1848 as professor of mathematics and acting President, Ewell was appointed President 1854. Overseeing the all male student body, numbering on average from about sixty to nearly one hundred, "Old Buck," as he was affectionately known among students, was a staunch unionist, bitterly opposed to secession. He hoped to the very last, disunion might somehow be avoided, but his ideas were in a distinct minority in Virginia, especially Tidewater where some considered his views heretical. Only his cousin, William Reynolds, a William & Mary student, shared Ewell's opinion, but young William did not wait for

---

15 Hudson, pg. 15.

the faculty resolution before leaving college April 25, 1861 for his native Baltimore.[16]

As early as January, long before the firing on Fort Sumter April 12th President Ewell had reluctantly received a student petition to form a military company for the purpose of training. Among the student proponents was Richard A. Wise of Richmond who'd already devised the uniform, 'homespun pantaloons, red flannel shirt, and fatigue cap. Members are to arm themselves with Bowie knife and double-barrel shotgun, or rifle.' Although intended for training, the organization never advanced beyond an initial meeting and many felt President Ewell had gotten himself appointed "Captain" in order to control the situation and prevent its ever becoming organized. 'Old Buck' was good at dealing with student issues having done so many times over the years. Breaches of the peace were relatively few and generally harmless, and on the whole, they were a studious lot. One thing they were all quite serious about however was living in accordance with the Southern 'code of honor' under which they'd been raised.

William & Mary students, like their brethren throughout the South, held that males must always display duty, respect and honesty. These characteristics were considered an essential part of education by which they'd grow to 'honorable men.' Faced with war the students now sensed this duty to defend their homeland and way of life, often feeling superior to Northerners. Any failing to behave honorably was considered cowardice and reflected poorly on proud family lineages, many dating to the colonists. Dishonor was not an option, so whether fearful, or simply uncertain, everyone put up a brave front, determined to behave honorably even in crises. If they harbored any doubts, they refused to allow them to surface.

Along with this deep sense of honor many students shared growing frustration with their view of the emerging world. Politics were readily discussed, sometimes heatedly.

"Get everyone together for a meeting," student Thomas Mercer instructed friends, Robert Armistead and John G. Williams, and the trio quickly sought out remaining students. About a third were from the city and immediately surrounding York and James City counties,

---

16 While sixty-one classmates, seven faculties, and President Ewell served the Confederacy, William Reynolds enlisted in the 1st Maryland Infantry Regiment. The only William & Mary student to serve in the Union Army, his name was omitted from a plaque dedicated by the Board of Visitors, in 1914 honoring student's military service. (Heuvel Sean Michael. 2006, The Old College Goes to War: The Civil War Experiences of William and Mary Students, Faculty, and Alumni, M.A. thesis, Univ. of Richmond.

while the remainder, some forty in all, hailed from throughout the Old Dominion including nearby areas such as Norfolk, Northern Neck and Middle Peninsula, as well as Richmond, Orange County, and other western areas. A handful were from outside Virginia, including William H. Day and Sterling H. Bess from North Carolina, and F.M. Wyman all the way from Mississippi. Henry D. Ponton was from Maryland, which though remaining in the Union, harbored strong ties to the Confederate cause, especially in the southern and eastern portions. Regardless of the geography of their birthplace, they shared ancestral beliefs and aristocratic views from the very pinnacle of a slave-based, agrarian economy.

Thomas S. Beverly Tucker, local student and grandson of St. George Tucker, spoke first, as additional students; brothers James and Henry Dix, Henley T Jones, Jr., J.D. Myers, L.P. Slater, J.V. Bidgood and W.H.E. Morecock[17] joined them at the tavern.

"Gentlemen, as we have discussed many times we have many proud traditions, not the least of which is leadership in politics and governance. Yet, of late, I fear our beloved Old Dominion has slipped from its former and I might add, rightful place of leadership in these matters. Our state's premier role dates to, if not predates the Revolution, and we must act now to restore her as leader." The present state of the nation presents us this rare opportunity to show how Virginia can, and must again lead. Gentlemen it is up to us," Tucker concluded, his fervor bringing a hearty round of cheers accompanied by great toasts of ale.

Next, Richard Wise, son of Virginia governor Henry Wise chimed in, "Yes, and just look at within our own lifetimes, since our childhood we have seen a period of rapid technological innovation. Railroads, the telegraph and large-scale manufacturing are being installed everywhere in the North, but here in the South these advances are far less accomplished, if at all. In many areas, we have nothing but dirt, crops and livestock. Our tardiness in adopting innovation means the South is being left behind, every day fallin' further behind the North, and under its domination, economic and otherwise. We need not look North to see that with development and technology come wealth, status and power." Lately, these have all been going to the North, have they not?" Catching his breath, he continued, "We've all grown up with the expectation, if not duty and birth-right, to take our places as leaders of society and with it, our rightful privileges!" This brought another round of cheerful agreement, and again more ale. "But I fear everything our ancestors built and what

---

17 op. cit.

we've strived for is threatened by Northern invaders and their abolitionist supporters. Gentlemen, as long as the South is denied the progress enjoyed by the North, we lose any promise of wealth, influence, or even status quo. We stand to lose all, and I do not intend to stand idly by," his conclusion bringing the wildest cheering yet.

"So what do we do?" Thomas Barlow asked after noise subsided enough to be heard.

"I'll tell you," Wise volunteered, "First, we activate our student company. If 'Old Buck' wants to remain Captain he's going to have to allow us to train. There's so much to do; marksmanship, drill and ceremony, military customs and courtesies, I say we must be ready for the inevitable. We can't let 'Old Buck' stand in our way any longer."

Tom Tucker who'd called the meeting to order, again spoke up, "So we agree about this Northern threat, and hearing you all today, can we now conclude the threat, no let us say, the reality of Civil War in our lives is both a calamity and an opportunity. This is our chance to honorably lead Virginia, free her from damn Abolitionists threatening our traditional way of life, and the industries taking our natural resources and the fruits of our hard labors for a mere fraction of their true worth, then turn around and demand we buy their finished goods at ridiculously inflated prices. Long ago the threat was from England, but now it's from the North. Gentlemen the birth of the Confederacy is our opportunity to assume our rightful role and lead the new Southern nation. And, I hasten to add, this is entirely consistent with the tradition of our founding fathers. Virginia will be re-established as a leading state and home of opposition to foreign tyranny, and Gentlemen, we are the ones to make this happen." His conclusion brought more cheers, seconded by all with another round of ale.

Although a consensus was emerging that war was imminent and they were going to do something; exactly who was going to do what and when was far from clear. Many spoke longingly of returning home to join up, but whether this was just idle boasting made easy by drink among friends, remained to be seen. Gradually the meeting began to break up as anyone who had anything to say did so, and funds for ale ran low. Tavern keepers learned of the college closure and wasted no time in cutting off credit they extended students. They feared, with good reason, the difficulty of ever collecting accumulated debts once closure sent students packing.

Down Main Street another meeting was getting underway at Charlton's coffeehouse. President Ewell invited faculty members to discuss some of the very issues the students argued. Joining Ewell in the large front room and spilling onto the adjacent broad porch were professors Edward S. Jones, Thomas P. McCandlish, Hanover County native Charles Morris, professor of law, Robert J. Morrison, professor of history, and Thomas T.L. Snead, professor of mathematics. Had he still been on campus, Professor Edwin Taliafero certainly would have attended, but he'd been the first to sign up, joining Confederate ranks the month before, where his brother, William Booth was a Brigadier General.

The gentlemen were soon invited into the rear private meeting room, at the insistence of Mr. R. Charlton, proprietor. "Welcome kind Sirs, here you may attend to your business, unbothered by the overly curious passersby. There is much gossip about these days, and as always, I endeavor to provide the best service, Gentlemen" placing a bottle of brandy on their table.

Opening, President Ewell offered, "Gentlemen, I greatly appreciate your efforts during these difficult times. I know all are quite busy and promise I'll not detain you any longer than necessary. I have a long list of tasks myself in order to close this college in a reasonable manner, but I am concerned our students remain dangerously naïve regarding events of late that set us irreversibly on a path to war. They are overzealous in their support of secession. How can I, or we, urge restraint, get them to think first, and talk things through, before jumping in. This whole affair is a giant bubbling cauldron about to boil over."

Jake McKenzie

Figure 9. College of William & Mary Professor Edwin Taliaferro, first faculty member to sign up as a Confederate officer. (date unknown), Courtesy, Special Collections, Special Collections Research Center, Swem Library, College of William and Mary, Williamsburg, Va.

"It is indeed a witch's brew we stir," someone seconded and much discussion ensued, fortified with coffee enriched with liquor, both of which would soon become scarce due to wartime shortages. Their conversation was lively as usually the case when the topic included politics or students. Though many insights were offered, like their students, not much was specifically agreed upon that Ewell could use to dissuade the student's unbridled zeal to join the fight.

Professor McCandlish, an 1857 graduate of the College, closer in age to the students than most of the faculty, reminded, "Gentlemen, I was educated here at William & Mary, while most of you and the balance of the faculty, took academic training at Northern institutions, in some cases, many years ago. Your thought and philosophy reflect those roots, quite naturally, and that era. Gentlemen, I mean no criticism, rather, this is fact and it shapes, even unconsciously, students' views, and yours of them.

McCandlish's views were seconded by Professor Thomas T. L. Snead, another William & Mary graduate, the year before McCandlish. "While students are indeed zealous," Snead agreed, "perhaps sometimes overly so, and some may seem naïve, you must consider their background and upbringing. Their expectations are quite unlike anything you experienced, either in the north or during your youth. Most students have never traveled north, not even a short visit, so have no firsthand knowledge of what you take for granted. For that matter, many have never even been anywhere outside the South. Most of you have lived, worked, and gone to school throughout the nation and many abroad. Our students have simply had no such experiences. In their youthful enthusiasm, they tend to see things as absolute, not taking time to appreciate nuances of complex issues. They do not appreciate subtleties, and what they perceive as a problem or shortfall, they endeavor to fix. They'd rather implement their solution right away, than take time to analyze, or wait for someone else to develop a better solution."

Although President Ewell and some of the other faculty were gaining a somewhat better understanding of their students' position, their discussion reached the point where little more was to be gained and the meeting was adjourned. President Ewell headed back down Main Street towards campus returning upstairs to his office to receive a friend from West Point, Colonel John. B. Magruder, finding him already waiting.

"Good to see you, Colonel," President Ewell said warmly.

"Likewise, Ewell, I am sure. You've done well, President of the College." Not waiting for Ewell's response, "Do you offer theatre? Perhaps I might provide a dramatic reading? Some say I have flair, you know," Magruder kidded, "that I fancy myself a frustrated actor, can you imagine?"

"Yes, Colonel, so I've heard and I well recall you favored oratory. Care for a drink?"

"Don't mind if I do. Yes, those were the days," Magruder reminisced. "What brings me here today, besides the pleasure of renewing old friendship, has precious little to do with acting. On second thought, perhaps this does belong in the theatre of the absurd…. I'm tasked with trying to stop the growing Union Army with a handful of hard luck farmers. Anyway, Ewell, I need your help. Since late last month I'm charged with defense of the Peninsula. The Yankees are building up Fort Monroe to launch an attack on Richmond. How many blue bellies they plan to send God only knows. Press called it, 'the stride of a giant,' or something to that effect. Now, Ewell, what I am about to share with you, must not leave this room. Do I have your sworn secrecy?

"Why, yes, of course."

"Very well, Ewell it is my considered estimation, and do not repeat this, that we'd be hard pressed to fend off an attack, our manpower being so woefully short."

Such a pronouncement from the commander of Confederate forces of the Peninsula caught President Ewell by surprise. Understanding the ramifications, including possible loss of Richmond, and early demise of the Confederacy, not to mention loss of the College, brought a rise to Ewell's bushy eye brows, "My God, what are you going to do John?"

"Well couple of things, Ewell. Some, I'm not at liberty to discuss at this time, however, suffice it to say, I am here to ask your assistance."

"Yes, of course," Ewell exclaimed, "but what, what could I possibly do?"

"A couple of things actually, so don't underestimate," Magruder replied. "First, manpower. As you can hopefully appreciate, I've requested additional troops from General Johnston, repeatedly in fact, but for a variety of reasons we won't discuss now, even if Johnston should send me all the troops he can spare, it's only a fraction of what's required, and, no tellin' how long before any of 'em actually arrive. I can't man defenses with empty promises! Benjamin, we can't wait for what might eventually arrive from somewhere else. I need you to form up a local unit, a kind of home guard, if you will. A lot of men have already signed up, but there's still quite a few around that haven't. And your college students – a bunch of them are ready to go I expect," Magruder speculated.

"Indeed! Ironic you mention that. I was just meeting with the faculty on this very point. The students strike me as hot heads, many of them, anyway. They really don't have much patience for reason and caution," Ewell lamented.

"Good," Magruder interrupted. "That's the very sort I need in the ranks, Benjamin. The time for debate is long past. This is war. That damn Yankee Dimick fella down to Monroe has turned all the big guns around, aiming 'em at Hampton! And they brought in a new General, politician, not real military. He's already stirring up trouble with a new policy that runaway slaves are no longer returned to their rightful owner, but become 'Contrabands of war,' he calls it. Can you imagine? Damndest thing I ever heard. Why they'll be no South as we know it left anymore Benjamin should these Yanks prevail, God forbid. Who knows what they'll do to your college?" Magruder posited, confident this not-so-subtle barb would hook his friend. "I need you, Ewell to lead an effort to get the remaining men from these parts, your students included, to form up a local unit. Without every man the Yanks could roll right up the Peninsula, take Yorktown, Williamsburg and your college, and continue right on in to Richmond."

Ewell's brow furrowed deeply, "John, I shudder to think what may happen should they get their hands on the college. Everything so many have labored for since 1693 would be lost. I cannot allow that to happen. I can't be the last president of the College of William & Mary! Some students came to me months ago wanting to form a unit, said it was just for training and several faculty have spoken of joining, and Professor Taliafero did so last month. Okay, I will do it. Form a local unit and help stop this madness," Ewell agreed.

"Good!" Magruder exclaimed. "Benjamin, the students are right about the training. It takes a long time to turn out a soldier. We can't in good conscience put school boys still wet behind the ears on the firing line without ensuring they're ready. Benjamin, you'd not believe how long it takes just to get troops equipped. Better you get right on it while there is still time. We'll talk more about this later, but at the same time the unit is forming I also need you to oversee layout of the town's defense. You remember, earth redoubts along a line, actually a couple of lines between them and us. Someone that knows what they are doing has to manage this. We can't afford to have 'em sited incorrectly. If fields of fire are at the wrong angle, anything could put us in jeopardy. Come ride with me and I'll show you what I have in mind for a defensive line just east of town. I've had a preliminary look and what I propose will provide defense of Williamsburg, and your College. It would run along a line connecting the head of College Creek over to Queens Creek. That way ravines and waterways reduce the length we have to defend.

"Sure, glad to help, but John it's been many years since I've done military terrain analysis and preparation of the battlefield," Ewell cautioned.

"Benjamin, it will come back to you naturally. I remember at West Point you were one of the best. You always had a good eye for topography."

"Yes, I can do that," Ewell volunteered, glad to be entrusted with such an important role. There was no longer anything he could do to prevent war. They were here and more were arriving daily. All they could do, like everyone on the Peninsula, was try to prepare for whatever was coming.

"Benjamin, thank you," Magruder said, rising to leave, their firm handshake turning into a bear hug. "Good to see you again my friend. I knew I could count on you, Ewell."

"Of course, I'll do whatever I can," Ewell replied, realizing he had to take a stand, and just had. Much as he wished this whole secession business would disappear, he knew it wouldn't. He could watch everything he'd worked for his entire life destroyed, or he could do what he must in order to try to preserve it. "John, about that dramatic reading, well yes I am sure the students would enjoy it, someday. But for now, I am sad to say, college's closed."

"Very well, I'll look forward to returning, after the war, when you've reopened, bigger and better than ever. Hopefully, won't be that long. We'll teach the Yanks a lesson and drive 'em back north for good. Once we do, we can get back to life as it's supposed to be. I tell you Ewell, I don't aim to let them dictate action on the Peninsula. I'm going to take the fight to them. That's another reason we'll need your unit just as soon as you can pull it together and train 'em. I'll send the Captain around to manage day to day tasks getting everyone signed up, equipped, trained, etc."

"And who serves as Captain?" Ewell inquired.

"Right now it's Captain Henley, John Henley, I recall, but I've heard he's not in favor. The men elect their leader you know, so by the time they reorganize, Henley might be out. Regardless, we need your backing and leadership to make the unit successful, as well as your expertise in design and construction of the defense works."

"Very well, and you shall have it," Ewell declared. "And John what is the name of this new unit?"

"Company C, 32nd Regiment, Virginia Infantry. But we'll call it,

'Williamsburg Junior Guard'." And with that Magruder turned and strode from Ewell's office, rejoining his aide outside, and riding off at a full gallop, plume and gold sash flying.

Though he'd taken no notice in his hurried departure, Magruder had ridden right past one of the young men he'd referred to in making his case to President Ewell. Enjoying the shade of massive oaks surrounding the Wren building, young Thomas J. Barlow sat thinking about what he and the other students had discussed. At fifteen years of age, one moment he'd been one of the sixty students at the College, but now, he and his fellow young gentlemen were putting aside Latin, natural mathematics, and philosophy to take up arms. Thomas was both excited and keenly disappointed. He'd enjoyed the intellectual stimulation and the camaraderie of fellow students. As privileged sons of landowners whose holdings were the size of counties, Thomas and friends were being groomed to assume their rightful place as leaders of commerce and society throughout Virginia and the South. Now, their opportunity for status and power at the apex of aristocracy were threatened.

What am I supposed to do? Thomas pondered. Many of his friends had already left, making their way home, mostly throughout the Old Dominion but a few to the Deep South. Some had already signed up to serve in Confederate ranks and many more hastened to do so. Even College President Benjamin S. Ewell, West Point class of 1830 and anti-secessionist, had finally decided to serve and Robert E. Lee himself appointed him a Major of volunteers.

No matter how long Thomas thought answers eluded him. *Was armed conflict the way to solve political disagreement? What would College alumni like Thomas Jefferson think of the current state of the nation's affairs? It hadn't been that long since the founding fathers struggled to throw off colonial rule and lay down founding principles of democracy. Rather than healthy civil discourse, the young nation is split apart. What is to be my role in this?* Thomas wondered.

Pulling out his lap desk, ink bottle, and quill, Thomas wrote his former classmate and good friend, Dessie Barziza in the hope that putting thoughts to paper might clarify things. Thomas penned…

"My good friend, Dessie,

Where to begin? So much has changed since you graduated. Today, I fear marks a dark day indeed in the history of our beloved alma mater. President Ewell announced the College is closed. Not suspension, mind you, but closed, and most of the students already left, those remaining making haste to return home straight away. Many are signing up and though I fear father may not approve, I hasten to join myself and come serve alongside you. Wherever are you now posted? Pray you'd show me what I need to know to be a soldier and if we might, by God's good grace, serve together. We'd surely keep one another safe. Do advise my friend, on how I might pursue that eventuality? Rumors this very day are that President Ewell is to become a Colonel and form a grand regiment from locals and students for the defense of our fair town. Can you imagine Yanks tryin' to destroy this ancient seat of learning? Such affront we shall not endure!

Dessie I am torn. Though I am not one to fight, I dare not sit idly by and watch our very way of life and all that we hold dear, destroyed.

But enough thoughts of war, allow me to close on a happier note, I have of late; found a great fondness, indeed I would say, infatuation, with Miss Victoria King. You recall she is the beautiful daughter of Dr. and Mrs. King. I hear the good doctor himself will soon be 'Colonel' as the army has a great want of surgeons. Many here say Dr. Kings' medical skills will be in dire need soon, but I do not mean to dwell on war. Rather, my heart is smitten with Miss Victoria, and must close now to call on her, begging she will hear me out when I ask that she await my return. Everyone says the war will be over quick as we drive the blue devils back north. Yes, good Sir, I must this very day bare my heart and thereby hope to learn her true feelings. Oh, but if they'd never started this fight!

Signed,
your most obedient servant,

Thomas Barlow"

Though several years older than Thomas, Dessie had befriended him when he arrived on campus and they became fast friends. His parents, Philip and Cecilia had actually named him, 'Decimus et Ultimus,' or '10th and last' but everyone knew him as 'Dessie.' His father came to America in 1814 to claim his inheritance of the Ludwell-Paradise house and gained citizenship marrying Williamsburg native, Cecelia Amanda Bellette. Later, he served as keeper of the insane asylum, and despite the large family, Philip and Cecelia somehow managed to send Dessie, who showed great promise, to the College of William & Mary. After graduation Dessie, like many young men of his day, sought adventure and headed west. Later as the threat of war mounted, Dessie obtained a commission as Lieutenant in his county militia in Texas, "Robertson's Five Shooters."

As Thomas finished his letter, his slave interrupted. "Master, here's dem biscuits you wanted," returning from running Thomas' morning errands. It was not unusual for students to have their personal slaves with them at college. Who else would look after them? While intended to free young masters from daily chores allowing their full pursuit of intellectual endeavors, the arrangement seemed to have failed in this original purpose. A quite different effect resulted when earlier there had seemingly been no end to nightly mischief, most carried out in the wee hours before dawn. The slaves, often carefully instructed and coached by their young masters, became convenient scapegoats to blame for the nightly pranks, despite their guilt being limited to following master's orders. But, the time of youthful foolishness was waning. Closure of the college, departure of friends, and threat of war; curtailed previous frivolity.

"There up ahead, that's Captain Cook," Thomas exclaimed, guiding fellow students towards the commotion. A throng of men and boys gathered under cover of several large shagbark hickories in the Wren Building yard. "And there's Dr. King."

"Hello Dr. King," Thomas called out, "I'm here to sign up." Like Ewell, Thomas concluded there was no point in delaying, and there was some sense of satisfaction in joining up with his peers. They were all in this together and would see each other through.

"Very well, Thomas. Captain Cook, I can vouch for this young man, Thomas Barlow," Dr. King announced.

"Good day young man. A student at the college I expect," Captain Cook inquired, already mentally separating Thomas from the mostly illiterate, poor whites that were every bit as 'slaved' to marginal sharecropped lands, as the blacks.

The Captain had very practical reasons in drawing distinctions among his new troops. He'd need an aide-de-camp, trustworthy messengers, those who could read a map or transcribe orders. He also needed to know who'd run off at the first sign of danger or the moment the Sergeant Major wasn't watching. But, whether illiterate backwoodsmen, dirt-poor share croppers, or privileged sons of wealth and means, Captain Cook knew he had precious little time to mold them into soldiers. Creating a cohesive force capable of doing anything, including defending their homes, would take time, which he knew he had precious little.

"Sir, yes and my studies were progressing well enough, if I may say Sir,"

Thomas replied. "But now it's closed and everything's changed," Thomas observed wistfully.

"Not as much change as you're gonna see presently," the Captain responded dourly. "Get in line to sign enlistment papers. We'll get you equipped and then you'll have one last chance to go back, get your affairs in order and report back here as soon as possible. You'll be in Colonel Ewell's unit, the 'junior guard' we call 'em. College lads and professors -only time will tell what kind of soldiers y'all make. Slave coming?"

"Why yes Sir," Thomas stammered, having never thought otherwise, though it now occurred to him they'd never spoken a word of it between them.

"Very well, then have him wait with your belongings over there with the other slaves. You understand Private Barlow, once in camp your slave works for me, doing whatever needs to be done. He's no longer your personal servant."

"Yes Sir," was all Thomas could manage. Overhearing the Captain's instructions, his slave had a feeling of impending doom, dragging his master's heavy trunk over to where others of his lot waited. The pile of belongings; trunks, chests, and carpet bags had grown into a small mountain. Fortunately, the army had wagons, having commandeered just about everything with wheels for miles around, and a small train approached presently. These and the recruits would have to wait, for it was not yet time to depart.

"Fall in!" Sergeant Major shouted as all scurried to comply with their new master, the army of the Confederacy at war.

"First order of business is getting you outfitted. There're two Quartermaster wagons yonder with supplies. That'll do for some. The rest have to make to do 'til we see about supplies from the general store. Whatever can still be had? As soon as the wagons are emptied that's our next stop."

While Sergeant Major was addressing his new recruits, Capt. Octavius Cook, newly elected commander, Company C, 32nd Virginia infantry was trying to compose a note to send to the town's store keepers. He was concerned, and rightly so, based on past experience, the Quartermaster would fail to furnish supplies and equipment needed by his men, and prove unable to make good on back orders. Captain Cook was looking out for his men, trying to ensure they had the equipment needed to not only fight but live in the field.

Civil War Comes Home

"Dear Mr. Vest, Mr. Greenhow, et. al.

Regarding recent news, on behalf of the Army of Virginia, and as leader of the Williamsburg Junior Guard, I regret to inform that Army Quartermaster issue items for our men are in woefully short supply. I therefore urge your generous sale or donation of such supplies and equipment that may be available from your inventory for our mutual defense and support of our Southern cause.

> Signed
> your most humble servant,
> Capt. O. Cook"

"Here Sergeant, have one of the aides make a copy for each merchant in town. We require their support in equipping the men. Quartermaster wares won't go far," Capt Cook explained.

"Yes Sir," the Sergeant replied, impressed his boss was planning ahead for the men's well being. *Not all the officers were concerned about the ranks,* the sergeant knew.

"Private Barlow isn't it" the Sergeant called out, not yet sure of everyone's identity with so many new faces, "You know this town right?" Not waiting for an answer, "Come here, into the headquarters tent and in your best penmanship copy this letter. One for each merchant in town, Mr. William Vest, Richard Greenhow, and any store that may have supplies we'll need. Then deliver the message quick as you can direct to each.

"Yes Sergeant," Pvt. Barlow replied, eager to perform his first task in uniform. Well, he wasn't exactly in uniform yet, as they all still wore their civilian clothes, and though he'd not yet taken the oath of allegiance, he already thought himself a soldier. "Certainly, I know the shops, and the general store," Thomas replied.

"Good, then get busy and return here post haste."

Pvt. Barlow immediately made the copies in his best handwriting and set out as ordered. It was not a particularly challenging task, but it was his first and Thomas strode Main Street with a new sense of purpose. It was a fine day, the hint of coming Spring in the clear bright still-winter chill, the red maples just budding. Thomas wondered what Victoria would think of him now that he was as soldier?

He hadn't long to day dream for soon came to the general store and was surprised to find the door locked. Despite repeatedly pounding and calling out, there was no answer. Discouraged at being thwarted in his first task, Thomas went on to the next shops, figuring he'd return later. He was spotted by Mr. William Peachy whose law office was but a short distance from the general store. Seeing the lad hurrying about with sheaf of notes, Mr. Peachy's curiosity got the better of him.

"Young man, may I be of assistance?"

"Thomas Barlow Sir, err, begging your pardon Sir, Pvt. Barlow. I have a message from Captain Cook, commander of…"

"I know who Captain Cook is!" cutting him off. "Here let me see that." Peachy snapped, opening the note, he read as Thomas, shifting his weight from side to side, waited patiently. Peachy thought, *war is going to bring significant business opportunity. Government contracts will buy all manner of goods. Prices are going to go up, way up, especially when women start runnin' out of things. With factories shutting down or switching to production of war materiels and the blockade, prices will be driven ever higher. Why, one could make a substantial profit in coming months off an inventory of just about any general merchandise. A very profitable margin is to be made selling every last item off the shelf. Folks will be outbidding one another. But, I sure as hell don't want to become a storekeeper. I could sell the entire lot and clear a tremendous profit.*

"Sir, I have to give this message to Mr. Vest. Do you know where I might find him?" Thomas inquired, almost pleading.

"Yes, so I see," Peachy replied

"I've been by the store but it's locked tight."

"I'm not surprised. My wife said something about Mrs. Vest wanting to quit this place to return to her family home in Henrico. But they can't have left just yet," Peachy offered. "Try going round back, the stairs lead to the Vest home above the store. You might find 'em there."

"Thank you Sir."

"No, it is I who thanks you," Peachy muttered under his breath, thinking, *I shall call on Vest myself after he's read the Captain's note. Then I may pay a call on the good Captain so I may better know his requirements. But all in due time,* Peachy concluded.

Thomas, though puzzled by Peachy's sudden interest in the Captain's note, headed to the store straightaway; relieved to see this time it had reopened. After showing Mr. Vest the Captain's note, Thomas wasted no time rejoining his unit. Though tempted to detour via the King residence to see Victoria, he took his new duties too seriously to delay.

When Thomas got back, most everyone in the unit, except slaves, had brogams, blanket, and a firearm. Some, especially slaves also carried an eclectic but necessary assortment of odds and ends; from pots, pans, and ladles, to horseshoes, hammer, and nails.

"Fall in!" the Sergeant Major bellowed, preparing for their first in ranks inspection. He and Captain Cook personally checked each soldier, with particular emphasis on adequate shot, powder, and ball. Noting the men's shoulder-slung haversacks filled with everything from salt-cured smoked hams to sacks of flour, salt, cornmeal and coffee, the leaders were pleased. Having troops well-fed led to good morale. Although they were well-stocked now, they knew it was a temporary condition. But having adequate supplies was only the first step in establishing camp life.

Most of the men didn't know the first thing about cooking. Nor did they know much about caring for themselves. Many of the youth had come directly from mother's care, while older fellows were equally helpless, having grown accustomed, though refusing to admit it, to being more or less dependent upon doting wives, slave cooks, and in some cases, mistresses for their meals, laundry, and hygiene.

"All right move out," came the order once the leaders satisfied themselves with enough inspecting for the moment. Certainly more would follow. The rag tag formation headed out of town, not east towards the enemy as many naively expected, but the opposite direction. They strolled more than marched, down a winding farm lane through a large grove of towering long-needle pines –their massive trunks the makings of ship masts down at the boat yards of Yorktown. The dark green crowns swayed in the bright blue early Spring sky, a circling red tail hawk screeching displeasure at having his hunt disturbed.

Thomas' slave wondered about their direction of march, daring to question his master in a cautious whisper, "Suh, ain't we headed the wrong way?"

"Shush, remember now," Thomas counseled, "we're soldiers. Don't be questioning the leaders or you'll find yourself in a mess of trouble and I can't help you. Just do what they say. You don't expect we're ready to face the Yanks yet do you? Why we ain't even fired our weapons, and we are just now marching, if you call it that, for the first time. We got a lot of training 'fore we see any Yanks," Thomas patiently explained. "And don't be talkin' in ranks," Thomas advised, lest you want the Sergeant Major on your case."

As Thomas hoped, they weren't going far carrying all their gear. Just west of town the farms and pastures supplying the college's kitchens were just far enough -beyond prying eyes of curious townsfolk, but not so far that messengers couldn't be sent to town. With pending college closure, no crops had yet been planted, leaving plenty of open space to encamp the entire company with room nearby for drill and target practice. The college's few remaining hogs, poultry, and cattle would soon be dispatched, adding to their food supplies. Hardly anyone was around to care for livestock and Captain Cook knew the importance of feeding troops well. Feasting made a great start for unit camaraderie and reducing absenteeism. Besides, many lads hadn't been eating all that well even in the best of times, and though some may get homesick, with a full spread of victuals, no one thought of leaving. Captain Cook also knew their good fortune in availing themselves of this largess, and that it was most certainly a temporary windfall. Hunger and deprivation would haunt them soon enough, but for now they feasted.

Pitching tents and setting camp took a while since there was a military way by which this and everything had to be accomplished, and these requirements were unknown to the recruits. Though it took repeated attempts to pitch tents, eventually camp was made and it was on to other matters, marksmanship topping Captain Cook's list.

Though he'd managed to arm each man, whether anyone could hit anything remained to be seen and he was anxious to determine how well his assemblage of college boys, clerks, slaves, and share croppers could shoot.

The men huddled within assigned squads, while others set up the firing range –the split rail fence around the pasture adorned with assorted bottles, tins, and such, the men stepping off 50 paces for the firing line. Even at that comparatively short distance their weapons were not particularly accurate. Squads took turns firing, and the training took on a festive air, bets placed among competing squads. Both Captain Cook and Sergeant Major were pleased when nearly every trooper demonstrated he could reliably hit targets even from increasing distance. However, both leaders knew stationary targets were one thing, moving ones quite another, especially when they fired back! Slaves watched their masters, placing side bets of their own, but did not participate of course for it was unheard of to arm a slave.

Balancing their supply of ammunition against the need for target practice, Sergeant Major called a halt to the shooting. This elicited howls of protest from squads needing just one more round to better their score and win all bets. Although firing practice was now concluded, Sergeant Major allowed shooting to continue at moving targets.

"Bird, squirrel, rabbit or other game is fair target," he pronounced, which brought an onslaught that soon cleared surrounding environs of everything bigger than a field mouse. It was a wonder no person was hit. As firing for the day drew to a close, camp fires were stoked and stew pots and skillets broken out, soon receiving freshly dressed small game. Arguments as to who was the better shot persisted, but were soon replaced by who was the better cook.

Initially, slaves kept their own camp fire, separate from white troops, though in time this would change largely as a practical matter, for there wasn't always that much firewood to be had. Thomas' slave gazed into the embers, wondering what his friends were doing, and what following Master Thomas into the army would hold for him, not that he'd had any say in the matter.

That night they all got an introduction to camp life as winds picked up, rustling tall pines and tent flaps all night. By morning temperature dropped, bringing a light frost and many didn't want to get out from under blankets when reveille sounded. *And so damn early too*, they noted. "Rise and shine, we got work to do," came the unwelcome call of the First Sergeant. Thomas stirred, wishing he was back in college. *There we could get up whenever we wanted, and go to the tavern*, he recalled fondly. Turned out from comforts of hearth and home, they were just beginning to understand what it meant to be a soldier. They wouldn't have to wait long to learn of the exploits of brothers in arms.

***

June 1861
First Fight: The Battle of Big Bethel

Virginia's Lower Peninsula

While General Butler's Union forces had scant information on the enemy's strength and disposition, or anything else beyond Fort Monroe's walls, such was not the case for Colonel John B. Magruder. The Confederates utilized a network of sympathizers and informants including businessmen with legitimate travel between the lines, as well as newspaper boys. Transiting Union lines at will, young lads had no problem selling out the papers, for the troops far from home eagerly sought any news. Under this ruse the boys were not suspect, or at least not often, until one senior Union officer caught on, annotating his journal,

"The rest of the day we remained…undisturbed…and reading the Richmond journals, two small newsboy's commendable enterprise having come through our lines from the Confederate capital to sell their papers. They were sharp youngsters, and having come well supplied, they did a thrifty business. When their stock in trade was disposed of they wished to return, but they were so intelligent and observant that I thought their mission involved other purposes than the mere sale of newspapers, so they were held till we (had moved) and then turned loose."[18]

Between newsboys, traveling businessmen, and sympathetic local

---
18 Markle, D. E. pg. 65.

residents, Prince John kept abreast of Union developments, especially the reinforcement of Fort Monroe and satellite Camps Hamilton and Butler. While keeping close watch and trying to anticipate Federal plans, Magruder kept his men busy preparing defensive works at several sites across the Peninsula. The men busily felled trees but mostly dug, hurriedly constructing a strongly fortified outpost at a cross roads in the eastern area known as Big Bethel. The site was purposely far-forward of the planned main defensive line and close enough to Fort Monroe to keep a watchful eye on the Yankees. West of the Big Bethel outpost Magruder had his men preparing the first of several defensive lines spanning the width of the Peninsula, about a dozen miles or so. Verdant landscape was soon scarred by long trenches, connected to form a network of overlapping firing positions. Avenues of approach were strewn with felled trees, their sharpened branches facing the anticipated enemy. Damming or diverting small streams made them too deep to ford and flooded pastures and fields turning them into marshy quagmires, no longer passable by man or beast. Huge mounds of excavated soil were turned into redoubts and redans with multiple gun emplacements surrounding a central bomb-proof powder magazine. Long days of hard labor stretched into weeks, Magruder pushing his troops relentlessly. The net result was a completely transformed landscape.

When the line was finally complete, the men thought their weeks of 'spade work' as they called it, were finally over, but celebrations were cut short, as they were ordered to move on, beginning work anew creating another line further west. There was to be not just one defensive line, but three such works, each successively further west. By incorporating natural terrain features, especially rivers, tidal creeks and marshes, Magruder shortened the distance requiring pick and shovel work by a good two-thirds.

The western most defenses, just east of Williamsburg, surveyed and laid out by his friend Benjamin Ewell, consisted of fourteen earthen bastions connecting College Creek, draining southerly to the James, to Queen's Creek flowing northeastward to the York. Magruder hoped they'd never need the Williamsburg line but it was a good fall-back position should they be forced to withdraw from the main line running from the Warwick River in the south, northward to the revamped Revolutionary War earth works surrounding Yorktown.

The Confederate lines were designed to allow defense in depth, i.e. the occupied line would be held as long as possible until defenders withdrew to prepared positions further in the rear. As the Peninsula was the Union's direct land route to Richmond, Magruder knew it must be defended at all cost. General Lee's plan to trade distance for time, slowing the attacking superior force was strategically sound, but others had differing opinions as we shall see.

However, the pressing matter now was firepower, specifically the lack thereof. There remained far too few troops to man the line, and most gun emplacements remained empty. There was a severe want of artillery for either it was already deployed elsewhere, or had yet to be forged, despite Richmond's Tredegar iron works going to three shifts, seven days a week. With these critical shortages of men and armaments a strategic plan to give up terrain to gain time in fighting a delaying action was the only practicable means of dealing with overwhelming Yankee troop strength and firepower. Lee, Johnston, Magruder, and their subordinate officers understood they could never fight a war of attrition against the industrialized North with its many factories and endless supply of immigrant troops.

Colonel Magruder was not shy about his need for troops and weapons when he proudly showed the results of his men's labors to visiting dignitaries. General Robert E. Lee and later, Magruder's immediate commander, General Joseph E. Johnston were duly impressed. Although the defense works were pronounced more than adequate, no matter how stalwart, the nagging question remained, would there be troops enough to man them? Despite the confidence Magruder and Lee shared, General Johnston and President Jefferson Davis remained vexed. Even the best defenses were useless when emplacements remained empty and trenches so thinly manned, soldiers could barely hear a comrade on either side. From Magruder in Yorktown, Johnston in Manassas, to Lee in Richmond; all worried, would Yankees take advantage and attack?

Colonel Magruder determined he'd not allow the Yankees to make the first move and his staff and subordinate commanders carefully developed plans to conduct their own reconnaissance. *It was one thing to have intelligence on the enemy but quite another to see how he reacted when tested,* Magruder knew.

After reviewing plans most of the night, early the morning of the 6th Magruder announced, "Colonel Hill, your Tarheels will occupy a forward position at Big Bethel, three miles southeast of Half Way House. Your position commands the intersection of local roads and the bridge over Marsh Creek close by the church. You'll be supported by Major Randolph's Richmond battalion of light artillery." Magruder's staff had chosen terrain well, the outpost controlling local roads in several directions, and Magruder chose equally well in selecting Colonel Daniel Harvey Hill and Major Randolph.

Colonel Hill's 1st North Carolina Volunteers, anxious to see action after arriving two weeks prior, quickly set to work. For three days, they rotated using axes and shovels for they had more men than tools and by sunset the 9th had constructed a four-sided redoubt, on the north bank of Marsh Creek well-sited to cover the bridge and roads. "We also constructed a smaller defensive work on the south bank, fearing the slightly higher ground there could afford some advantage, and we leave nothing to chance, Sir," Colonel Hill noted. "Major Randolph placed his guns so as to sweep all approaches...."19

Even as his men dug, Colonel Hill's scouts reported two small enemy raiding parties in the vicinity of Little Bethel, a road intersection some three miles southeast on the road to Fort Monroe. Colonel Hill immediately ordered two companies, each augmented by a howitzer, to engage and the Tarheels soon found the Yankees plundering a farm house of what little food remained. Despite General Butler's prohibition of foraging and depredations of all kinds, Yankees helped themselves. The Richmond Howitzers quickly limbered, sending a shot close by the farm house but without striking it -enough to send surprised Yankees running. Hill's men gave chase, the enemy barely making it back to New Market Bridge entering Hampton. The other Tarheel Company soon engaged in a similar foot race with remaining Yanks with the same outcome.[20]

Later that evening Colonel Magruder received Colonel Hill's report. "Sir, earlier this afternoon, elements of the 1st North Carolinians got word of two Yankee patrols in the vicinity and sought to engage promptly. We found 'em plundering the farm but they ran full stride, just beating my men to New Market Bridge on their way back to Fort Monroe. This being the second race on the same day, over the New Market course, in both of which the Yankees reached the goal first. Afterwards, my Tarheels found a few local men fed up with having farms plundered and slaves stolen, and wanting to join us. Also, we found a few more slaves, seemed like they was making for Fort Monroe but we put them to work on our defenses, Sir," Hill explained.

Though disappointed Yanks had escaped, Magruder resolved, "Very well, Colonel. We'll catch 'em next time. By now, Butler is probably receiving

---

19 Britton, R. op. cit.
20 op. cit.

their reports," Magruder postulated. "Colonel Hill post additional sentries tonight, lest the Yanks dare return."

Fort Monroe, Virginia

Receiving reports on the encounter, General Butler stormed out of his office cursing a blue streak, infuriated his troops were chased all the way back to Fort Monroe. "Convene a meeting of commanders. We must retaliate!" Despite no military experience, Butler estimated he had enough troops to act, and reinforcements were arriving daily. However, whether new troops were ready for action was another matter.

Augmenting the approximately eight hundred 3rd and 4th Massachusetts Volunteers garrisoned, 2nd New York Volunteers arrived the 24th of the previous month but their recently issued uniforms, so shoddily constructed, began falling apart within days. Colonel Carr, Commanding, noted his men, "appeared on parade with blankets wrapped about them to conceal lack of proper garments." Colonel Carr, like General Butler, Lieutenant Colonel Dimick and other commanders, battled seemingly never-ending logistics problems. Accomplishing anything was repeatedly delayed by supply shortfalls that frustrated General Butler's military and political timetables.

Close on the heels of the ill-clad 2nd New York, fellow New Yorkers of the 5th Infantry, under Colonel Andrea Duryea, reported for duty. Their uniforms were also notable, but not for cheap thread or poor tailoring. Quite the opposite, for the 5th wore blousy, full-cut red trousers with white turbans, after the gaudy French style of the Crimean War. Duryea's Zouaves, or "red-legged devils," as they were known, were followed within weeks by 1st Vermont volunteers, and the 1st, 3rd, and 7th New York Regiments, each with their own distinctive uniforms. The 7th New York's grey, rather than traditional Union blue, was adorned with bright white crossed belts which one astute private noted were, "whitened with infinite pain and waste of time, and offered a most inviting target to the foe."[21]

With these reinforcements, Butler's command exceeded sixty-seven hundred troops which far exceeded what could be accommodated at Fort Monroe. Fourteen hundred remained garrisoned there while the balance occupied Camp Hamilton, three miles west under the command of Brigadier General Ebenezer W. Pierce, Massachusetts Volunteer Militia, and Camp Butler in Newport News overlooking the James. With this considerable force at his disposal and irate at the outcome of the recent

---

21 op. cit.

encounter, General Butler was spoiling for a fight. He also saw military action as the best means to advance his political agenda which included grandiose plans to conquer the South and win the war.

Figure 10. Colonel Andrea Duryea, Commander, New York Zouaves (date unknown). Courtesy of the Library of Congress, Washington, D.C.

Figure 11. Colonel Duryea's Zouaves. Courtesy of the Library of Congress, Washington, D.C.

Butler was further enraged to learn, contrary to his recently proclaimed contraband policy, Confederates were seizing slaves, then working them to improve Rebel defenses.

"Tell me again gentlemen," General Butler asked, "how good is our intelligence?"

"Well Sir, we learned the Rebels are close at hand and they're spoilin' for fight, but clearly we need better information," Lieutenant Colonel Dimick offered, wondering, *what's he have in mind now?*

"As I expected," replied Butler. "We must run them out of the area."

Turning to Colonel Duryea, commander of the 5th New York Zouaves, and Brigadier General Pierce, leader of the Massachusetts volunteers, "I want operations mounted as soon as possible. Let 'em know we mean business."

"Very well Sir, I'll set it up," Colonel Duryea responded. "General, it takes time to prepare and there's a lot to be worked out." General Butler wouldn't hear it; he wanted action not excuses.

"Colonel, I'm not talking about a long term operation. Big Bethel is only eight miles northwest. Infantry on the march supported by mounted artillery, resupplied from here if need be. So, when can they be ready?" General Butler inquired, exasperated by the prospect of delay.

"How soon can your Zouaves be ready Colonel?" Not waiting for his answer, General Butler continued, "Sir, Washington sent me here to ensure a strong Federal presence and Fort Monroe has fast become the most secure Union post in the entire South, thanks to the good work of Lieutenant Colonel Dimick." General Butler finally recognized the considerable effort well underway long before his arrival. "But, we'll not win a damn thing staying inside; while Rebels encroach within miles, kidnapping and impressing local men into Rebel service and stealing slaves to work on their defense. Gentlemen, the battle is outside the walls, yet we don't even know enemy strength, or position, save for Big Bethel, let alone his intent. After this recent insult, we know they are far too close. We must drive the enemy from the area," General Butler stated unequivocally.

Lieutenant Colonel Dimick listened carefully. Not in his wildest dreams had he expected a political general to employ his troops. *Now, just weeks since arriving, he's ordering movement against an enemy of unknown strength occupying fortified positions. He's going to get people killed.*

After much wrangling, Colonel Duryea and other commanders formulated a plan in response to Butler's edict. It wasn't particularly detailed or cohesive. In fact, it was merely a collection of individual unit plans rather than comprehensive, but General Butler continued to press and they felt they had to agree on something.

"General, we can be ready on the 8th" Colonel Duryea finally offered. "We'll attack before dawn, catch 'em asleep. My Zouaves will lead off at 2:00 a.m. crossing New Market bridge and we'll be behind Little Bethel." Then Colonel Frederick Townsend added, "I'll follow two hours later with 3rd New York headed to Big Bethel."

"Very well," General Butler replied, "but that's only New York units. What about others? This is not 'New York against the Rebels.' We have other states and they're just as anxious to engage," Butler enjoined, not about to allow Massachusetts volunteers to be left out. Apparently, Duryea's planning involved commanders he knew personally and quite naturally, those were fellow New Yorkers. He hadn't thought to advise those he didn't know, and besides, informing a rival unit reduced one's own chance for glory, and all commanders, Butler included, were anxious to see their names in the print.

"What other units are ready?" Butler asked.

Not wanting to speak for, or against other units, most commanders remained silent despite his direct question. Then Lieutenant Colonel Dimick volunteered, "Sir, that'd be 1st Vermont. They've gotten themselves pretty well-equipped, and for the most part, remain healthy."

"Very well, 1st Vermont, it is. Send for their commander."

"Sir, Colonel Phelps commands. J. Wolcott Phelps, good man, no nonsense New England type," Lieutenant Colonel Dimick replied.

"Sounds like the right man. Best I speak with him directly since he's apparently been left out of planning," General Butler remarked disparagingly, casting a penetrating stare at Colonel Duryea. "Have him alert his unit so the men are getting ready whilst we meet."

"Yes General. Right away, Sir," Lieutenant Colonel Dimick replied, heading out to send a messenger to track down 1st Vermont.

A short time later...

Saluting sharply, Colonel Phelps' inquired, "Sir, you sent for me?"

General Butler turning in his chair, not bothering to return the salute, motioned for him to be seated.

"Pleased to meet you Sir," Colonel Phelps replied, uncertain why he'd been summoned to immediately appear before the Commanding General.

"Colonel, I'm advised your 1st Vermonters are not only healthy and equipped, but ready to go," General Butler opened.

"Indeed Sir, that is correct. I would not have it any other way, Sir." Colonel Phelps said proudly.

"Good, then I need you to march with us to a local crossroads, Big Bethel. The mission is to show the flag, let 'em know we're here and mean business, but also to conduct reconnaissance, gathering information on the enemy's numbers, defensive works, and disposition." Lieutenant Colonel Dimick noticed that General Butler left out the part about retaliating for Rebels having chased his men all the way back to Fort Monroe.

"Yes, Sir," Colonel Phelps replied.

"With your men we'll have nearly forty-four hundred in all, more than sufficient in my estimation to engage and destroy this marauder, should we encounter them under favorable conditions," General Butler explained. "Any questions?"

"No Sir, perfectly clear," Colonel Phelps replied, but wondering, *if he's talking about 'gathering information' why also, 'engage and destroy?'* but thought it best not to question, and went along with the General's initial comment. "I understand Sir. We need better intelligence on what these Rebs are up to. First Vermont is proud to do its part, Sir."

"Good" Butler pronounced, not waiting for further comment. It was clear he was focused on retaliation. Other more experienced officers, more analytical and less emotional, like Lieutenant Colonel Dimick were gravely concerned the planned multi-pronged reconnaissance and attack against both Little and Big Bethel was far more complicated than need be. *There are too many moving pieces*, Dimick thought. Having seen Butler's head strong nature, however, he knew, *Butler would neither wait, nor hear opposing views, no matter how well founded.* Dimick kept his thoughts to himself, while Butler continued.

"General Pierce, you will have overall tactical command, and hold the balance of 7th New York in support, along with three other regiments at Camp Butler as reserves." This surprised not only Brigadier General Pierce but all the other officers present.

"Sir, as you prefer," General Pierce replied, "but I assumed you would be commanding Sir?"

"No, General, I am going to orchestrate the action from Fort Monroe. From there I can send advice and order reinforcements as needed."

"Yes Sir," General Pierce replied, the others silent at this surprising turn of events. *First he is anxious to mount operations as soon as possible, even before units are fully ready,* Dimick considered, *then immediately stakes his claim to the safety of the Fort, whilst others do the fighting.*

"3rd New York will tie white cloth on their left arm," General Butler continued, "and the Zouaves will do likewise. They can use strips from their damn turbans. There's too many different uniforms among these units and I dare say recognizing one another would otherwise prove confusing, especially at night. In addition, troops will use the watchword, 'Boston,' my birthplace, and no attack should be made until the watchword is shouted. When the attack is made the men are to fire a volley then charge with bayonets," Butler instructed.

Shaking his head in disbelief, Lieutenant Colonel Dimick wondered, *where did he get these ideas? He's probably right about units not being able to identify one another, but a volley followed by a bayonet charge in the pitch black? He's going to get a whole lot of people killed!*

In the hurried confusion organizing the operation, General Butler's staff failed to inform Colonel Bendix, commanding officer of 7th New York Regiment, of either the requirement for his men to don white cloth bands on their left arms or use the watchword. The 7th New York continued their preparations without this key information.

At the prospect of an imminent operation, after long months of training, equipping, and waiting, troops and their leaders were both nervous and excited. Colonel Duryea wanted his Zouaves assembled early and ordered 4th Massachusetts and 1st Vermont to fall in several hours ahead of the previously agreed upon schedule. Although many troops were still figuring out how to wear all their gear, 4th Massachusetts managed to assemble by midnight, but 1st Vermont was nowhere to be seen and Duryea became frantic. "Send messengers to find the Vermont outfit!" he was ordering when Lieutenant Colonel Peter Washburn, 1st Vermont suddenly showed up at his tent.

"Sir, begging your pardon, Colonel Phelps sends his regrets."

"What? What do you mean, 'sends his regrets?' We are trying to fight a damn war?"

"No Sir, Colonel Phelps is quite indisposed at the moment. Bad case of the 'Virginia Quickstep,' I regret to inform. "Colonel Phelps has been dancin' all day."

The men laughed at Phelps' plight for they'd all been through it. Diarrhea was a common, if not constant complaint throughout the camps among both officers and enlisted.

"Given this turn of events, I guess you'll lead the Vermonters," Colonel Duryea observed.

A surprised Lieutenant Colonel Washburn couldn't very well object. Besides, he wanted to be in the fight and distinguish himself, like everyone else.

Despite last minute substitution of Vermont commanders, remaining units formed up and were ready to march, also several hours ahead of schedule. Waiting anxiously, it wasn't long before they convinced themselves there was no point in standing around, and headed out. In their haste, they failed to inform anyone of their early departure and this remained unknown to Generals Pierce and Butler and anyone else that was part of the operation. Butler hadn't even bothered to see the departing units off, instead, remaining at his desk. While he was burning the midnight oil signing logistics forms, the long blue line filed out, twisting forth from the sally port.

The men's nerves on edge in the pitch black, 3rd Massachusetts headed west then north toward Little Bethel, General Pierce and staff at the head. After several hours of uneventful marching in the dark, a large number of men were just spotted up ahead, emerging from dense woods along the road, unlimbering an artillery piece.

Before General Pierce or anyone else could understand what was happening, Boom! Suddenly they fired. Volley after volley of murderous musket and cannon fire came screaming down the dark lane directly into the Union soldiers.

"Take cover! Into the woods!" General Pierce screamed, men falling all around him. Momentarily, 3rd New York began returning fire as seconds stretched into timelessness. No one had expected to encounter the enemy until reaching their last known position at the Bethel cross roads, Big or Little. Both were still miles away. Yet, here they were suddenly heavily engaged in a pitched fight. It was not Rebels they faced but Colonel Bendix's 7th New York's murderous fire.

For a full quarter hour, self-inflicted carnage raged. The 'defending' Colonel Bendix and his men knew nothing of the watch word, "Boston," and nothing about identifying friendly forces by white-marked left sleeves. They did recall, however, that according to plan, Union troops would not depart for several more hours. They therefore reasoned these must be enemy and the previously untested troops, kept up a frantic rate of fire in their nervous fervor. Meanwhile, Confederates, in the safety of dug in positions a short distance northwest were now well-warned by prolonged Yankee firing.

Finally, Colonel Bendix whose men had opened fire realized their horrible mistake, frantically calling, "Cease fire! Damn it, Cease fire!" Eventually the trigger-happy troops stopped but not before twenty-two casualties, mostly from Pierce's 3rd New York, lie prostrate, their life-blood staining the sandy soil. Several grievously wounded expired in a matter of minutes. Others writhed in pain as calls went back for the regimental surgeon. The doctor remained at Camp Butler for no one had thought to involve him in planning, nor even inform him the operation was underway. Meanwhile compatriots watched helplessly as there was not a bandage among them and none knew what to do to stop the bleeding.

By the time the surgeon grabbed his medical bag, mounted, and galloped up, many casualties no longer required his services.

Noise of the fire-fight fully alerted the Rebels, eliminating any possibility of a Federal surprise. Other Federals on the march also heard the shots being fired in their rear. As it was still long before their own troops were scheduled to be on the move, they assumed the firing represented an imminent enemy threat and feared they were in danger of being cut off. One error begat another as inexperienced leaders prematurely ordered a hasty retreat. The skitterish units quickly rejoined the reserves even before the operation had begun, effectively removing themselves from subsequent action. They were not the only forces to withdraw, however.

A small Confederate party occupied hasty earthworks at a lone outpost at Little Bethel. Upon hearing the prolonged distant firing, they also thought themselves badly outnumbered and in this, they were correct. Rather than waiting to be overrun and captured, they beat a hasty retreat, vacating their encampment just ahead of the invaders –all but three who tarried too long trying to gather their belongings and were captured by Zouaves and sent to the rear for interrogation.

Given the night's casualties and confusion, and having by now fully alerted the enemy, Colonel Duryea and Lieutenant Colonel Washburn argued against continuing.

"General Pierce, with all due respect, we must retire to Fort Monroe, regroup and try again another day," Colonel Duryea advised.

"General, I concur," Lieutenant Colonel Washburn quickly added. "By now the Confederates are lying in wait somewhere to ambush. Should we continue, we'll surely suffer many additional casualties, but if we withdraw, we preserve our forces to fight another day."

"Gentlemen, we will press this attack! There's no valid reason to fall back now. Regrettably, we suffered casualties yes, but these losses, though costly, are small and our force is well over four thousand. Such losses are NOT, as I need not remind you, a result of enemy action, but stupid mistakes! We cannot retreat without so much as even finding the enemy. I am determined to gain advantage and press on to victory. Now see to your men." Seeing General Pierce was not about to be dissuaded, both commanders did as instructed.

"Very well Sir, but I am on record as opposing," Colonel Duryea added.

"Noted," General Pierce snapped. "Now send a rider to Camp

Butler fast, carrying my orders to bring up 1st and 2nd New York from reserve."

"General, I think it unwise," Duryea again argued. "As you just mentioned Sir, we are over four thousand strong. Part of the reason for the disaster on the road to Little Bethel was we have too many different units on the move and no one coordinating overall operations."

"I thought General Butler was supposed to be doing that!" Pierce snapped angrily.

"Adding more troops now would only increase confusion," a frustrated Duryea postulated, refusing to comment on General Pierce's barbed comment on General Butler's uselessness parked safely behind Fort Monroe's massive stone walls.

"Colonel, I have had quite enough! Were you not a principal planner of this operation you are now so quick to abandon?" General Pierce snarled. "The first defenses we came upon were abandoned in our path. Does this not suggest enemy weakness? We have sufficient troops to force a retreat all along his line and I intend to be the victor in this! Now, can I count on the Zouaves?"

"Of course, General, begging your pardon Sir," Duryea concluded, speaking no further of his differing opinions. Although General Pierce heard the caution, he refused unsolicited advice. More determined than ever, Pierce scurried from one unit to the next, reorganizing his floundering force; still certain glory would be his.

Shortly after 7:00 a.m. Pierce finally had his troops ready to move again. Despite Colonel Duryea's reservations, the Zouaves led the contingent preparing the delayed assault against Big Bethel, supported by two pieces from the 2nd U.S. Artillery under command of Lieutenant John Greble. Because horses had yet to be requisitioned for Greble's unit, their heavy, rifled pieces had to be pulled everywhere by his men. With the friendly fire incident, then General Pierce's hurried regrouping, the artillerymen were already exhausted. Shortly, the sun was fully raised and already building towards the heat of the day and Greble's men inexplicably wore their heaviest woolen uniforms. As Lieutenant Greble's parched men rotated turns performing hard work usually done by horses, word was passed, "I hear there's more than four thousand of 'em entrenched at Big Bethel." This approximated the size of the Union force. Although most of the men lacked combat experience, they understood intuitively that an attack against entrenched troops required a superior force. They also understood that in attacking prepared defenses many among them would soon be casualties. Thus, already nervous troops were understandably on edge about advancing in the open while taking fire from several angles of defilade from prepared, alerted defenders. Only the few veterans among them appreciated how unlikely it was their return fire would find intended targets safely dug in behind dirt and logs. Fired upon at will while approaching fully exposed was not how the Yanks had envisioned their first action.

Simultaneously, a few miles north, Confederate Colonel Magruder was also planning an offensive. He'd ridden hard the thirteen miles south from Yorktown to Big Bethel the evening before and conferred with Colonel Hill and other trusted commanders late into the night. Emboldened by the previous chase of two Yankee units to New Market Bridge, Magruder was determined to take the fight to the invaders. His planning meeting scarcely concluded before he had the entire camp roused at 3:00 a.m. Soon, some six hundred men, not the rumored four thousand the Yanks thought he had, were on the march towards Little Bethel, supported by two artillery pieces. Marching southeast at quick step, they were surprised to see a distraught woman running towards them. Miss Nicholson, daughter of the Elizabeth City County surveyor, was coming from Colonel Mallory's place a few miles above New Market bridge on Sawyer Swamp Road. [22]

"Stop! Yankees is coming!" she shouted.

Quickly brought before Magruder, the young woman tried to explain in between catching her breath, what she'd seen. "Sir, there's several thousand Yankees on the road ahead."

Taking her startling facts as truth, Magruder immediately ordered, "About face!" Although curious, he wondered what business she had alone on a country road in the middle of the night. He was simply thankful for her timely warning and would not risk losing men by being surprised, caught in the open by a far superior force. Without a moment to waste, Magruder had his entire force countermarching back from whence they'd come. One officer, referring to the brave Miss Nicholson who'd risked her life, noted someone, "ought to have a monument erected to commemorate her action."

---

22 West, pg. 65.

Figure 12. Burned out bridge to Hampton, Va. Courtesy of the Library of Congress, Washington, D.C.

In short order, Colonel Magruder's main body was safely back inside their earthworks and soon augmented by some two hundred men of Lieutenant Colonel William Stuart's 15th Virginia Militia occupying the forward earthworks south of Marsh Creek. The "tobacco worms," as Virginia troops were referred to by soldiers from other states, were soon joined by two companies of Tarheels, from Colonel Hill's 1st North Carolina Regiment. Major Edgar B. Montague's battalion of Virginia infantry arrived on the run from Yorktown, taking up positions on the right flank. Here Marsh Creek looped in a wide bend and they hastily threw up a redoubt on the west side of Big Bethel church. Magruder oversaw the hasty reinforcement of his position. With these additional units streaming in at the last minute he'd more than doubled his original strength, to fourteen hundred fifty-eight men. Although his force was doubled, Magruder still had but a third the strength of Pierce, who, fortunately for Magruder, still believed his opposition to be much larger. Otherwise, he may have attacked immediately even as Magruder's men completed last minute preparations.

Just a mile south of Magruder's main defenses, a company of Zouaves, under Captain Hugh Judson Kilpatrick, overran the Confederate picket guards, continuing forward until within sight of Big Bethel. Captain Kilpatrick quickly extracted a scrap of paper from his coat pocket and penciled a crude diagram of what lay ahead.

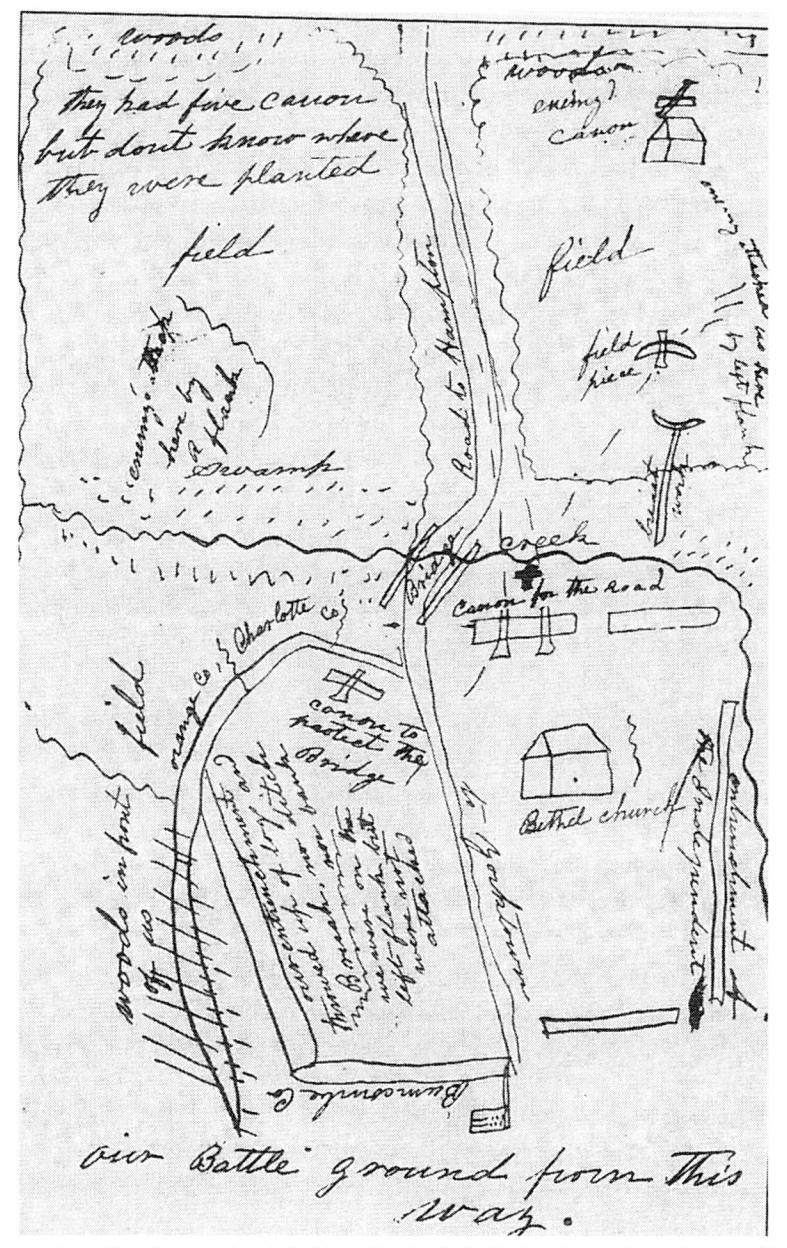

Figure 13. Sketch map, battlefield at Big Bethel. Variously attributed to the Daily Press Newspaper, Newport News, VA or the City of Hampton, VA.

"Quick man, get this to General Pierce immediately," the Captain ordered his messenger. The quickly drawn sketch showed the main enemy body dead ahead dug in behind Marsh Creek, flowing west to east. The road to Big Bethel, known locally as Sawyer Swamp Road, ran straight ahead due north, and a bridge crossed nearly perpendicular the creek directly under Magruder's guns. When Pierce received Kilpatrick's sketch of the enemy disposition, he saw the field as divided left and right by the road and bridge, both well-controlled by the enemy. On the right, Kilpatrick had penciled in dense woods and the swampy fields and marshes which Pierce estimated would become a quagmire stalling any advance. To the west, left of the road, prospects appeared somewhat better as most of the ground was open except for a large peach orchard and several farm houses and associated small out buildings. These were serviced by a farm lane intersecting the main road and continuing westward for a mile to a natural ford of Marsh Creek. Some concealment might be found in the orchard for the peach trees had recently leafed out, and the buildings offered cover to Federal sharpshooters. Otherwise the area was completely dominated by the strength of the Confederate position.

Acting on Kilpatrick's map, General Pierce ordered, "Kilpatrick, take three companies of Zouaves down the road, rest of 5th New York advance on the right in the woods." While Duryea's men moved forward on the right, Colonel Townsend's 5th New Yorkers advanced into the orchard just west of Kilpatrick's forces and the road. Lieutenant Greble's men, laboring to the point of collapse moving heavy pieces across soft soils, made for the intersection of the farm driveway and the main road, a position approximating the center of Magruder's line.

By 9:00 a.m. Magruder's men gawked in amazement at the heretofore unseen enemy, now in substantial numbers across their front. After months of training and equipping, not to mention days and weeks of digging, the war was right before their very eyes.

"Steady boys," leaders cautioned, lest their green troops fire prematurely.

Once the enemy was within six hundred yards, the Richmond Howitzers, under Major George Wythe Randolph, opened up. "BOOM!" The first shot, personally aimed by Major Randolph, a ten pounder from a Parrot gun, was right on target and "struck the center of the road a short distance in front of their column and probably did good execution in its ricochet."[23] Colonel D. H. Hill, observing from the main Confederate

---

23 op.cit pg. 38

works, recorded artillery fire had, "completely broken up" the advancing Union forces.[24] An artillery duel opened in which Lieutenant Greble's exhausted men commenced to counter engage. In their haste however, the Yankees did not have Randolph's careful aim, and their shots, high and wide, fell harmlessly.

On Magruder's right flank Major Montague soon had reason for grave concern for with the bend in Marsh Creek they were almost perpendicular to Lieutenant Greble's guns busily sending shots down the length of their line. Although his forces were dangerously exposed, Montague later recorded, "the major part of the enemy's shot had sufficient elevation to pass over our heads...One ball passed under my horse between his fore and aft feet; several others passed within a few feet of his head, and few buried themselves in our breastworks."[25]

As artillery grew hot from continuous fire, the Zouaves let out a cheer and charged headlong against withering fire from the 1st North Carolinians. The Zouaves continued to push forward, until as Captain Kilpatrick noted, "we reached a point just on the edge of the woods, where the fire was so hot and heavy we were compelled to halt…My men ... falling one after another."

Their compatriots, 3rd New York, were likewise advancing along the west side of the road and approached to within two hundred yards of Confederate lines. Seeing his men falling on both sides of the road before him, General Pierce belatedly wondered if he shouldn't have heeded Duryea earlier and called the whole thing off. It was too late now as it quickly became grievously clear Butler's simplistic, 'fire a volley and charge with bayonets' would never carry the day.

"Go forward on the left," Pierce ordered the 7th New York and 1st Vermont, "Support the attack by the 3rd!" They too immediately came under direct fire by the Richmond Howitzers, Major Randolph's aim holding true. Colonel Bendix, 7th New York reported no sooner than his men formed up they came under fire, "striking a man down by my side at the first shot."[26]

Seeing effective fire decimating the planned attack even before it could be mounted, Pierce ordered both 4th and 7th New York as well as 1st Vermont, "Go across the field, west to east and join 5th New York in the woods to attack the Confederate left." Simultaneously, skirmish units

---

24 op. cit.
25 op. cit.
26 op. cit.

in the vanguard were ordered in the opposite direction, while Colonel Townsend's entire regiment was ordered forward against the center of the Rebel line. General Pierce explaining, "Townsend you will attack directly forward and thereby fix Magruder's attention, whilst the Zouaves make good on our right." It was risky at best and confused.

Figure 14. Scene from the Battle of Big Bethel Courtesy of the National Archives, Washington, D.C.

As ordered, Townsend formed his men on line, advancing through the orchard with color guard forward as if the entire six hundred fifty men were on parade. Supporting Townsend's advance, Lieutenant Greble somehow spurred his men to increase their rate of fire, but most of shells still sailed harmlessly overhead or plowed into the muck in front of the Confederate earthworks. When one round landed close by, Colonel Hill pointed an accusing finger down range, shouting, "You dogs! You missed that time!!"[27] Seeing his Tarheels duck at overflying shells, Hill jovially shouted, "Boys, you have learned to dodge already. I'm an old hand at it,"[28] and as they did so, jumping for protection at each screaming ball, they appreciated their leader's wisdom in forcing them to prepare stout earthworks. "Colonel Hill knows more about good banks and ditches than we do, and we'll never grumble at pitching dirt again!"[29]

---

27 op. cit. pg. 39.
28 op. cit.
29 op. cit.

As Yanks approached within two hundred yards, Rebels continued blasting away, cutting them down left and right. Still the Yankees came on as Major Randolph's pieces were leveled and loaded with canister shot, taking a horrific toll on the remaining 3rd New York. As litter bearers ran forward to retrieve countless wounded, the Albany men attempted to return fire but many of their shots zipped through the branches high above. While carnage continued unabated, the flanking force to Pierce's right finally made its way through the thick underbrush, emerging nearly a mile downstream where some two hundred yards further, Colonel Bendix's troops discovered a natural ford across Marsh Creek. It was then guarded by no more than forty Tarheels or somewhat less than one-fifth their own numbers. The Rebels behind trees and stumps initiated sufficient fire to keep Colonel Bendix fixed in place and sent a swift rider to Magruder warning they were in immediate danger of being overrun at which point the Confederate left flank would be turned. Colonel Bendix, apparently overestimating the opposing force, failed to press his attack, while Magruder wasted no time reinforcing.

"Captain Werth, take the Chatham Greys double time to the Tarheels and hold the left flank at all cost! I'll send a howitzer from Randolph to support," Magruder immediately ordered. That was all the instructions needed as one platoon set up a prepared ambush should their defense falter. The trailing howitzer soon found a perfect spot a hundred twenty yards upstream within range for canister shot.

One round of such munitions decimated Bendix's line which was quite enough to cause him to order an immediate withdrawal back to the cover of the woods. Although the Confederate left stoutly defended and Bendix's men were pulling back, the attacking threat continued elsewhere.

Despite murderous losses, the 2nd and 5th New York pressed forward in the center to the point where 3rd Virginia had to fall back as Union forces momentarily occupied the vacated advance redoubt. Though now in position to press the attack, Colonel Townsend hesitated, fearing he'd be counterattacked and flanked, and ordered withdrawal from the positions they'd just paid for dearly. Seeing Yanks withdrawing, Confederates mounted a quick counterattack, regaining their previous positions.

While Union forces fell back on the right and center, Major Theodore Winthrop organized an attack on the Confederate left, leading Vermont and Massachusetts troops across Marsh Creek despite deadly fire. Gaining the far bank, Major Winthrop mounted a log, rallying his men for the final charge, brandishing his sword overhead, urging them on, when shot clean through the heart. Disheartened seeing their gallant leader fall, his men abandoned the difficult charge and withdrew. Only a few making it back across the creek they'd just crossed with such difficulty. On seeing fleeing Yanks, it "decided the action in our favor," Colonel Hill noted, later recording Major Winthrop "was the only one of our enemy who exhibited an approximation of courage that day."[30] Major Winthrop's heroic but short-lived attack was supported by Lieutenant's Greble artillery, but Greble also fell mortally wounded and his men too began falling back in a disorganized general retreat. With valiant officers killed at the front, the Union left was in full retreat, joining the right and center as forces fell back all along the line. Confederate fire had proven too accurate. With retreat turning into rout, the Union object quickly changed to returning to Fort Monroe by the most expeditious means. Yankees lost seventy-six in all; eighteen killed on the field of battle, fifty-three wounded, and five missing in action, presumably drowned in Marsh Creek, or having run from the carnage. Confederate losses on the other hand, were one killed and seven wounded all of whom recovered.

The northern press had a field day with this first Union venture against the enemy. General Pierce was found incompetent and forced to resign, while Butler was faulted for remaining in the safety of his office and ordering troops forward without knowledge of enemy disposition. While the North vilified Pierce and Butler for a costly defeat accomplishing nothing, Magruder was immediately glorified throughout the South, the sudden hero of a grand, lopsided victory. The entire battle had not lasted even thirty minutes during which only about three hundred of Magruder's men were simultaneously engaged. Southerners cited the decisive action as clear evidence of the superiority of their fighting men. Many now spoke of a short and victorious war and promoting victorious Colonel Magruder to Brigadier General for defeating an invading force triple the size of his own, with minimal losses.[31]

Having again proven himself and now a commanding general, Magruder's urgent requests for more troops were reconsidered. Had he possessed such numbers at the time of Big Bethel, Magruder may have pursued the routed Yankees to great advantage. Finally, men and units were ordered and gradually moved from north and west. While few disputed

---

30 Quarstein, pg. 40.
31 June 17th 1861, followed by his promotion to Major General, October 7, 1861

Brigadier General Magruder's needs, some considered the relocation a futile exercise in 'robbing Peter to pay Paul.'

With troops, both blue and grey, continuing to move to the Peninsula, residents noted the battle at Big Bethel as indicating it was high time to leave. A massive flight of refugees from the Peninsula, heading west to safety ensued. Among them, George Benjamin West who recorded,

"After the barrel of [Big] Bethel, June 10, we did not feel so safe in Williamsburg, and brother and father thought it best for us to move to Richmond. Soon after the fight we went out to the farm of Mr. William Burk on the Chickahominy, and remained a day or two. From there, mother, Mammy Watson, Sue, Lizzie, Bettie, and the baby of Hannah took a steamboat to Richmond, and the rest of us, together with Aunt Liza Tabb and Shields, her son, drove up to Richmond. We had to pass one night on the road and expect to spend it at a Colonel Lacy's, to whom we had a letter of introduction, but by mistake we passed Colonel Lacy's and when we reached the next house it was after sunset. We drove up to the house to ask for accommodations for the night, and on account of our dirty and not very respectable appearance, there was some hesitancy on the part of Mr. Appleton to take us in. But we were soon made at home and treated very kindly by all the family. We did not unpack anything, so I remained in the carriage all night to guard our things.

The next day we passed Bottom's Bridge about noon, and the first house we came to was a small dilapidated one on our right, in a shady yard, so we stopped to eat our dinner and to buy forage for the teams for we did not have any. An old man seemed to be living alone at the place, and everything showed he was very poor. He had very little corn or fodder but let us have all we wanted, so we took some with us besides what the horses ate. When we asked him the price, he said he made no charge and was glad to furnish it, and we insisted on his taking the money he said to father, 'Even if you had an abundance of money, yet I would not take a cent from your under any considerations, as you have had to leave your home and are now casting your lot with the South.'

This was only a small thing, and yet it has made me think better of mankind on account of it, and I still like to think of it and I hope it has made me better and more willing to help others and to sympathize with them. We can never tell the far-reaching effect of a small act of kindness.

That afternoon the latter part of June, we reached Richmond and

attracted as much attention and curiosity as an army corps did a year or two after. We were not an attractive sight driving through the city, and I had to often reply to inquiries as to where we were from and why we were moving. I suppose some of them got an idea of what war was.

In a few days we rented a house on thirty-fourth and P Street from a Mrs. Hill, at $12.00 a month. It was a large two-story brick house, with a large two-story brick kitchen and also a smokehouse and stable. Soon Mr. Ned Parrish's family rented part of the house.... We lived as two families, but in the closest kind of intimacy. One can imagine how we had to live with so many people living in a small house.

We did not form many intimacies with the Richmond people. We refugees were poor and kept very much to ourselves and visited seldom outside ourselves."[32]

***

---

32 West,

October, 1861.
SUMMONED TO COMMAND
General George B. McClellan

Washington, D.C.

"Come hither without delay,"[33] the President's telegram concluded. Upon receipt, General George B. McClellan rode hard for sixty miles to the nearest railway station. The day after arriving in Washington, the 31st he commanded the entire Union Army.

That night he poured his heart out in a letter to his wife, "The people call upon me to save the country. I must save it, and I cannot respect anything that is in the way. I was called to it. My previous life seems to have been unwittingly directed to this great end." This confidence, pompous arrogance aside, was exactly what President Abraham Lincoln sought -a leader who'd organize the army, develop plans, and most importantly, win battles. After the disastrous rout of first Big Bethel, then Manassas a few weeks later, and with the Capitol's populous and nation's business under constant threat from Confederates across the river, Lincoln, Congress, and the nation were increasingly concerned with prosecuting the war. This "get on with it" sentiment rose to a fervor when the press revealed that much of the Confederate armaments holding the nation's capitol hostage were in fact, 'Quaker guns' –logs positioned and painted black to look like cannons. For months, all of Washington had been duped as logs not cannons loomed menacingly and harmlessly from the nearby heights of Arlington. Union soldiers, their Commander-in-Chief, and the nation were desperate for a strong military leader who would take charge and

---

33 Foote, Shelby, 1958, The Civil War a narrative, Fort Sumter to Perryville." Random House, New York, pgs. 86, 99.

decisively save the Union. With his record of command of an engineer company in the Mexican War, it seemed President Lincoln had finally found such a leader in George Brinton McClellan.

General McClellan again penned his wife boasting just ten days after arriving, "I have restored order completely."[34] There'd been no doubt, languishing Yankee ranks lacked good order, and McClellan was a strict disciplinarian. The troops also lacked supplies and equipment, but McClellan was the consummate logistician. He organized the day-to-day functions of the massive army in minute detail and had them fully equipped for the first time. While these reforms were necessary, they alone were not sufficient.

What the Army needed, and President Lincoln demanded, was a war plan. General McClellan knew his predecessor, General in Chief Winfield Scott had been relieved, in part, because his 'Anaconda Plan' to choke off the enemy by blockading Confederate ports and sending an entire army aboard gunboats down the Mississippi to New Orleans would take years. President Lincoln could not wait and General McClellan needed a viable plan, and he'd soon have it.

***

---

[34] op. cit. pg. 101.

Figure 15. General George Brinton McClellan. Courtesy of the Library of Congress, Washington, D.C.

Making his rounds on Capitol Hill one day McClellan spotted an acquaintance. "Colonel, a word if you please," General McClellan addressed Colonel Rush Hawkins, 9th New York, who approached in the hallway having just completed testimony to Congressional staffers about Union progress in the Carolinas.

"Yes Sir, of course Sir."

The General's aide-de-camp scurried to open the double doors to an ante room off a grand parlor, in order the men might speak privately, out of earshot of prying reporters and staff, which filled the Capitol these days.

Taking time to trim and light his cigar, offering one to the Colonel, McClellan inquired, "Colonel, your briefing on amphibious operations at Cape Hatteras, how was the information received?"

Before the Colonel could answer, the General continued, "I've word of the victory, of course, and the operation's success, but the official report is somewhere mired in bureaucracy. Might as well be at the bottom of the Potomac for all the good it does me," giving his aide a stern look. "Even should I demand that report this very day who knows how long before it would make its way through the staff," the General complained, his aid hurriedly scribbling a note to have the after action report forwarded immediately. Otherwise, his aide knew he'd face a similar fate –buried somewhere in Washington.

Colonel Hawkins declined the offered cigar but was grateful for the intervening moment to compose his thoughts. "Sir, the news was received rather well, I'd say. Of course, given our victory, people are anxious to hear good news as you can well imagine, Sir," Colonel Hawkins explained.

"Yes, of course, but get to the details." McClellan said gruffly, recalling his days in Mexico. Under his predecessor the old war horse, General Winfield Scott, McClellan commanded a company of engineers in an amphibious landing. This allowed siege lines to be established and after a few days shelling Vera Cruz surrendered, McClellan clearly recalled the lessons of his own amphibious operational experience years prior and was anxious to hear report of a similar success at Cape Hatteras[35]

"Yes Sir, some particularly noted the cooperation of naval forces in this victory. The naval bombardment under Admiral Stringham proved most effective."

---

35 Dougherty, Kevin, and J. Michael Moore, 2005, The Peninsula Campaign of 1862, a military analysis, University Press of Mississippi.

Civil War Comes Home

"Old Silas, I'll have to get in touch with him again, it's been years," McClellan volunteered, his aide already taking another note.

"So what did you and Old Silas accomplish down there at Hatteras Inlet?" McClellan continued, anxious for every detail.

"Yes Sir, with three hundred nineteen officers and troops ashore, while under the protection of naval bombardment of Confederate positions from Admiral Stringham's fleet, we captured six hundred and seventy prisoners and thirty-five cannons, Sir" Colonel Hawkins explained proudly.

"And what were your losses, Colonel?"

"Sir, just one casualty."

"Indeed, Sir, this is a grand victory," McClellan complimented.

Although Colonel Hawkins understood the interest in the recent lopsided Union victory in North Carolina, he sensed there may be more to the General's questions. Colonel Hawkins ventured, "Sir, permission to speak freely Sir?"

"Of course, Colonel," McClellan replied, intrigued, as was his aide.

"Sir, as I have already had occasion to discuss with General Wool at Fortress Monroe, there are strong parallels on the Virginia Peninsula with regards to Federal gun emplacements and bombardment of Confederate positions. We might advantage ourselves there, similar to Hatteras," the Colonel offered.

"You have my full attention," McClellan replied eagerly.

"Sir, if I may" and Colonel Hawkins began sketching a map in remarkable detail of Virginia's Peninsula flanked by the James on the south, and York River to the north. He filled in Norfolk and Portsmouth, Fortress Monroe, and the additional batteries being constructed on the shifting shoals of Hampton Roads channel on what would later become Foot Wool. After drawing Camp Butler with its excellent twin wharves at Newport News, he added what was known of enemy positions behind earth works from the vicinity of Lee's Mill northeasterly to Yorktown.

"I am not good at drawing Sir, but you can see my point," Colonel Hawkins explained. "From points currently under our control and from selected emplacements forward, one could bombard enemy positions from a distance, and I dare say take the field, without substantial losses," Colonel Hawkins offered hopefully. He had thought it through, had seen it work on Hatteras Island and now laid out what he felt was a sound strategic plan. He was stunned, however, at the General's reaction.

"Very well, that will be all Colonel." General McClellan sternly advised, without any further comment. He allowed no hint either way as to the feasibility of what had just been proposed and remained staring at the hastily sketched map lying on the table. McClellan's reaction also caught the adjutant's attention, both men wondering about the General's demeanor. General McClellan continued staring at the map, deep in thought. He'd just heard of a spectacular, one-sided victory at Hatteras Inlet using naval bombardment to support ground troops to great effect. He recalled his own similar experience at Vera Cruz fourteen years prior in which again, an amphibious assault followed by siege proved victorious, also with few losses. Pounding the table "By God, that's it!" McClellan exclaimed. Though outlined in only the most preliminary terms, McClellan instantly grasped the merits of the concept of such an operation, quickly adding, "And Colonel, you will speak of this to no one!"

"Yes, Sir," the surprised Colonel replied. He'd expected some comment, whether positive or otherwise, on the soundness of his proposal, yet the General offered not a word.

"And you too Major," McClellan directed to his aid. "No one is to know a word of this."

"Yes Sir, of course Sir," the Major as stunned as Colonel Hawkins.

From this brief, chance meeting McClellan now had his campaign plan. That it was drawn up by a Colonel not on his staff mattered not. It fit McClellan's thinking and was consistent with his Mexican War experience. He knew myriad details would have to be worked out, but that was his specialty and he had a large staff he was not afraid to use.

"Gentleman, I hope you understand," the General offered after an awkward silence. "There are spies about, and those whose loyalties aren't known. We'd jeopardize our soldiers should a map such as this or any word of it fall into wrong hands."

"Yes Sir, of course," Colonel Hawkins quickly agreed, the aide nodding. Both subordinates understood and had heard his chief of intelligence, Mr. Alan Pinkerton speak of the risks. What neither grasped however, was that in their short meeting, McClellan had just adopted key points of the strategic campaign to carry the war to Richmond.

"This will show Lincoln and his civilian cronies that think they know how to run a war," thought McClellan. *"How dare they propose attacking Rebels head on, such a waste. What do politicians know of war-fighting? "*

Seeing the General deep in thought, the Colonel inquired, "Will that be all Sir?"

"Yes, dismissed," barked McClellan, muttering a barely audible, 'thank you,' then adding as the Colonel reached the door the aide had just opened for him, "Not a word to anyone, Colonel, to do so would be espionage. Do I make myself clear?"

"Yes Sir," both officers replied simultaneously, and with that McClellan carefully folded the Colonel's map placing it inside his breast pocket and strode out, down the stairs. Once outside he mounted before the aide even knew where they were heading.

General McClellan spent most of that evening in his residence office, having instructed both, aide and wife he did not wish to be disturbed. The former dared violate the General's instructions in order to convey the after action report on the Hatteras Island amphibious operation. Bringing the requested report to the General's desk the Major spotted the hand-drawn Peninsula map now accompanied by several pages of notes in the General's hand.

"Will there be anything else Sir?"

"No, Major that will be all."

"On second thought, inform my wife not to wait up for me. I'm busy tonight."

"Very well Sir. Good night General." He didn't wait for a reply for he knew his boss' mind was some two hundred miles south on Virginia's Peninsula -gateway to Richmond, and the nerve center of the Confederacy.

***

December, 1861- January 1862
Frozen in Place

The White House, Washington, D.C.

"General McClellan, in your estimation how many men would be required for a combined front assault and flank attack on Confederate forces at Manassas, and Sir, how soon could these troops be ready?" President Lincoln asked. Frustrated by the lack of any word from his senior general, he was proposing his own plan for prosecuting this war. The mood of the country called for action and the political winds swirling Washington this holiday season were as biting as those of frigid Illinois.

"Mr. President, to attack Manassas or Centerville against the enemy's greatest strength is sheer folly. Losses would be far beyond what the Army or the nation could bare. Such an attack, ill-advised as it would be, could not be mounted by fewer than one hundred thousand men, at a minimum. A force of that size takes months to equip and assemble. The losses from such a blood bath could not be tolerated Mr. President, I cannot approve of such a plan," McClellan exclaimed. "I have now my mind turned actively toward another plan of campaign that I do not think at all anticipated by the enemy, nor by many of our own people,"[36] McClellan offered without explanation.

President Lincoln had no idea what McClellan had in mind, nor did anyone else. McClellan was ever distrustful of politicians, especially

---
36 Foote, pg. 154.

Lincoln, and made no effort to explain anything. Their meeting adjourned inconclusively, Lincoln more frustrated than ever. Yet, he somehow found encouragement there was now a plan, whatever it might be.

For days, torrential cold rain kept everyone indoors except the lowest ranked messengers. It gave the women, children and slaves time to decorate. Holly, pine, and juniper boughs were fashioned into wreaths and affixed everywhere and anywhere space could be found; fireplace mantle, stair banisters, above and around doorways and windows. The Christmas tree, decorated with small candles, homemade ornaments and little paper cups filled with nuts, dried fruits and other treats was placed on a table which also held a few unwrapped presents. The abundance of greenery provided not only a festive look, but also a fresh scent. Houses and buildings were kept closed as much as possible against the cold and the fresh pine aroma masked the musty smell of body odor and stale cigars.

While house slaves kept busy with holiday preparations, many field hands were given time off from their usual chores. One task they didn't mind, however, was preparing the Yule log. Tradition held that as long as the Yule log burned, slaves would have a light work schedule. Thus, the field hands searched far and wide to fell the largest tree possible. Then as if massive size was not enough, the men took turns making sure the sawed log was kept wet. The saturated wood could barely be got to burn at all initially and the slaves tending the fire made sure it burned as slowly as possible.

While most slaves, except house servants, enjoyed a reduced work schedule, so did their masters. There were concerts and oratorical performances, a great number of caroling parties, often sung in neighbors' homes, and the exchange of small gifts or remembrances. As the festivities and horrible weather deferred most work, it also deferred military planning meetings, and in the midst of holiday preparations, General McClellan took to his bed with typhoid. Both his physician and his severely weakened state kept him there three long weeks. With Christmas and New Year's holidays filling what remained of the calendar, little, or truthfully, no work was accomplished. What planning went on was for balls and parties, not prosecuting the war, as the commerce of the capitol went into full production of gay events despite war time concerns.

Near the top of peoples' worries, at least among those whose family members had enlisted, was how their loved one was getting along in camp at Christmas. Unfortunately, like their Commanding General, many troops were ill, but unlike McClellan, none had a warm bed in which to recover. Although men did everything they could to make winter camp survivable, it was a cold miserable existence. As they went into winter encampment, they scoured the country side for every scrap of lumber or fence rail that could be carried off. This was not firewood but construction material for they built little cabins or in some cases little more than lean-tos. Piecing scrap wood together best they could the walls often consisted of more gaps than solid. Once erected, beams held their tents stretched out to form a roof or wall against winter wind. The empty tins in which the received their hardtack and salted pork, consumed only because they'd otherwise starve, were flattened and fashioned into a crude smoke stack, allowing a small fire in a futile attempt to heat their mean habitation. With dry wood, oiled and waxed tent canvas, crude stoves improperly connected to haphazard smokestacks, and high winds, the risk of fire was considerable especially crowded together.

Despite the hardship, troops kept up their spirits. With the holidays, they'd spend many a dull winter day dreamin' of Christmases past. Few could obtain a pass to go home for most were on ninety day enlistments and the time and distance involved in travel home were too great to allow a visit, even brief. Instead, men mostly made the best of it, trying to think of better times ahead and comforting one another through the long cold nights. Those that could write composed letters to loved ones. For many this was the only gift they could send. Mail was a great morale booster, involving a great deal of camaraderie when news from home was shared. Along with letters, families sent boxes, packed with everything their loved ones might need; from knitted wool socks to hams and baked goods. Sometimes the contents did not survive the rough handling of the postal system and Quartermaster. Soldiers often found carefully prepared baked goods saturated with something that had spilled, a cake soaked in ketchup for instance. Presents from home were also subject to pilferage. One private thought he had the best gift when he spotted a bottle of brandy in his box. Inviting cabin mates to share in the good fortune with a nip, all were sorely disappointed to find someone had beaten them to the contents. The bottle had been opened, brandy removed, replaced with water and cap resealed. Thirsty disappointed lads cursed their luck, the army, the war, and anything else they could think of. In some camps spirits were served, even egg nog, and most drew extra rations Christmas day. Drilling was foregone for once, and on both sides, cold lonely men tried to make the best of it.

***

Civil War Comes Home

A few weeks later,

"If General McClellan does not want to use the Army, I would like to borrow it provided I could see how it could be made to do something,"[37] President Lincoln remarked. Only half joking, his comment set the tone for the meeting, his patience worn thin. Despite having tried, on numerous occasions to impress upon General McClellan the need for action, nothing was forthcoming and week after week, delays drug on. While President Lincoln understood the necessity of the Army going to winter quarters, he also knew planning must go on long before the Spring thaw, if troops were to move when the weather finally broke.

The Commander-in-Chief's mood became increasingly gloomy, like the heavy winter clouds hanging low about the White House. His concern and the mounting political pressures for when and where this unwelcome war might be prosecuted were increasing. General McClellan, for reasons kept to himself, did nothing to help the situation; in fact, in large measure he'd caused it by failing to inform the President or any of his advisers of an emerging plan for a Peninsula campaign. Even after goading by a White House proposal to attack the Confederate flank and front near Manassas, McClellan failed to reply. Exasperated, Lincoln could wait no longer.

"Gentlemen, its ten days into the New Year and we must move forward with a plan of attack," the President announced solemnly to gathered Cabinet members and General officers, the later including two of McClellan's' division commanders, Major General Irwin McDowell and Brigadier General William Franklin. The former outlined his plans for an overland offensive, not unlike the President's proposal prior to the holidays. This direct assault was to drive Confederates from their stronghold around Centerville and Manassas, simultaneously reducing the threat on Washington, and sending Rebels scurrying pell-mell back to Richmond. Then, Brigadier General Franklin offered a counter plan involving amphibious operations. Unbeknownst to anyone, it was not that dissimilar from McClellan's secreted plan, but McClellan was neither attending nor even aware the meeting was taking place. He remained ill at home. As the evening wore on, the pros and cons of the two plans were debated and Lincoln sensed they were now re-hashing old arguments about the merits of land versus amphibious operations. Their points were not based on any recent evidence from the field, but on long-held opinions which were seldom swayed no matter how long the Generals kept at it.

---

37 Bailey, 1983, Forward to Richmond; McClellan's Peninsular Campaign. Time Life, Alexandria, VA, pg. 68.

They'd sooner run out of cigars than admit their concept of how to fight might be out of date. Frustrated, Lincoln adjourned the meeting without a decision -except to meet again. It would take more than one session to develop the Union strategy.

After several more White House sessions, word of what was going on reached General McClellan. Despite lingering weakness, he forced himself from his sick bed, attending their next meeting, Jan 13th.

On seeing the emaciated McClellan, a surprised President Lincoln offered, "Welcome back General, I hope you are feeling better than you look?"

"Yes Mr. President, considerably weakened just now, but not dead yet, my good Sirs," General McClellan responded sarcastically, casting a perturbed glare at everyone in the room. President Lincoln was not sure whether McClellan was referring to his weakness from protracted illness or his leadership of the army. "Mr. President," General McClellan continued, his voice unwavering though he had to steady himself by holding the back of a chair. "How do we expect to fare if plans are made while I am excluded?"

"General McClellan," Lincoln responded, "we had word of your late illness and with your subordinate Generals present, desired to proceed so that operations may someday begin once you recover, stars align, or whatever it takes to move the army to action."

Seeing McClellan readying what undoubtedly would be a sharp rebuke, Treasury Secretary Salmon Chase, one of the few Cabinet members regularly attending the largely military meetings, intervened. He meant to spare his friend McClellan from embarrassing himself by being dressed down or otherwise humiliated in front of his staff by the Commander-in-Chief. Skilled at Washington's politics, Chase also meant to spare the President the indelicacy of a public challenge by his senior General to the point of having to either acquiesce or remove him for insubordination.

Despite his friend Chase's timely intervention, McClellan refused to provide his plan for the war, declaring instead some present "were incompetent to form an opinion and others incapable of keeping a secret."[38] "I can assure your gentlemen," McClellan finally offered, "I have a fixed schedule for this advance."

In providing no details, McClellan irreparably weakened whatever frail thread of friendship that remained with Secretary Chase. With other engagements pressing, and seeing the impasse created by McClellan's

---

38 Dougherty and Moore, pg. 39.

stonewalling, Lincoln adjourned the meeting. Unhappy with the failure to reach agreement and the continued foot-dragging by McClellan, even if he had been gravely ill, the President remained convinced of the necessity of moving ahead with his own, or what would soon become known as, the Administration plan. He could hardly be expected to conclude otherwise as still, no one else, even his subordinate commanders, had a clue what McClellan had in mind or when it might eventually take effect. Thus, in Special War Order number 1, on Jan 31, 1861, the President directed the Army of the Potomac, "after providing safely for the defense of Washington, should move forward, on or before February 22nd and seize and occupy a point upon the railroad south-west of Manassas Junction."[39]

Not one to acquiesce to politicians, even written orders from the Commander-in-Chief, McClellan petitioned the President to present reasons for preferring his own plan over the administration's. In a letter Feb 3rd McClellan carefully reviewed the military situation, finally revealing a plan to "descend the Potomac, sail up the Rappahannock to Urbana for a base and by rapid march, gain West Point at the head of the York, thus threatening Richmond before Johnston's army at Centerville could fall back and meet him…."[40] Operationally, this was the shortest land route to the Confederate capitol, and it would shift the center of military operations from the outskirts of Washington to Richmond. Explaining his position to Secretary of War Stanton, McClellan offered, "The total forces to be thrown upon the new line would be, according to circumstances, from one hundred and ten thousand and one hundred and forty thousand. I hope to use the latter number by bringing fresh troops into Washington and still leaving it quite safe. I fully realize that…time will probably be the most valuable consideration." He went on to caution, "it is highly probable that the weather and state of the roads may be such as to delay the direct movement from Washington… The roads have gone from bad to worse. Nothing like their present condition was every known here before, they are impassible at present. We are entirely at the mercy of the weather." Adding to the advantages of his plan, "we demoralize the enemy by forcing him to abandon his prepared position for one which we have chosen, in which all is in our favor, and where success must produce immense results. Nothing is certain in war but all the chances are in favor of this movement. So much am I in favor of this southern line of operation, that I would prefer to move

---

39 http://myloc.gov/Exhibitions/lincoln/presidency/CommanderInChief/BattlingIncompetence/ExhibitObjects/DraftGeneralOrderNo1.aspx
40 Webb, Alexander S., Campaigns of the Civil War: The Peninsular. pgs. 18-19.

from Fortress Monroe as a base, as a certain though less brilliant movement than that from Urbana, than to an attack upon Manassas"[41]

Despite McClellan's points, the merits of the Administration's plan remained; it was a direct not indirect advance on the enemy, it kept the army between the enemy and Washington rather than leaving the capitol exposed, and it required less time and resources. Finally, should things not unfold as planned; a retreat could be accomplished while still defending Washington.

Whether looking to counter any Administration plan or simply misinformed, McClellan was convinced he faced no fewer than one hundred fifteen thousand at Manassas. Based on this erroneous information, he was certain the enemy's works could not be taken or turned at any cost. This drove him to his far more complex plan, despite the President's stated urgency that, "If something was not done soon, the bottom would be out of the whole affair."[42]

---

41 op. cit. pgs. 19-20.
42 op. cit, pg. 17. Foote, pg. 156.

MARCH, 1862
Spring Thaw…

To break the impasse, Lincoln convened a 'council of war' - a dozen top generals who'd finally discern a viable Union strategy. After seemingly endless cigars and posturing, eight had sided with McClellan, while Generals Sumner, Heintzelman, McDowell, and Keyes, all his corps commanders, dissented. Although Lincoln was disappointed the frontal attack plan he'd proposed months earlier was rejected, he was nevertheless relieved there was finally a plan and a majority agreed. On the basis of their vote March 8 he issued:

"*Presidents General War Order #3,*

Ordered, that no change of the base of operations of the Army of the Potomac without leaving in and about Washington such a force as, in the opinion of the General-Chief and commanders of army corps shall leave said city entirely secure.
That no more than two army corps (about fifty thousand troops) of said Army of the Potomac shall be moved enroute for a new base of operations until the navigation of the Potomac from Washington to the Chesapeake Bay shall be free from the enemy batteries and other obstructions or until the President shall hereafter give express permission.
That any movement as afore said, en route for a new base of operations, which may be ordered by the General-in-Chief and which

may be intended to move up on the Chesapeake Bay, shall begin to move upon on the bay as early as the 18th of March instant; and the General-in-Chief, shall be responsible that it so moves as early as that day.

Ordered, that the army and navy co-operate in an immediate effort to capture the enemy's batteries upon the Potomac, between Washington and the Chesapeake Bay."

Signed, ABRAHAM
LINCOLN[43]

***

Mysteriously, at virtually the same time, Confederates were evacuating Manassas and Centerville.

McClellan was furious. "This is no damn coincidence!" Later, in sworn Congressional testimony, he'd testify the Rebel withdrawal was the result of a traitorous leak.

Whether due to a Union leak, better Rebel intelligence, coincidence, or some combination thereof, General Johnston had been contemplating just such a move for weeks. When information arrived March 5th about unusual activity among the Federal division opposing them (one of Hooker's divisions in Dumfries), Johnston correctly assessed the situation: Federals were finally taking to the field to launch long-delayed operations. In preparation, on March 7th Johnston ordered all his troops east of the Blue Ridge to move to the south bank of the Rappahannock River, about half the distance to Richmond. Some forty-two thousand effectives quickly occupied prepared works where a depot of food and other supplies awaited.[44] "We should be better able to resist the Federal Army advancing by Manassas, and near enough to Fredericksburg to meet the enemy there, should he take that route, as well as unite with any Confederate forces that may be sent to oppose McClellan, should he move by the Lower Rappahannock or the lower Bay,"[45] Johnston reasoned. He was taking prudent action to cutoff a Federal advance, and defend Richmond. "We had to regard four routes to Richmond as practicable for the Federal army: that chosen last July via Bull Run, another east of the Potomac to the mouth of Potomac Creek and from there by Fredericksburg; the third and fourth by water —the one to the

43 http://www.classicreader.com/book/3766/263/
44 Dougherty and Moore, pg. 45.
45 Webb, pg. 25.

lower Rappahannock, the other to Fort Monroe, and from these points respectively by direct roads (west to Richmond)."[46] Johnston's massive movement was completed in just four days without enemy interference or apparently even their knowledge. Upon learning the Rebels had slipped away, McClellan directed his own relocation to Fairfax Court House but refused to consider pursuit. By this time, Rebels safely occupied the area from which McClellan had proposed to begin his operations, necessitating his change of plans to less preferred alternative.

Frustrated, McClellan's staff, numbering nearly two dozen, including two French noblemen who'd volunteered, Comte de Paris, pretender to the throne, and his brother Duc de Charles, dubbed "Captains Parry and Chatters," by the troops, busied themselves planning relocation to Fort Monroe.

Adding to his woes, the very day McClellan took to the field, March 11th, Lincoln relieved him of command of the Union Army. Although his demotion could have been in response to letting Johnston slip away, Lincoln was trying to make the best of a difficult situation. Relieving McClellan of responsibility for the entire Army would allow his full attention to the Army of the Potomac.

Although furious at being stripped of power and at Lincoln for not bothering to inform him personally, McClellan directed his energy and his staff to the task at hand. Their 'Urbana plan' was now defunct with Johnston occupying dug-in positions from which any Federal move could be blocked.

Calling his own war summit, McClellan met Corps commanders; Generals Sumner, Heintzelman, McDowell, and Keyes at Fairfax Court House, March 13.th He explained, "should circumstances render it not advisable to land at Urbana, we can use Mob Jack Bay or the worst coming to worst, we can take Fort Monroe as a base and operate with complete security, although with less clarity and brilliancy of results, up the Peninsula."[47]

Due to Johnston having stolen a march, the generals had no choice and quickly adopted without dissent, McClellan's less preferred option, moving to Fort Monroe. The proceedings of their meeting were summarized and sent to the War Dept. which approved the same day but added stipulations for the defense of Washington – a perennial sticking point.

---

46 op. cit. pg. 26.
47 op. cit.

WAR DEPARTMENT,   March 13, 1862

"The President having considered the plan of operation agreed upon by yourself and the commander of army corps makes no objections to the same, but gives the following direction as to its execution:

1. Leave such force at Manassas Junction as shall make it entirely certain that the enemy shall not repossess himself of that situation and line of communication.
2. Leave Washington entirely secure.
3. Move the remainder of the force down the Potomac, choosing a new base at Fortress Monroe, or anywhere between there and here: or at any event, move such remainder of the army at once in pursuit of the enemy by some route.

EDWIN M. STATON,
Secretary of War."

President Lincoln, realizing only too well that time was running out, acquiesced after a clear majority of the military council approved the modified plan. Even then, stipulations added that Manassas Junction and Washington must be "entirely secure" -as if that could be guaranteed in wartime. Lincoln reflected, "Even should I somehow find, or be able to generate support among my senior cabinet members to reverse the council of generals' approval, the responsibility for any subsequent action would be mine alone. Best we move forward with this plan, late and imperfect as it is, for we cannot continue to do nothing while Rebels operate with impunity, war debt skyrockets, and calls for results increase." Plans for a Peninsula campaign were finally born, after long and difficult labor.

In addition to stroking the egos of several generals, each adamant that their plan alone could win the day, the President was dealing with increasingly fractious national politics. Despite acts of violence, especially over the free soil movement for newly joining states, the President managed to rise above the furor of the day, urging calm and unity.

"I have no prejudice against the Southern people. They are just what we would be in their situation. If slavery did not now exist amongst them, they would not introduce it. If it did now exist amongst us, we should not instantly give it up."[48] His conciliatory view was in the distinct minority.

48 Roble, George. C., 2010, God's Almost Chosen People: a Religious History of the American Civil War, The University of North Carolina, Press. pg. 22.

The President was one of few in Washington with the backbone to express his wisdom publicly.

Union embarkation finally began March 17th with Heintzelman's corps, Hamilton's division thereof first, and Porter's following on the 22nd. The first of the following month General McClellan and staff left aboard the steamer, *Commodore*, sailing overnight, arriving Fort Monroe the following afternoon. Once settled, McClellan soon reported the following forces "ready to move;" two divisions of Heintzelman's Third Corps, two divisions of Keyes' Fourth Corps, and one division of Sumner's Second Corps, a separate infantry brigade, reserve artillery, and three Cavalry regiments. However, being reported as 'ready' and actually moving out were two entirely different matters.

***

APRIL, 1862
STRIDE OF A GIANT[49] — PREPARATIONS FOR WAR

Along the road from Yorktown

"The Yankees have landed!" The old slave, Isom heard, awaking from the commotion. Quick as his stiff bones allowed after sleeping on the cold ground, he crawled out from under the ancient buckboard. "I be getting' too durn old fo' dis. Marsa wants his oysters and this late in the season too. Why I always gots to be da' one, driving that durn mule all the ways down here to fetch oysters?"

Interrupting his steady stream of grumbling, he asked another hurrying past, "Excuse me young fella, what's all dis hub bub?"

"Why ain't you heard ol' man? The fleet landed down to Ship Point? The Yanks have come to free us. Don't you know?" With that he was off, joining the growing throng on Yorktown's working water front.

Squinting to see across the wide water, flat calm and silvery in the early light, Isom couldn't make out anything. It was the wrong direction from where he stood, though others milling about claimed they'd earlier seen a forest of masts punching through morning mist. The fleet was actually anchored a short distance east on the Poquoson River. As the Yanks were coming up the Peninsula, there'd be no point in landing at Gloucester Point across the York River.

---

49 Hastings and Hastings, pg. 8.

"Yes, Suh, Lord God almighty, theys more ships ever I laid eyes on," one of the wharf hands commented to anyone within earshot.

Isom thought, *I gots to tell Marsa straight away.*

"Git along mule! Marsa's got to know 'bout dis, and da sooner da better." He couldn't have gotten any oysters anyway for the entire waterfront was in turmoil. The entire U.S. Navy and a fleet of contracted and commandeered civilian transports were anchored nearby it seemed.

Isom hadn't made but a few miles northwesterly towards home when pickets emerged from the shade of the tree line. "Halt!"

"Where ya headin' 'ol Tom?" the taller of two skinny lads called out, not in a friendly tone.

Yanking the reins, Isom was immediately compliant, ever deferential -a behavior he'd learned to quickly employ in such situations over his nearly three score years. "Beggin' you pardon Suh, I be headin' back to my Marsa' onliest I ain't got his oysters."

"Let me see your papers," the boy-turned-soldier gruffly demanded, barely as tall as the flintlock with which he struggled. The old slave immediately presented a well-worn note his master had penned, recalling his master's careful instructions; *'Isom, you must keep this on your person at all times when errands take you off the plantation.'*

"Here ya are, Suh. All signed right proper in the Marsa's hand."

Impatiently grabbing the document the Private feigned reading but Isom knew otherwise. He could tell from the pattern of stains on the document he'd memorized he'd been carrying it so long, the lad held it upside down.

"Who you'd say your master was?" the boy private snarled, tobacco juice drooling from rotten teeth.

"Suh, that's be Mr. William Peachy, esquire. At your service, Suh."

"Well you don't say. I hear old man Peachy's some kinda big shot lawyer," the private noted. "You best be gettin' along," he instructed, returning the slave's well worn pass, not wantin' to cross Mr. Peachy. "Seen any Yankees?"

"Yanks? Why no Suh, not on de road, but dey be comin' fo' show. I heard 'dem big ships now lying to anchor. 'Round 400 in all they say."

"We know about the ships, ya damn fool. Why the hell you think Prince John got us out here in the middle of damn nowhere guarding this sorry strip a dirt road?"

"Suh, yes Suh, you's right," the slave replied wanting to remain ever agreeable but wondering are *they going to detain me much longer just 'cause they got nothing else to do.*

The private and his compatriot, bored with standing in the sun harassing a harmless old slave, eyed the shade of the embankment and finally let Isom pass. The picket boys would rest in the shade 'til they saw the next traveler approaching. They had a lot to learn 'bout soldiering.

"Git up mule, we best not be sittin' here all day. Sooner we git news to Marsa da better," Isom said to the braying mule, the wagon creaking into motion.

***

Williamsburg

Handing over the sack of fresh-baked biscuits, the last they'd enjoy in a long time as they were due to report back to camp, Thomas' slave added, "Master, there's news… word about town is Yanks landed down to Ship Point. Folks seem mighty stirred up."

"Are you sure? Where are they comin'?" Thomas demanded, adding, "I must get over to see Miss Victoria. Remember, I helped you read in the Gazette about our College regiment forming? Quick go buy a paper, then finish my packing. Take everything this time includin' remainin' clothes, and books, all of it. We can't be leavin' anything at the College any longer. I must figure a new plan," Thomas thought out loud, handing his slave back the sack of biscuits they shared.

In the excitement Thomas had momentarily forgotten his slave was not allowed to read. Sent to buy a newspaper, the slave would naturally explain should anyone ask, 'it's for my Marsa'. It was illegal for slaves to read or write, or for anyone to teach them. Thomas could be fined and his slave punished if the fact the slave could read became known. In the past such indiscretions were sometimes overlooked, but these days with the war on, folks were a lot more anxious. Rumors of slave rebellion spread fast and far, even if they were just rumors. Although Thomas knew both the law and the consequences of violating it, he'd nevertheless secretly taught his slave as much as he could. For his part his slave proved a ready and capable student, reading and writing, but still at a beginning level. Thomas also confided closely with his slave on personal matters, as he might a white friend, for they'd grown up together, inseparable.

Returning shortly, the slave announced, "Well Suh, you right, them papers did say, President Ewell be holding a meetin' to organize the home

Civil War Comes Home

guard. Suh, what's this 'organize' mean? You ain't taught me that one I reckon," the slave asked, taking another biscuit.

"How can you eat at a time like this? I need you to go and get all my stuff packed. I don't know where we'll be headin' though most likely off to war and no doubt a lot sooner than anybody imagined."

Wolfing down the biscuit, his slave gathered his satchel to depart, not harboring a second thought about following his master's instructions, even if it meant going off to war. Where Marsa went, slave followed. They'd grown up boyhood friends, into their teens and young manhood. Their lifelong friendship was at extreme odds with their legal relationship; master and chattel, owner and property.

"Whilst you're finishing packing, I'm goin' to head over to the King's residence. I gotta pay my respects and call on Miss Victoria. Tell you what, you run by the King's house on your way back and let the housekeeper know I want to come calling, this very day on a matter most urgent," Thomas instructed. He hoped Victoria's mother would agree to his seeing her on short notice. Folding his letter to 1LT Dessie Braziza, Thomas had decided joining up was the right thing to do. Even if the letter never got mailed, writing it down helped formulate his plans, now made urgent with the breaking news of the Union fleet.

Thomas' slave stuffed the remaining biscuits in his satchel, *no tellin' when we might get hungry*, hastening from the cool shade of the Wren yard into the hustle and bustle of Main St. *It does seem busier now, or is it just my imagination?* Striding quickly to do his master's bidding he heard his name and turned to see his friend, W.B. Nelson, slave to Captain Octavius Cook.

"Hey, where you headin' in such an Almighty hurry?"

"I didn't see you. How you been doing W.B.?"

"Well I been 'round, you know my Marsa got me doing all kinds of errands to get ready. He sayin' we got to prepare for war. Give me the chills. Do I have to go off an' be his slave in the army? Ain't this here war supposed to be 'bout making us free?"

"I don't know W.B. Why, just a few minutes ago my Marsa told me to go pack all the rest of his stuff as we likely be movin' out though he don't have no idea in all God's Kingdom where that may be."

"Wait a minute, if you going to pack all his belongings, why you headin' away from College? Where you going?" W.B. questioned.

"W.B. First he tells me, 'pack everything' then says to first go over to Dr. Kings' and axt them can he call on Miss Victoria, real urgent. Why

I don't know what Marsa Thomas is up to. He don't tell me what he's plannin'."

"I know what you means, but I will tell you, my Marsa,' Captain Cook he be taking all able-bodied men, and some not so able-bodied if you axt me. Some of 'dem young white fools ain't nuttin' but peach fuzz boys, I swear. Theys paying cash money for new recruits, white folks that is, us coloreds they just take."

"I know W.B. Marsa Thomas he done already sign his self up with Captain Cook, and me along with him! Marsa Thomas got 'dis friend already in the military, officer too, and he been writin' him 'bout what to do. I don't rightly know. All I knows is, wherever he goes, I go. So I pray, sweet Jesus he don't go and get us both kilt in this here war," a chill running down his spine at the first he'd spoken of this possibility.

"What about you? Where you going?" Thomas' slave asked, wanting to change the subject.

"Ain't you heard? Yankees' landed down to Ship Point. Marsa Captain Cook told me go straight away to deliver this message to the editor of the Gazette, handing Thomas's slave the note, W.B. glancing around ensuring no one was watching.

"Here, let me take a look," unfolding the paper. Fortunately, the customary sealing wax had not been applied, the author assuming its confidentiality, given the messenger's illiteracy. Looking around furtively to ensure no one was observing, Thomas' slave hurriedly read,

April 1, 1862

To the Honorable Mr. E. H. Lively,
Editor-in-Chief, Gazette.

Sir, Greetings and salutations! I bring most urgent news. This date certain the large Union flotilla carrying a great mass of troops and all manner of war provisions anchored at Ship Point.

I beseech you make haste to warn residents, the danger of invasion of our fair town is fast upon us. With such notice, women and children may yet escape the coming fury. Able-bodied free men and boys hasten to your Christian duty and answer the call to arms. Discharge your sacred duty to the Great Almighty and repulse these invading blue devils.

Your most humble servant,
Capt. Octavius Cook,

Commanding, Williamsburg Junior Guard

On reading this, Thomas' slave paused. *All this talk of Yankees is true,* he realized, trying to fathom the momentous changes war would bring. Handing the note back to W.B. he explained, "It's says, make ready for war 'cause Yanks is a comin' soon. This'll be the biggest dam fight ever. You best git to 'dat newspaper office like your Captain said." *And I best high tail it to the Kings and get back to packin.' Marsa Thomas got a ton a books and all his clothes, we're gonna need a wagon. He's got too much, everything I own fits in this haversack with room to spare for vittles.*

"OK, I hear you. I got to go. Take care of youself," W.B. offered, "and may the good Lord keep us both safe."

"Amen, W.B. So what you gonna do?" Thomas' slave asked.

"After I deliver this message I ain't rightly sure," adding before turning to go, "but I heard the Yanks is looking for slaves to fight and I aims to be free, someday."

Alongside the kitchen building behind the Peachy home, old Isom pulled up as Til, the cook came out to inspect. Spying the empty buckboard instead of the anticipated load of oysters, she laid into poor Isom before he could even bid good day.

"Where you been old man, don't you know Marsa done got his heart set on dem fine York River oysters and heres you come rollin' up, empty and late. You got some explaining to do."

"Morning Miss Til," Isom unflappable. "Well, there's no oysters this day, Miss Til, nor anytime soon I expect. Onliest thing theys gots down to the waterfront is Yanks."

"What? Oh Lord God," Til fairly shrieked.

"Yes Mam, it's the Gospel truth, the Yankee fleet's sittin' at anchor down to Ship Point. Folks from there to here are mighty stirred up, saying all kinda things, like, 'The Yanks gonna invade.' 'We going to war.' 'Slaves gonna be freed.' Yes Mam, talk is runnin' wild, though I doubt anyone knows what it means. Why I was stopped by Rebels, boys really, on the road back. They so lookin' for a fight 'tis a wonder they don't shoot me just on general principals."

"Oh, I'm sorry," Til realizing her mistake in chastising him earlier, "You best be gettin' inside to tell the Marsa this news," then adding, "when you done, comes back out here and Til fix you breakfast."

"Yes Mam," Isom smiled. The only thing he'd eaten since the evening before was a piece of stale cornbread, and he'd already had more than enough excitement on an empty stomach what with them Rebel lads. Isom hoped Marsa would be more concerned with news of the Yanks than his failure to procure the desired oysters and resolved not to bring up the latter. *Best let Marsa focus his attention.* Meanwhile, Til sent one of the kitchen girls to fetch her husband Jake. Nearby, the slave everyone called Yellow Jim, was hoeing the kitchen garden, taking it all in. A careful observer of comings or goings at Marsa's house, Jim had seen the commotion and sensed something amiss. Extricating himself from between long rows of recently sprouted seedlings, Jim made for the tool shed, where he exchanged hoe for satchel, under the ruse of needing to make a delivery. Although he'd long-ago adopted the demeanor of an illiterate field laborer, supposedly too dim to even know when to come in from working the fields without overseer's explicit instructions, in reality, Yellow Jim was both observant and astute.

His master's assumption, shared by a majority of slave owners, held their slaves too stupid to understand much of anything. This afforded Yellow Jim ample opportunity to carry out clandestine business completely unsuspected. He knew the newly arriving Federals would be desirous for any information on enemy fortifications, troop disposition, and local roads. Although he'd not yet personally viewed the defense works, Yellow Jim had kept his ears open, gathering information from diverse sources. While the tid bits seemed random or insignificant, taken as a whole his information was valuable, especially as Federals had precious little to go on otherwise. Now with news of their landing, he knew he had to pass along what information he had and that it was perishable as Til's cookin'. Yellow Jim also understood that word of the Yankee fleet would spread rapidly, and once that happened, his movements would be curtailed. Thus, he endeavored to devise a means for passing essential information without having to travel or raise suspicion, and came upon a unique solution as later recorded by a Union officer.

"There came into the Union lines a Negro from a farm on the other side of the river…who was found to possess a remarkably clear knowledge of the topography of the whole region…. When he first saw our system of army telegraphs, the idea interested him intensely, and he begged the operator to explain the signs to him. They did, and found that he could (readily) understand and remember the meaning of the various movements.

Not long after, his wife… expressed a great anxiety to be allowed to go over to the other side as a servant to a 'secesh woman…. The request was granted…and in a few days was duly installed as laundress and was soon found to be wonderfully well informed as to all the rebel plans. Within an hour of the time that a movement of any kind was projected, or even discussed, among the rebel generals, (we) know all about it...which corps was moving, or about to move, in what direction, how long they had been on the march, and in what force; and all this knowledge came through her husband and his reports always turned out to be true. Yet he was never absent, and never talked with the scout, and seemed to be always taken up with his duties....

How he got his information remained for some time a puzzle...at length, upon much solicitation, he unfolded his marvelous secret to one of our officers.

Taking him to a point where a clear view could be obtained...he pointed out a little cabin... and asked him if he saw that clothes-line with clothes hanging on it to dry. 'Well, that clothes line tells me in half an hour just what goes on at rebel headquarters. You see my wife over there; she washed for the officers, and cooks, and waits around, and as soon as she hears about any movement or anything going on she cones down and moves the clothes on that line so I can understand it in a minute. That grey shirt there is one general; and when she takes it off, it means he's gone down about Richmond. That white shirt means Hill; and when she moves it up to the west end of the line, Hill's corps has moved. That red one is another general. He's down on the right now, and if he moves, she will move that red shirt.

One morning (he) came in and reported a movement over there, (adding) But it won't amount to anything, They're just making believe.

An officer went out to look at the clothes-line telegraph through his field-glass. There had been quite a shifting over there among the army flannels. But how do you know there is something in it?" the officer asked.

"Do you see those two blankets pinned together at the bottom?"

"Yes, but what of it?" the officer replied.

"Why, that her way of making a fish-trap' and when she pins the clothes together that way it means they is only trying to draw us into their fish trap.

With the clothes-line telegraph, the slave and his wife continued to be one of the most prompt and reliable of intelligence sources.[50]

***

---

50 Markle, pg. 60-62.

Mr. William Peachy and Captain Octavius Cook met this time at the old Charlton coffeehouse. Both lawyers, they were more professional colleagues than close friends. With few social peers, they tolerated one another as a kind of forced company, rarely seeing eye-to-eye on much of anything. Although expressing support for the Southern cause, Peachy was more pragmatic, voicing reservation about disrupting their way of life, most particularly his status as a principal beneficiary of the daily labors of large populations of slaves and indentured servants. Their talk today quite naturally involved news of the morning.

"My good Sir," Peachy continued, "I do expect a businessman could turn a handsome profit from this war, or even the uncertainty of it. I dare say wagons, blankets, not to mention munitions, medicine and foods; all manner of your materiel of warfare will soon be quite dear, would you not agree, Captain?"

Captain Cook, more idealist and patriot, may have agreed with the facts, but he objected vehemently, "But should one profit at the expense and suffering of fellow citizens, even as our patriots fight to preserve our rights? The Southern gentleman is duty-bound to preserve the sanctity of our way of life. Indeed, gentleman of our class must lead commoners in this great struggle, not profit from it. We set the example, and it's every Southern male's solemn obligation to defend his home and women folk. It is our job, so help us God. I don't see any need nor any justice in profiting from war."

"Well, I'm too old to fight," Peachy countered, his convenient excuse, though many his age and older had signed up. What Peachy meant, but could not bring himself to say, was he had too much to lose to be caught up in soldiering, what with wartime profits to be made. By whatever means, supplying the Army, or taking advantage of citizens fallen on hard times, the opportunities, were endless. And, they were further increased by the lack of competition, with most males gone to fight.

Captain Cook, tiring of Peachy's endless speculation, and refusing to grant why any male claiming Southern lineage should be granted an excuse from serving, made his apologies and beat an early departure, "I bid you good day Sir. In these trying times, I have much to accomplish and many preparations wait, none of which involve speculation or profiteering."

***

Civil War Comes Home

Figure 16. Portrait of the William Peachy family and slaves at home in Williamsburg, Va. Courtesy of the Colonial Williamsburg Foundation, Williamsburg, Va.

On the way to the King's, Thomas stopped at the garden of another house, quickly picking a handful of early daffodils. He knew better, usually purchasing his presents for Victoria but it was not market day and he had no time. He figured no one would mind just this once and besides daffodils were common 'round these parts. Surely they'd forgive him a few flowers for his girl friend given today's circumstances. Straightening his clothes, smoothing his hair, Thomas rapped firmly on the massive door. Momentarily, a house slave opened, and as previously instructed, invited young Master Barlow to please make himself comfortable on the front porch. Trying to see past inside Thomas could make out very little for the house remained shuttered against sun, as was the custom.

"Very well," Thomas replied, taking a seat on the wide porch. *Dr. King had prospered indeed*, he contemplated, though marrying wealth had never entered Thomas' mind. As he waited, he watched the song birds flittering among the emerging shoots and buds in the Spring garden, but was brought back to reality on hearing the door creak. To his surprise it was not Victoria, but her father. Jumping to his feet, Thomas extended his hand offering a hearty, "Good morning Doctor King,"

"Hello, Thomas, good morning young man. Looks to be a fine day, wouldn't you say?" foregoing the obvious, *what brings you here?*

"Ah, yes Sir, fine indeed, at least the weather," Thomas answered awkwardly, trying to think of what else to add. "Fine weather, though the day's news may not be so good, I fear."

"Why whatever do you mean?" Usually the doctor was well informed for traveling surrounding counties seeing patients afforded him more news than most town folk had. "I was out rather late last night delivering a baby. The midwife was otherwise occupied and I haven't heard. I was so busy yesterday I didn't even glance at the Gazette."

"Well Sir, I trust mother and baby are fine, thanks to your expert care," Thomas offered. "Sir, there's no small amount of speculation around town about the war and what Mr. Lincoln intends to do but this very morning brings word the U.S fleet sailed up the York and anchored and is even now offloading troops. I have no reason not to believe it is true, yet I pray its not."

"Indeed, invading already? I dare say I hoped we'd be spared this war. I'd not heard this development, forgive me, young man." Not waiting for Thomas to reply, Dr. King continued, "I met with Captain Cook and others concerning the need for medical care, but I thought such discussions were for the future, down in the Carolinas." The doctor's voice trailed, realizing those conversations were no longer hypothetical. War was closing fast, long before he or anyone had expected, let alone had time to prepare.

Dr. King's medical practice consisted mostly of childbirths when midwives weren't available, tending to fevers, and care of the elderly. His trauma experience was limited to an occasional overturned wagon, falling off a horse, or an accident involving farm implement or other cutting device. *I must send to Richmond for textbooks on surgery*, he realized. Dr. King also knew he'd need medications for his supply was barely adequate for local day-to-day needs and entirely inadequate for armed conflict.

Seeing the doctor deep in thought, Thomas hesitated to interrupt, finally finding the courage. "Sir, if I may, I came to call upon Victoria. I am quite taken with her charms," Thomas offered, not sure what or how to explain his feelings to her father.

"Indeed, young man you hardly know her," Dr. King replied preoccupied, still shaken by the thought of doctoring wounded, having heard accounts of the carnage at Big Bethel.

"Well, yes Sir, that may be true but what I meant was I hoped to come to know Victoria better, but I fear I may be delayed in such matters, what with signing up and all. In any case, I am more than charmed by fair Victoria. I could not bear to sign up and leave without letting her know my true feelings."

"Young man, Victoria's feelings are a matter of speculation, especially for us men, but you have my permission to call upon Victoria as she may see you, if that is your mind."

"Yes Sir, thank you. It is indeed my sincere wish, in fact, it's the only thing on my mind," Thomas volunteered, wishing even as he'd spoken, he could recall the words. Blushing and embarrassed, he quickly changed the subject. "Sir, you do know with the College closed, and the Yanks nearby, I'll soon be gone off with Company C, 32nd Virginia." Voicing for the first time what had replayed over and over in his thoughts for days, Thomas was stunned but continued. "In fact, I sent my slave to pack all my belongings, so I am ready whatever service may be required." He was unsure what duties might await, though he had the basic prerequisites; an accomplished horseman and accurate marksman. He was also a quick and willing learner.

"I'm proud of you young man. Even my old bones will soon be draping a uniform I expect, as doctors will be needed. Now excuse me young man, but if the news is as you describe, I must again speak with President Ewell about a surgeon's commission." And with that Dr. King rose, turning at the door adding, "Victoria will be out presently. Good luck young man." Thomas was left to ponder his first conversation with Dr. King, in which he'd just announced his infatuation with his daughter, Victoria, and his imminent departure to soldier for the Confederacy.

After a brief pause, the door re-opened, this time Mrs. King and Victoria emerging, the latter wearing a pale yellow dress with matching shawl and bonnet. Thomas was again immediately on his feet, offering the purloined daffodils to Victoria. Mrs. King signaled for Thomas to join Victoria on the joggling bench, while she took her favorite rocker and resumed her embroidery in the sunshine. The two youngsters stared into each other eyes, whispering to the point where Mrs. King cleared her throat, reminding them of her presence. Thomas explained what he'd told her father adding "if you would be so inclined, Victoria, will you write me often and await my return? "

Victoria allowed, "I will, but I can't imagine you'll be gone all that long Thomas? After all, the college will resume in fall as always, won't it Mother?"

"I'm sure it will dear," her mother replied, while Thomas, though hopeful she was right, was less certain. Despite his inclination and preference to remain in their company, Thomas knew he must go. He was pleased he'd obtained what he'd sought -Victoria's promise of devotion.

"Ladies, if you will please excuse me, I must depart to make my preparations." Lingering as long as he could, he finally broke a kind of strange magnetism seemingly holding him to the porch. As Thomas waved from the gate, it never occurred this could be the last time he'd see Victoria. Everyone was speaking of the war as short and victorious –like a brief interruption before things returned to the way they were supposed to be, the way life had always been. Little did Mrs. King suspect she'd soon be similarly bidding farewell to her husband.

***

Meanwhile across town, W.B. made it to the Gazette, proudly informing the clerk, "I got a message for Mr. Lively."

"Yes, thank you, I'll be sure to give it to him right away."

"Yes, Mam," W.B. thanked, his enthusiasm instantly deflated by completion of his task.

As W.B. departed, the clerk headed to the back room which served as Mr. Lively's office. She knew he was busy with a visitor, the Revered Thomas Ambler, Bruton Parish, but as she'd been instructed, news can't wait, so she knocked on closed doors, apologizing for the interruption.

"Yes, enter."

"Begging your pardon Sir," nodding to Rev. Ambler, "but this message just arrived, Sir."

Seeing the note was from Captain Cook, Lively offered, "If you will please excuse me Reverend."

"Of course," the Revered agreed, equally interested in hearing the news.

"My God! Excuse my language Reverend, but Yanks have landed!"

"Oh my," Reverend Ambler let out. "What else does he say?"

"He's calling on all able bodied men to do their Christian duty" as he says, and for women to evacuate children to Richmond and points west. He wants a special edition to spread the news."

"Stop the presses!" Lively shouted, loud enough to be heard through closed doors above the din. "Reverend, I am afraid I must conclude our meeting due to this urgent news."

Civil War Comes Home

"Of course," Reverend Ambler replied, already gathering his hat. Humming, "Onward Christian soldiers," he was suddenly inspired to write his next sermon, *denouncing the invasion as the devil's work, and how it was every man and woman's Christian duty to rise up against this affront to God.*

***

"Marsa, what's with you Suh, runnin' in here all out of wind," Thomas' slave asked. Thomas noted little progress on the sorting, packing and loading of his possessions while he'd been calling on Miss Victoria. *Where do I ship it?* Not knowing where or when, they'd be going, or end up, Thomas wasn't sure.

"Come on, fetch the steamer trunk, it'll hold my books."

"Suh you put all 'dem books in one trunk, nobody can lift it," his slave observed, no doubt from experience.

"Well then put half books, the rest clothes, and what about your stuff?"

"Marsa everything I got is right here in this haversack."

"Very well, as soon as you have the trunk packed, go down and hire a cart and horse. Nothing too costly, just something to get us to camp."

The slave neatly arranged a bottom layer of books, carefully folding clothes on top while Thomas sat down, pulled out his lap desk, ink, and quill to begin another letter.

"Marsa, you writing at a time like this? I just took your last letter."

"Not another letter, just a note to Miss Victoria. She said she'd be waitin' for me when I got back."

Looking at Thomas, the slave shook his head, trying to conceal a smirk, "ain't my Marsa smit by love. Just come in from paying her a call, and already writing her."

"It's a farewell letter, now let me be so I can think of what to write," Thomas instructed, frustrated at his loss for words not his slave's good natured teasing.

Thomas's slave returned to packing, managing to fit all the master's clothes into one trunk then departed to arrange transportation. He thought about asking Thomas if he must accompany him, but didn't bother for he was certain he knew the answer. On the way to the livery, he again bumped into W.B. Nelson, this time talking with Yellow Jim.

Surprised, they quickly asked, "Where you off to in such a rush?"

"Well, Marsa gonna be a soldier and I got to get a wagon on account he be takin' so much books and clothes. What he be needin' all dat whilst fightin'?"

"You going ?"

"Expect so," Thomas' slave replied, uncertain if he had any other option.

"Damn fool, why you fightin' da white man's war? You like being slave?" W.B. questioned sharply, Yellow Jim looking on with quite interest. Though a man of few words, he understood far more than he let on. He was just more circumspect than most in what he shared.

It bothered W.B. his friend would accept going to war with his master. W.B. had invested considerable time thinking on it while working the fields. "Look, as slave you up at dawn, mostly likely earlier or whenever Marsa says you gots to be up, and he don't care a lick whether you tired, sick, or hungry. Everybody; man, woman, and child gots to do his bidding and you best be jumpin'. No grumbling, or delay for if you tarry, you feel the sting of his whip. You breaks your back all day, whether freezing cold, or burning sun, 'til exhaustion, and you consider yourself lucky if you get anything to eat, even slop not fit for hogs. Finally, you collapse on the dirt floor of a cabin crowded with others, if lucky sharing a blanket between you. And for what, Marsa gets richer, and you gets up and does it all over again da' next day and every day for the rest of yo' life. That what you want?"

"No, course not. We all want better and I sure don't wanna get killed, Lord no," the slave replied. "What choice is there?"

"Fool, you need to decide fo' yourself. Me, I'm planning on joining up, but I'll be fighting for me and all the slaves, not fo' white Marsa. I heard they gonna be forming up units just for us so we be fightin' too," W.B. explained.

"That's right," Jim agreed, "I heard ol' man Jeff Davis is madder than a hornet over it too. "

"Now hows you know a thing like that," W.B. asked, surprised to hear Yellow Jim mention the Confederate leader.

"It was writ up in the Washington paper," then quickly adding, "so I was told," not wanting to reveal to even trusted slaves, he was literate. "You know 'bout Mr. Lincoln needing more soldiers don't you? Dem first seventy-five thousand boys joined for three months. Hell, by time the short timers learnt marchin' and they finally got weapons, it'll be time to be headin' home."

Civil War Comes Home

"How you planning on going about joining up, W.B." Thomas' slave asked.

"Well, I don't rightly know jest yet, but do you swear on your Momma's grave to keep secret? Now if you ever breathe even one word to anyone, most surely you'll be the cause to get me kilt, and I swear my ghost will take up in your bed. You'll get no peace for the rest of your days," W.B.'s genuine fear readily apparent. Both Yellow Jim and Thomas' slave, anxious to learn of W.B's plan, promised silence.

"OK, I'll tell you. On the next full moon I'm making a run for freedom, - headin' into 'ol White Oak Swamp and lay low a few days. Then after the heats off, I go up the Chickahominy River and then to the Underground Railroad, and keep making my way north. Steady north, not stopping 'til I make Boston. Yes Sir, Boston is the most welcoming place for freed slaves. Abolition folks help you find a place to live, give you food, and a payin' job. Not dis slavin' for the Marsa from time you old enough to walk 'til your tired whipped bones is laid in a grave."

Yellow Jim cautioned, "I don't know W.B., White Oak Swamp is right treacherous, and ol' Chickahominy River's drowned many a folks over the years. Folks enter the swamp are never seen or heard from again. Place is full of snakes, quicksand, evil spirits and such. You best not set foot near it. You better off headin' the other direction, go east to Fort Monroe. They building a whole city right outside the fort, 'Slabtown.' Thousands of runaways is there —everyone of 'em now 'contraband.' Army pays 'em to work. Good too, $11.00 a month, same as privates, and they get fed good every day. Go there, where you got food, a place to sleep, and job, not no White Oak Swamp."

"Well I heard such tales about the swamp too and so what? Folks lived in there for years and know secret paths and how to stay alive. I take my chances in there 'fore I spend rest of my born days in chains of slavery or git kilt trying to sneak past Rebs to make it to Fort Monroe. The Rebels got dogs hunting down runaways, treein' 'em like an ol' 'coon. Besides, I ain't gonna live in no Chickahomony swamp, just passin' thru to catch the Underground Railroad on the way north. Like I said, I be working and living a free man whilst you fools is still down here getting' whipped whenever Marsa's got a mind to when he's not having his way with your womenfolk."

"We know that ain't right, but nuttin' we can do 'bout it," joined Thomas's slave. Yellow Jim was hurt by W.B.'s reference to the ongoing affairs of many masters with their younger female slaves. *It ain't right,*

Yellow Jim seethed. At this disturbing thought, "I gotz to be movin' on," Yellow Jim remarked. He was on his secret mission to pass the news about the Rebs to the Yanks. In the unlikely event anyone questioned him, he had his Marsa' pass and would claim he was on an errand, and feign simple ignorance. Yellow Jim, like W.B. supported the Union. They'd risk their lives to pass information to officials at Fort Monroe. The slaves knew mostly they'd want to know troop strength, identities of commanding officers, and how and where forces were positioned. But with so little knowledge Union leaders gladly took any information they could get, and relied on cunning slaves who formed the 'Legal League,' -an organization of slaves acting as spies, gathering and transmitting information from local sources, often by courier to Union lines.

While both militaries, blue and grey, engaged uniformed espionage agents, both sides also drew upon extensive networks of civilian agents, formal and informal, including slaves like Yellow Jim, children, sometimes as newsboys, and foreigners. Yellow Jim and other slaves could sometimes easily pass critical information with little suspicion, such as the close line laundry signaling system. Other times, information was passed from behind Confederate lines in what became known as the "Black Dispatch." In time these came to be effectively used by several Union generals in Virginia and Carolina as well as the western front. General Rush Hawkins, the Union Commander at Cape Hatteras, North Carolina, who had advised McClellan on an amphibious plan for the Peninsula remarked, "If I want to find out anything hereabouts I hunt up a Negro; and if he knows or can find out, I'm sure to get all I want."[51] Frederick Douglas similarly espoused the contributions of slaves to the Union war effort,

"The true history of this war will show that the loyal army found no friends at the South so faithful, active and daring in their efforts to sustain the Government as the Negroes. It will be shown that they have been the safest guides to our army and the best pilots to our navy, and the most dutiful laborers on our fortifications, when they have been permitted to serve. Gen. Burnside in the difficult task committed to him of feeling his way in the intricate rivers and creeks of Virginia and North Carolina, has found no assistance among the so-called loyal whites comparable in value to that obtained from intelligent Black men."

In addition to gathering and transmitting intelligence, the Legal League secret slave organization helped Yankees that had escaped from

---

51 op. cit.

Confederate prisons to return north, much as white abolitionists operated the Underground Railroad assisting runaway slaves to freedom.

Yellow Jim had the good sense not to divulge his secrets to anyone, even fellow slaves. He had no faith in promises of silence, as W.B. had invoked, having seen first-hand how even the strongest could be forced to talk. Mostly, Yellow Jim weeded the kitchen garden, biding his time close by the main house, listening and observing, all while remaining unseen himself, hidden in plain sight. Periodically, he'd disappear into the night to tend to Legal League business, but he was always back before dawn. Yellow Jim thought about W.B.'s plan to escape, resolving to considerate it again but realizing he was contributing to freedom through his clandestine activities, decided to stay in place. Besides, successful operatives were not easily replaced.

As Yellow Jim slipped into shadows making his way through dangerous territory enroute to Fort Monroe, W.B. and Thomas' slave bid farewell. Each faced danger, one soon to fight the white man's war, the other continuing the larger struggle against slavery, neither certain how long they had.

***

"'Bout time you returned," Thomas remarked to his slave. "What took so long? Did you bring the wagon?"

"Marsa, I done checked everywhere but there's no wagons to be had, not a cart, horse or mule available, not anywhere, at any price. You see Suh, all of a sudden like, everybody's got to have a wagon, headin' outta town.

***

"Damnation. Well then, we just got to carry it."

Struggling with the large, loaded trunk, his slave was quiet, burdened also with thinking about why he had to go off to fight this white man's war. *Was W.B. right? Was now the time to rise against it? There's nothing I can do at the moment. If I drop the trunk and run, I'd immediately be captured and severely whipped, though Thomas has never once struck me. No, I got to bide my time and wait, like W.B.'s doin'. Wait for just the right moment.*

Jake McKenzie

Figure 17. The Christopher Wren building, College of William & Mary. Rear view Courtesy, Special Collections, Special Collections Research Center, Earl Swem Library, College of William and Mary, Williamsburg, Va.

Figure 18. The Christopher Wren building, College of William & Mary, front view Courtesy of the Colonial Williamsburg Foundation, Williamsburg, Va.

Eventually the pair made it back to the Wren building where a few students were still preparing to travel home. Inside, President Ewell continued preparations for shutting down.

Closure of the college did not mean Ewell's work was done. Far from it, there was as much or more to be accomplished preparing for closure than required to operate day-to-day. Ewell had the foresight to ensure the necessary arrangements were accomplished in a logical and thorough manner for this would be essential to reopening as quickly as possible. There was far more to it than bolting shutters and locking doors. Contracts for faculty, staff, and support services had to adjusted or renegotiated and historic and legal documents had to be shipped elsewhere for safekeeping.

Besides responsibility for the College which included faculty and students in addition to buildings, Ewell also took his commitment to long time friend John Magruder quite seriously. Ewell's concurrent military obligations focused on two principal duties; the design and construction of the Williamsburg defense line, which would protect both town and College, and, organizing and training the 32nd Virginia infantry which would do likewise. The new unit included several faculty, the majority of his students, and many life-long friends and neighbors, from all walks of life. Although Captain Cook undertook day-to-day operations, Ewell was in overall command and ultimately responsible. To Ewell's way of thinking his dual military missions were inseparable; the manpower of his new unit was required to help build then man the defenses and the earthworks would protect and shelter his men. In a like manner, he viewed defense of the town and college closure as closely related. A man driven to accomplish all things well, Ewell was working seven days a week, often from before dawn to regularly well into the night.

The field work to design and layout earthworks was a huge undertaking for the line spanned the width of the Peninsula from College Creek to Queens Creek. It was crucial not only to the town's defense but to the South's grand strategy: Yankees had to be contained, if not defeated, short of Richmond. How far east of the Capitol this could best be accomplished became the central point of discussion and planning at the Confederate White House.

Jake McKenzie

Figure 20. The William & Mary faculty, 1862. Six joined as Confederate officers while the seventh worked in Richmond as a Confederate civil servant Courtesy, Special Collections, Special Collections Research Center, Swem Library, College of William and Mary, Williamsburg, Va.

While Ewell had full responsibility for preparing the defense, he knew better than to operate in a vacuum, and took care to seek and obtain repeated approvals of his plans as work progressed. Optimizing use of natural terrain features, Ewell's detailed drawings and maps for more than a dozen redoubts were reviewed and approved by no lesser authority on military engineering than Robert E. Lee. In itself this was no small accomplishment given the growing bureaucracy in Richmond. Then, came surveying and site demarcation, locating and contracting for labor and materials, followed by overseeing the work ensuring all was built according to specifications. This took considerable time, most of it on-site and while Ewell was spending long days in the field, his College closure tasks were delayed. Within this impossible schedule, he was also working to organize, man, train, and equip a new military unit – a task neither Ewell nor anyone else could accomplish single-handedly.

Because Ewell was, of necessity, spending so much time on the defense works, some men of the newly created 32nd Virginia came to view him as an absentee commander, a leader in title only. When Ewell often had to miss formations and musters, the men did not then appreciate it was only because he was overseeing construction of positions upon which their very lives would soon depend. Some became increasingly disenchanted, blaming every delay, disruption or disappointment in military life on the absent commander, and movement to replace him began.[52]

Although Ewell was disappointed when men of his unit voted to replace him, especially as he'd done all the ground work drawing up community support for creating the 32nd then scouring the country-side for enlistees. In other ways, however, Ewell was relieved to be free of one of too many duties. Commanding a newly forming unit had proven far more demanding than either he or Magruder had appreciated. Now, Ewell could focus on closure of the College and timely completion of defenses, the latter taking on increased urgency as word of the Yankee build-up on the lower Peninsula continued trickling in. Again, President Ewell would have no easy time of it.

Engineer officer, Captain Alfred Landon Rives was dispatched to check on the status of the defense works. Touring the line the young engineer found a number of reasons to criticize both its design and execution. Having worked tirelessly and having gotten approvals at every step, Ewell

---

52 By late May, 1862, Ewell was not re-elected Colonel of the 32nd and was replaced by popular attorney, Edgar B. Montague, then Lieutenant Colonel of the 53rd Virginia Infantry.

was understandably furious. He protested the works were already approved by everyone from Magruder to Lee, but to no avail. Apparently young Captain Rives was out to make his name, not caring who he offended in doing so. Rives persisted until somehow both Magruder and Lee were persuaded to order the alterations. Adding insult, these were to be implemented by Ewell with no additional funding, manpower, equipment or supplies authorized.

As disappointed as Ewell was about faults found with his work, he was more upset when he eventually learned of a change in Confederate strategy. Secret plans now called for withdraw from Yorktown, passing through Williamsburg on a grand march west, to defend the Capitol not from the Peninsula, but the very gates of Richmond. The strategy no longer included using the lines on which Ewell and so many others had labored so tirelessly. Ewell had understood Magruder's request as a valid need. *Certainly, so much labor and resources would not be expended for something unless it was critical,* Ewell understood. It had certainly seemed reasonable to West Point graduate Ewell, as it had to fellow alumnus, Robert E. Lee, President Davis' senior military advisor, that they'd fight the Yankees right here, where they had clear advantage. This was far less risky than repeatedly withdrawing, giving up prepared positions only to retreat to find somewhere else to stand and fight. *Why we could end up in the quagmire of Chickahominy River bottomlands between Williamsburg and Richmond.*

How would the town and college now be defended? When Ewell finally came to the realization there was neither plan nor interest in defending Williamsburg he was incredulous! The revelation, b*oth town and college are sacrificed* hit like a bolt. Women and children would be defenseless, subject to the ravages of the enemy. But, he tried to rationalize, *if we stay and fight, the town, and the college along with it, will be destroyed in the bombardment. Innocent women, children, elderly, and wounded will be killed, either in the explosions or the resulting fires. On the other hand, if we clear out, and there's no resistance, they may pass through, intent on the chase. With any luck, they may be in too much of a hurry to loot or pillage,* he hoped wishfully. *Maybe they'll pass woman and children by with a tip of the hat, 'How do you do Mam?'* Ewell hoped he was right, but there wasn't a damn thing he could do about it now. The situation had gone far beyond anything anyone could control.

Ewell turned instead to the one thing he could influence -closing the College of William & Mary. Closing it and leaving it undefended were completely different matters. *What else must I do so the buildings, historic records, and chance of someday reopening are not destroyed?*

Though disagreeing with the revised Confederate strategy, and discouraged the hard work of preparing defense works was seemingly for naught, Ewell neither faulted his superiors, nor waivered in continuing to do everything in his power to ensure success. While President Ewell remained burdened with his original responsibilities for the college, his friend General Magruder took on a different kind of task.

***

'Prince John', as Magruder was affectionately known, strode into the parlor full of ladies, bowing deeply, the plume of his wide-brimmed hat brushing the floor acknowledging polite applause. He'd grown accustomed to a hero's welcome and today's visit brought him to the temporary Williamsburg home of Mrs. Letitia Tyler Semple, late of 'Villa Margaret.' On the eastern bank of the Hampton River, it was once the fine estate of her father, former President John Tyler.

"My dear ladies," Magruder opened warmly, "how good of y'all to see me. Words cannot express the importance with which I hold the many contributions of the ladies auxiliary. The gratitude my men and I feel towards your noble efforts knows no bounds." Always theatrical, he continued in stage voice, "My dear mothers of the Confederacy, why if you could only see how much it means to our soldiers when your packages and letters arrive. I pray, do continue your efforts and now, in the face of these heathen invaders, double your efforts on behalf of our gallant fighting men."

While keeping a watchful eye on Yanks, Prince John also kept in touch with the women. Their support might well determine, at least in part, whether wounded soldiers perished or survived. There were some things Army logistics hadn't quite yet figured out, for example; bandages and dressings, replacement clothing, especially socks, and palatable food. Men in the field counted on women's auxiliaries to make up the shortfalls. No where would this become more apparent than in providing medical care.

Working the room like the lady's man he fancied himself, the plumed and groomed Prince John kissed hands and cheeks, making each feel the sole object of attention, if not affection. He usually drew a crowd, but it wasn't only the hero of Big Bethel that accounted for the turnout to Letitia's invitation. The Tyler family was well known in Peninsula social circles, her friends thronging to see her again on her return from up north. Letitia and her husband, James, until recently the U.S. Navy paymaster in New York, came back to Virginia as soon as the secession vote was tallied.

Figure 22. Villa Margaret, Hampton, Va. summer home of President and Mrs. John Tyler and their fifteen children. Courtesy History Museum, City of Hampton, Va.

During their flight from what would soon be enemy territory, a fellow traveler had Letitia's ear, and she heard more about the unsanitary conditions of camp life and more soldiers succumbing to disease than gunshot, than she'd ever imagined. This gave her the idea to establish a soldier's hospital and she wanted to enlist as many friends as would join her cause. Her compassion for the fate of Southern soldiers now matched the depth with which she despised Yankees, especially for driving her family from their home.

At Villa Margaret, Letitia had enjoyed an idyllic childhood, one of fifteen children of President John Tyler and wife Julia, the siblings spent their youth swimming, fishing, crabbing the waters of Hampton Roads and picking peaches on their six acre estate. As she grew to womanhood, there were fancy balls and dances at Fort Monroe, and the grand social scene, Old Point Comfort and its famous Hygeia hotel. Many young gentlemen called on Letitia and her sisters, enjoying evenings on the high veranda of the three-story Renaissance home on the Hampton River.

However, Letitia's family's life was shattered when 3rd and 4th Massachusetts took over Villa Margaret as their barracks, turning out the

Tyler children including Letitia's baby sister, Pearl. President Tyler was away at Richmond as a delegate to the Confederate Congress when this disaster struck and Letitia was already married and in New York, so it fell to Mrs. Tyler to protest the Yankee affront. Her impassioned appeals fell on deaf ears at Fort Monroe and the White House. Seeing what they'd put her mother and younger siblings through, Letitia harbored an unabiding hatred of Union soldiers. *They come all the way down here from Massachusetts just to ruin our home,* Letitia never forgot.

Her sad recollections fueled her resolve to do everything in her power for the Southern cause. As Letitia explained her purpose, Magruder grew increasingly uncomfortable. He did not share the ladies' fervor for convincing soldiers to live righteously or healthfully. After decades in uniform, he was convinced good ol' boys made fine soldiers who would curse, drink, swear, gamble, and smoke whenever and wherever they saw fit, and no wife, mother, or doctor would tell them otherwise. Nevertheless, *if they wanted to supply food and medicine why not,* Magruder rationalized. However, it was not only her friends and Prince John that Letitia wanted to convince.

Letitia had also told her father what she'd learned of the plight of soldiers, and as she pressed her cause, he recalled her headstrong nature, apparently undiluted by time or marriage. He knew she'd not easily be dissuaded. Finally, almost in self-defense, he agreed to use his reputation and authority as seated member of the Confederate Congress to gain her audience with Confederate Secretary of War Pope Walker.

***

Richmond

Ushered into the War Secretary's office, Letitia opened immediately, "There must be better medical care for our soldiers, and not just after a battle but every day. Who takes care of our 'boys' so far from home?" she asked rhetorically. "Why no one," answering her question. "These men have neither idea nor inclination to keep themselves clean, well fed, or healthy. The longer in camp, the sicker they get. Conditions are disgraceful. All the camps are a disgrace, and unsanitary in the extreme! When men take ill, which is inevitable given their slovenly ways and lack of nutritious food, they have no medical care. None!" After her harsh opening, Letitia paused to allow the War Secretary's reply, but he deemed response pointless.

Secretary Walker listened politely as Letitia stated her case, poignantly but apparently not convincingly. It was only out of respect for her father that he'd granted her an audience and he wasn't really even listening. "I do not see any need for more hospitals. Now if you will please excuse me, I really must attend to more important matters," he replied.

Furious at his dismissal, Letitia remarked in a voice loud enough for all to hear while being escorted out, "Pray Sir, what can be a more pressing than the health of our troops?" She'd inherited her father's fighting spirit and was not about to be put off. She could care less about clerks trying to quiet her, picturing instead the malnourished, sick, and wounded desperate for aid. Letitia understood better than the War Secretary and his legions of clerks, nutrition, sanitation, and medical care were so lacking as to be virtually nonexistent.

"Very well, Madam," Secretary Walker announced, seeing she'd not be put off, "I'll grant permission for you to set up this hospital you feel is so important, but we have no funds for such foolishness." The Secretary hoped this would end her strident pleas, and clear her from his office.

Surprised and elated, Letitia had the presence of mind to manage a respectful, "Thank you, Sir," then immediately adding, "and I will treasure your letter of authority on this matter." Letitia, having come of age among her father's White House staff, was wise in the ways of bureaucracy and had the good sense to know to get a concession or support in writing.

Secretary Walker grimaced. He'd not anticipated her tenacity and deflected her to his staff. A clerk, emulating the practice of apparently the entire office, tried to put her off again, "Yes, Mam, we'll be in touch when the paperwork has been drawn up."

Wise to the ways of government officials, Letitia was not about to depart without the War Secretary's signed promise. As she persisted, the clerk also capitulated lest he never be rid of her. "Very well Madam, as you wish." After another considerable wait he re-appeared, bearing a large rolled document. Letitia quickly but carefully looked it over ensuring all was in order including signature and affixed seal. Finally satisfied, she thanked the relieved clerk, turned on her heels and was off, more determined than ever to establish a Confederate soldier's hospital.

Hurrying back to Williamsburg, she found the road so clogged, progress was delayed. Traffic was unusually heavy in both directions; military personnel and their supply wagons headed east, while west bound was a steady stream of civilians burdened by their worldly possessions. Wagons piled high signaled flight from the pending conflict.

Letitia sought to enlist her friends, hence the invitations to her parlor. While the women mostly discussed the latest news, Letitia tried to keep their attention on plans for converting the Female Academy into a hospital. She proudly displayed her hard-won War Secretary document, not mentioning at this time, there was no funding authorized.

Meanwhile, having heard bits of Letitia's diatribe against the Army's failure to care for its soldiers, Prince John began to look in earnest for an excuse to extricate himself, seeking to avoid embarrassment should they ask him to address shortcomings in medical care. He found Letitia's circle to be unlike any he'd previously met where the ladies mostly maneuvered for his attention without all this 'storm' and politics. Letitia's band of sisters already had enough of hollow pronouncements and broken promises and were fed up with political double talk, none of which had ever improved any soldier's lot one bit.

Prince John was soon apologizing, mumbling, 'military matters demanding urgent attention,' when Letitia announced it was time they took matters into their own hands. "If we wait on politicians and Generals nothing will get done."

Her friends agreed for none had heard from their sons or husbands, and there was certainly no information about their health, welfare, or even whereabouts. Thus, with the sympathies of her friends and the War Secretary's support, albeit tacit, she found renewed impetus to move forward.

Figure 23. The Female Academy, Williamsburg, Va. Courtesy of the Colonial Williamsburg Foundation, Williamsburg, Va.

Among the gathered friends was Mrs. Durfey, fellow member of Bruton parish choir, accompanied by daughter, Margaret, though the latter had protested being part of that 'flock of old hens.' Only after Mrs. Durfey allowed Margaret to have her own friend, Victoria King, along did Margaret consent. While the women met, Margaret and Victoria carried on about what would they do with all the young men gone off to war? Victoria blushed when she told Margaret about Thomas Barlow, and Margaret was embarrassed, "I don't even have a boy friend and now they're all leaving."

"Don't fret Margaret," Victoria offered, 'just you wait, the right man will come along for you, probably when you least expect it."

Back in the parlor, Letitia, Mrs. Durfey and others continued discussing plans for the Female Academy and were soon expanding their consideration to include other private schools; Male Academy, Female Institute, Classical & Mathematical Institute, Mrs. Young's Female Academy, Mrs. Allen's Male & Female School, Mr. Blain's Mathematical & Classical School for boys, Miss Lindsay's Academy, and Miss Gilliam's seminary. While encouraged, Letitia worried, *how will we possibly obtain funds for such an undertaking?*

Eventually they adjourned, promising to meet again soon, as they had so much to do and little time. Though they felt the War Secretary's dismissal of soldier medical care as an insignificant woman's issue was wrong, they would not be dissuaded.

In coming weeks, Letitia and friends worked hard transforming the Female Academy into what resembled a hospital. All the school desks, tables and chairs had to be moved out and there were no longer any men, free or slave, around town to do the hauling. Then, beds, crates of linens and medical supplies had to be unloaded and carried up the stairs and set up. The women learned as they went and by the time they'd converted several of the classrooms to wards, they'd surprised themselves with their problem solving skills.

With a great sense of accomplishment and renewed determination, they were now anxious to show the results of their planning and labor to Confederate leaders. They were hopeful their example would be replicated elsewhere, and that funds might yet be made available for soldier medical care, and Letitia decided to host an open house. Among those calling was Confederate General Lafayette McLaws. He'd heard about her visit to the War Secretary and wanted to see the outcome. He also visited out of respect for his friend, former President Tyler. Referring to Letitia, General

McLaws remarked, "I hadn't been in the room more than five minutes, when if she had said to me, 'bring me a bucket of water from the spring,' I would have done it!"

Letitia exemplified the 'take-charge attitude' essential to the task before them. Her group and other women's hospital auxiliaries were noted for their accomplishments, often against very long odds. Their vision and hard work were fortuitous. The consequences of not having otherwise provided adequate medical care would soon become all too evident.

***

Figure 24. Confederate President Jefferson Davis. Courtesy of the Library of Congress, Washington, D.C.

Richmond

Confederate President Jefferson Davis ordered, "Make for Williamsburg with utmost speed and defend at all peril, lest the Capitol fall and our cause lost."

East bound, as Letitia saw, the road was jammed, hundreds if not thousands of troops, all hurrying at quick step. Among the regular units rushing from the Valley and northern Virginia, were a handful of home guard details consisting mostly of elderly, recovering wounded, and boys. Many of the latter were slowed down by lugging heavy old flintlocks. Though their firearms were more family heirloom than modern weapon, they'd nevertheless prove effective for they'd been relied upon for generations to put meat on the table. Regardless of vintage, every weapon was needed and what the irregulars lacked in firepower, they made up for in determination. For most of 'em, every day of their lives had been a struggle just to stay alive. With training, they'd eventually become soldiers -some more disciplined than others, but every one of them tough.

They came from diverse backgrounds; from prosperous families with lineage traced to the original colonists, to common laborers struggling to barely feed a starving family. Even share croppers working marginal lands long depleted by countless seasons of cotton or tobacco, supported the Southern cause, even if many of them may not have fully understood it or the ramifications of a slave-based agrarian society. Though these poor had not enjoyed society's benefits, they'd not allow Northern invaders to take anything from them —at least not without a fight to the death. Far as most knew, they were defending their way of life from foreign oppression and it was their God-given duty to do so.

Such unity of purpose was unheard of in the North where the war brought frequent protests, some violent. In marked contrast to Southerners, should a Northern man object to war, or simply prefer not to serve for any reason, he simply paid a replacement to stand in for him. Let someone else do the dying, was a common reaction. Such a system was incomprehensible to Southerners, including William & Mary students and who understood it was their God-given duty and a matter of honor to defend their homeland.

***

Strolling back to his office, William Peachy was deep in thought about his conversation with Captain Cook when he stopped, turned, and headed down Main St. to the general store, adjacent to Raleigh Tavern. Although the store had been completely destroyed by fire in 1859 it had been rebuilt much larger the following year by Mr. William W. Vest, proprietor.

Upon entering Peachy asked, "Sir, I hear you're planning to leave for your wife's family farm in Henrico?"

"Yes, with the children, my wife no longer feels safe this close to the front," Mr. Vest explained.

"Indeed, Sir it would appear the Yanks are at hand, but how can you leave your store?"

Civil War Comes Home

"That Sir is the crux of the matter. I can't leave for the people need my store and besides, all my assets are tied up. My inventory is extensive as you know."

"Indeed, it would appear so. Tell you what Vest, we've been friends a long time and I'm always one to help out. What if I offered to buy you out? Everything in the store, the entire inventory."

Vest was dumbstruck. "Sir, thank you but what do you know about mercantile? I can't picture you a store keeper." Though Vest knew his wife was anxious to leave, he couldn't just walk away from what he'd spent his life building. "Uh, well, I suppose," he finally managed.

"Vest, what's your inventory worth?"

"I don't rightly know off hand. Give me a few minutes," Vest stammered, scurrying behind the counter retrieving two leather bound ledger books, well worn, one for inventory, the other accounts payable. With war looming, he knew the latter would soon be worthless. The ability of clients to pay off accounts for seed and farming implements, not to mention cloth, thread, needles, pins, and other household goods, was problematic even when harvests were bountiful. Now, he estimated his chances of ever collecting were near zero. *Somehow it didn't seem right,* he thought. By extending credit for seed and farm supplies, Mr. Vest had singlehandedly underwritten a significant portion of the local economy. Despite the prospect of losing his life's savings, he wasted no time on what might have been, and tallied up his inventory. The long list included every manner of farm implement and household goods. Anything factory-made came through Vest's store, mostly from northern suppliers, which had already dried up since the secession. After pouring over his ledger, carefully rechecking figures, Vest announced, "My good Mr. Peachy, as you can see Sir, there is considerable inventory, both in the store and in several out buildings. In all, these total well over thirteen hundred dollars at my cost, and worth considerably more at current prices," Vest explained. "Furthermore, my accounts payable are worth at least that much if not considerably more. Are you proposing to purchase these just debts as well?" He wondered, *just what is Peachy thinking? If I can get him to pay half, I'll have to take it, despite the loss.*

In his best poker face, Peachy showed no reaction. He'd never fancied himself a shop keeper and had no idea how much inventory it took to stock a general store, or what it was worth. He thought, *now if I can get all this for a good price...I wonder how low he will go?*

In the awkward silence, Vest heard his daughter crying and his wife calling after their son from the cramped living space above the store. Momentarily, Peachy broke the quiet, "Tell you what Mr. Vest, in view of our long term friendship, I am prepared to offer you one hundred dollars cash for your inventory. As far as any accounts payable, I have no idea what records you've kept, nor what agreement you made with the debtors but that hardly matters. When the war arrives your accounts payable will be worthless. Many of the debtors may not survive and if they do, no one will be in any position to repay anything. No, I'll just purchase the inventory. You can keep your ledger books," Peachy explained harshly but Vest knew the truth in his logic even if it meant his business was ruined.

Vest was shocked and disappointed. He'd thought Peachy was his friend and trying to help, but on hearing his preposterous offer, imagined his real interest was war profiteering. Vest replied calmly as he could, "Mr. Peachy, as you probably know I've spent my life as a merchant supporting the needs of every citizen of this town. My 'accounts payable,' justly owed me, is more than the value of my entire inventory, which is far more than ten times your offer. It's taken all my life to build this business, and for the town's benefit and you would have me give it all to you for pennies on the dollar? Tell you what, give me half and its yours, all of it," Vest offered.

"I understand Mr. Vest, but no, I can't pay you half and no one would. The country is at war. It's your choice -leave inventory here and it's captured and used against us. If Yanks advance and take the town, you'll obtain nothing for the entire lot."

Vest remained silent, disappointed that his supposed friend was trying to take advantage of the wartime situation. At the same time he realized Peachy was right, and there was nothing he could do.

"Cash?" Vest inquired, "not a promissory note that'd be worthless in Henrico?"

"Yes Sir, allow me to return to my office and I'll bring the funds to consummate the deal." With Williamsburg too small to have a bank, business deals were either bartered, or limited to the few who had cash or gold. "Then, you'll be on your way with your family to the safety of Henrico."

Vest had no choice but to try to set the price. "All right, give me one-third the value and it's yours –all of it."

Peachy reconsidered, *one-third was a lot more than what I offered but I knew he'd not take the initial low offer. Even at a price of a third, there's still a wide margin for a considerable profit, and the army will buy up most of this inventory at inflated prices,* Peachy thought.

"Very well," Peachy agreed, "one third it is, of the listed inventory, but not the accounts payable. The property is worth something but the debt is worthless."

Vest remained silent. He sensed Peachy would not deal at one-half the inventory value, and he understood his concern about the accounts payable, hard as it was to accept losses.

"Okay, one-third of the value of my inventory. But I'm sad to have mistaken your friendship these many years." Just wanting to be done with the whole affair, Vest excused himself up the narrow stairs to his living quarters. "We're leaving as soon as possible," he announced to his wife. "We can't make it all the way by nightfall, but we'll get as far as we can and find somewhere to stay the night."

Mrs. Vest didn't question, silently continuing to gather, sort, and pack clothes and personal belongings. She was torn between wanting to bring everything and knowing there was only room for a fraction of it in the wagon. First, the family bible, then her daughter's christening gown her late mother had made. Meanwhile, Mr. Vest went back downstairs, again going through his inventory, prioritizing high value items, determined *not to give everything away to that damn Peachy. He's got no idea what's here. I'll pack these for my use and he'll never know.* Placing two crates in the wagon, which he'd not included in the inventory, he began loading rifles, powder, shot, and flints, filling the first with munitions. Next, he turned to the small apothecary, gathering herbs, healing salts and balms, knowing these would be in great demand. Next he added soap, sacks of flour and as many cured hams as he could cram in. Nailing both crates shut, he returned upstairs to haul down trunks his wife loaded, piling them atop the crates, determined to load the wagon carefully for safe travel but as full as possible. He didn't know what they'd face and wanted to be prepared. Besides, they'd be starting anew in Henrico, his hurried packing fueled by resentment towards Peachy.

Meanwhile, Peachy, returning to his law office fast as his gout would allow, saw opportunity in the midst of calamity and seized it. He was determined to secure a generous share of whatever profits were to be had from this war. As he sat at his desk thinking over this deal, one of his slaves approached, "Marsa, Sir, what you need me to do?"

"Wait a minute while I finish this note, then you can take it to Captain

Cook for me most quick, and only him, mind you," Peachy instructed hastily scrawling,

"My Dear Captain Cook,

Sir, subsequent to our meeting last, I have acquired a considerable inventory of equipments and finished goods, many of which no doubt, would be of great service to your army. Included for sale are every manner of customary implements from shovel to nails, tools, and of course shot, powder, and flints.

Your humble servant,
Wm. Peachy, Esq."

"Now take this to Captain Cook without delay. Most likely you'll find him about the Wren Building, gathering recruits." The thought of war profiteering hadn't entered Peachy's mind. He rationalized he was merely helping the Vest family get out of a jam, while simultaneously supporting the war effort by making supplies available to the army for which they might have urgent need. Peachy's message got to the Wren building where Thomas and his slave waited in the shade with many others. Several large supply wagons had arrived and there was a great deal of commotion. So much so that Thomas found it hard to concentrate, the din of simultaneous conversations drowning his thought. There was endless speculation about the war, varied opinions on the enemy, and many questions about what was going to happen and when? What were the Yanks up to, how long will the war last, and most of all, what is their fate as soldiers? Misinformation far outweighed fact.

"At ease," Captain Cook shouted in his command voice from astride his mount so as to be seen and heard by all. "Gentlemen, hear this! I am Captain Cook, Commanding Officer of the Williamsburg Junior Guard. You are now part of the 32nd Virginia infantry. You no doubt heard by now, Yanks are offloading down to Ship Point. It's up to us to stop 'em. If there be any here ain't up to the fight speak now."

His challenge was met with silence. Though more than a few had trepidations, none dared admit fear. "Gentlemen, and I use the term loosely, our purpose here today," Captain Cook continued, "is to get everyone signed up, and properly enlisted to defend our homes against the northern invaders. As you probably already know, there's a handsome enlistment bonus authorized by President Jefferson Davis himself, payable to new recruits. Once everyone is signed up, you'll take the oath of allegiance, swearing faith to our cause then be given your equipment. See the wagons yonder? They's from the Quartermaster –the Army's supply store if you will, But before we get to issuing your equipment, I got some questions for you gents."

"By show of hands, who's here with your slave?" Among the several dozen, nearly half raised a hand -including many former students. "Very well, gentlemen your slave can come with you, but they'll be the working party and henceforth no longer your personal servants. When there are trenches to be dug, everyman, slave and free, will turn to and work." The Captain wanted no confusion for what he was calling for was previously unheard of - master and slave performing manual labor side-by-side. Preparing for battle was not the time to be debating a new social order. On hearing this, Thomas' slave recalled his conversation with W.B. about his plotting to escape.

"Next, by another show of hands," Captain Cook continued, "how many brought your horse or have one to bring?" Fewer hands rose. Poor lads from the country, without so much as a mule let alone horse, just stared at the dirt, embarrassed by their poverty. "Very well, those with horses most likely will be scouts and messengers -the eyes and ears of the Army."

"Last, how many brought a rifle or other firearm?" At this, nearly every hand shot up for it was customary for free men to go about daily business armed. In reporting for duty everyone had come bearing at least one, sometimes several firearms. These ranged from ancient pieces carried against the Red Coats, to handmade knives with which they were fearfully adept. Although some had newer rifles, they were of every different manufacture and model, meaning it was up to each man to obtain the spare parts needed to maintain his weapon. Brothers from poor families had one musket between them -their family's heirloom handed down. Regardless of their weaponry, the men claimed proficiency and a readiness to demonstrate it against the invaders.

After considerable delay, Captain Cook finally ordered, "All right, Line up!" Each man was to sign the enlistment roster. Those that could write did so but the majority made their 'X,' each mark then initialed by the Sergeant Major. Every man enlisting, except slaves, received a hand shake and a Confederate $10.00 bill for promising to lay down his life, should it come to that.

Along with Thomas Barlow, fellow William and Mary students; J.V. Bidgood, brothers James H. and Henry S. Dix, Henley Jones, Jr., Thomas Mercer, W. H. E. Morecock, J.D. Myers, and L.P. Slater signed up.[53] Others would join later.

With enlistment completed for now, Captain Cook called his recruits to attention, directing they raise their right hand and repeat after him the oath of allegiance to the Confederacy.

"I, ..., do solemnly swear that I will bear true faith and allegiance to the Confederate States of America and that I will serve them honestly and faithfully against all their enemies or oppressors whomsoever; and that I will observe and obey the orders of the President of the Confederate States and the orders of the officers appointed over me, according to the rules and Articles of War."

This completed, a loud cheer went up, marking their new status as brothers-in-arm and signaling nervous relief in an uncertain future.

"All right, line up to draw your gear," the sergeant ordered as quartermaster soldiers untied and pulled back the canvas on their wagons revealing what appeared to the recruits as an odd assortment of goods. First, each man was given his 'box' –a knapsack of waterproof canvas stretched taught over a wood frame -uncomfortable to the point of unbearable. The stiff wood frame dug into backs and shoulders even before loaded. Next were shoes. Master Thomas, now Private Barlow was one of the few wearing his own boots. Slaves and share croppers were mostly barefoot. The former would remain so while the latter drew heavy leather brogams. These were coarsely, often shoddily made, one size fits all, left and right the same. For some, these were the first new shoes they'd ever owned and were eagerly donned. Later, blistered from the stiff new leather, they weren't quite so pleased.

Next, those drawing muskets got accompanying bayonet, cartridge box, and cap pouch. Everyone received blanket and water proof ground cloth, along with canteen and tin cup. There were no extra uniforms and any additional clothing they furnished themselves, usually stashed in a small haversack also containing personal items and food.

After their equipment they drew rations. By regulation, they would have an ample, if bland diet. Daily allowance consisting of three quarters pound of pork or bacon, or one and a quarter pound of beef, eighteen

53 Heuvel, op. cit.

ounces bread or flour, or twelve ounces hard tack, or one and one forth cup corn meal. In addition to these individual rations, every hundred men were issued eight quarts peas or beans, or ten pounds rice. When available; coffee, sugar, vinegar, salt, and fresh vegetables were issued, quantities unspecified. However, what they actually had to eat seldom followed regulation. Sometimes men foraged, adding game, seasonal berries, wild greens and roots, or sometimes if they happened to camped within hiking distance of lake, stream or river; fish and even turtles were added, though not commonly.

Despite perpetual hunger, the men did little to improve their diet for cooking was considered woman's work. Back on their farms and homesteads it was women who knew how to cook, season, and which native plants provided sustenance and flavor. Should a soldier seek to learn, he was teased about doing women's chores. Even in the best of times when they were issued all their rations, soldiers endured an inadequate, if not unhealthful diet, poorly prepared.

Between rations and equipment, every man was heavily burdened carrying the minimum essentials to live, however austerely. But the unit was also issued items for common use such as large cast iron frying pan, and kettle with lid. Although heavy and awkward to carry, these were essential for preparing stews, frying cornbread or scrappy game when available, or anything they found to eat.

With newly issued gear and considerable personal belongings loaded on wagons, the recruits began climbing abord, Thomas helping Dr. King, but before anyone was situated they heard Sergeant Major bellowing.

"What in damnation you think you're doing? You think you're riding? Well I got news for y'all. From henceforth, you march anywhere and everywhere I need you to go! You're ridin' days are over. Lest, of course, you plan on transferring to the cavalry and I doubt there's one amongst the whole lot, can ride decent enough for cavalry. Now git down and form up to march. What are you a bunch a women, packing all that? We'll soon see how much you really need!"

Presently, the wagons piled with gear followed the gaggle of new recruits, the whole lot showing no similarity to a military unit. Nevertheless, the bulk of Williamsburg's Junior Guard was now finally formed and was making its way west, away from town to the far edge of College land.

***

Meanwhile, on the lower Peninsula, General Magruder did not wait for far away units like 1LT Brazazi's to arrive or new ones like Captain Cook's to train. To continue buying time, ever-theatrical 'Prince John' ordered what would become one of the greatest deception campaigns in history.

"Get units marching, back and forth, into the night," Prince John ordered. "Have 'em be as noisy as possible. I want a company to sound like a division. How many bands do we have? Send to Richmond for more musicians, I want reveille and taps sounded all along the line even if it's one trumpeter riding back and forth! And drums, even if there are no troops marching I want drummers as if the whole Army is on the move. Detail some men to build campfires along the length of our lines. I want Yanks to see the biggest encampment ever. In day time, fit horses with branches dragging behind and run 'em back and forth to stir up clouds of dust. And get mess kits, pots and pans; I want them strung on mules banging around all day. Gentlemen, we have got to look and sound like the entire Confederate Army. Anything and everything has to be done to make our forces appear ten times actual strength."

"McClellan is cautious by nature. If we can convince him or even plant the seed that he is opposed by a sizeable force, he will delay. This would allow time for reinforcement. Our survival and Richmond's depends on fixin' McClellan in place long as possible. Should he get word of how thin we're manned, he'll attack our weakest points and all is lost."

His commanders fully understood, and there being no questions, were dismissed and returned to their units where drumming and bugling, marching and riding, and setting campfires soon created sights and sounds of an imaginary Army. With noisy demonstrations continuing, soldiers became more enthusiastic with each passing day, trying to outdo one another in reinforcing the ruse.

Meanwhile, planning for repositioning the reinforcing units continued in earnest in Richmond. Magruder's commander, General Johnston, wanted to see for himself and arrived with staff in the midst of the ongoing deception effort.

After riding most of the length of the easternmost line, General Johnston remarked, "General Magruder, your preparations have been considerable and take good advantage of nature's features."

"Thank you Sir, We could do more if we had more men and shovels. We're short tools General, as well as men. Every implement we have is in

Civil War Comes Home

constant use, the men work to exhaustion then hand off picks and shovels to the next man. There's not enough to go around, Sir.

"I understand General, but Tredegar Iron works is turning out canons these days, not tools. Even if you had more implements, the Yanks could easily take unmanned trenches and piles of dirt, soon as they figure out we don't have enough men. Despite my pleas to General Lee and President Davis we simply do not have the troops to man the trenches against the numbers McClellan is prepared to throw into the fight. Oh, they've promised more men, over and over, but can they get here? McClellan now has over one hundred twenty thousand! You've got maybe ten per cent of his strength?" Johnston posed the question, though knowing the answer.

"Actually, General, our fielded strength is about seven thousand," Magruder replied. "According to unit rosters, we have nearly ten thousand but that includes sick, lame and runaways. Men who can pick up a weapon, even the walking wounded, are several thousand less. General, we've done the best we can." Magruder offered.

"John, I know that. Lord knows we just don't have manpower. They've ordered units from all over the country to defend Richmond, even as far as Mississippi and Texas but I fear there may not be time."

Figure 25. General Magruder's headquarters, Yorktown, Va. Courtesy of the Library of Congress, Washington, D.C.

"Sir, I understand, but again and again, McClellan has shown his cautious nature. The 'Virginia Creeper' can't seem to act until every possible thing is perfect," Magruder said using McClellan's sobriquet. "Sir, despite our small numbers, Yanks think our forces much greater and given McClellan's cautious nature, I don't think they will attack -at least not for the next month. I am trying to get good intelligence, and one source which I consider reliable, speaks of their plans to lay siege. Well, if that be the case, it will involve a Herculean effort to build rail transport and emplacements for the mortars. My God, those things weigh tons and the soft wet soils around here will swallow 'em. General, allow me continue to defend in place, we've got strong positions from which we can keep an eye on McClellan. General, from everything I understand it will be quite some time before he's ready to move. Until then, I'll continue demonstrations as a larger force. We're effectively bottling up his huge army with just a fraction of his strength. Hopefully this will allow time for reinforcements to arrive," Magruder reasoned, almost pleading.

Figure 26. Confederate forces under Major General John B. Magruder fortified their strong positions, while effectively fixing Union forces in place through a series of ruses, deceiving the enemy into thinking the entire Confederate army awaited them, when in fact the Confederates were outnumbered by approximately six to one. Courtesy of the Library of Congress, Washington, D.C.

Figure 27. Confederate positions reinforced on the Yorktown line. Courtesy of the Library of Congress, Washington, D.C.

Civil War Comes Home

Figure 28. Refugee family flees pending battle. Citizens from all stations in life fled with what worldly possessions they could transport. Many headed west for the capitol, Richmond, Va. Courtesy of the Library of Congress, Washington, D.C.

Figure 29. Former slaves also fled, but in the opposite direction, east towards Fort Monroe and their new status as contrabands of war. Courtesy of the Library of Congress, Washington, D.C.

General Johnston considered Magruder's comments carefully. He had full confidence in him, but was also weighing the risks. If McClellan breached their defense, and he could do so on strength of numbers at any time at any of several points, he could be at Richmond's doorstep within a day if he pressed the attack, two at most. Johnston continued, "Fortunately, our naval forces and gun emplacements ashore defend against a water approach to Richmond, via either the York or James. So, if McClellan should move, disinclined as he may be, he'll attack by land, as your information about a siege supports. There are only two narrow poor roads from here to Williamsburg and a single one to Richmond. Yes, General, Williamsburg will be the cork in the bottle, but the question is how long can we count on McClellan to remain true to past performance? If he remains slow, methodical and deliberate, we have time. If not, we are doomed."

General Johnston paced, deep in thought, while General Magruder remained uncharacteristically quiet, out of respect for his commanding officer's deliberation.

"On the other hand, I cannot leave Richmond vulnerable much longer," Johnston continued.

Finally he decided, "All right, Magruder, keep up the defense here but only for another month, at most. Keep me advised of McClellan's actions, certainly if he shows any sign of moving, and even if he just remains sitting in place, I want to know. If he moves to lay siege to Yorktown or anywhere else along the line, you must withdraw immediately and fight a delaying action to conserve strength. We can continue to buy time with your charade of a larger force, but eventually they are going to realize they've been duped. With those hot air balloons above your lines, sooner or later, trees or not, someone's going to notice the lack of troops. Do not, under any circumstances, allow your forces to be drawn into heavy engagement as we cannot win against so many and we'd risk losing all," Johnston explained. General Johnston had given his orders. Defense of the Peninsula was to be a classic delaying action, employing successive lines of defense, withdrawing up the Peninsula towards Williamsburg.

"Yes, General, thank you Sir," Magruder replied, "Rest assured General, I'll send a messenger immediately on any action, or intent, and we will prevail Sir.

***

While both Generals Magruder and Johnston continued to work to put more men in the field, the urgently requested troop movements could not be accomplished as quickly as either expected or required. Transportation was simply not available. While the men marched everywhere, their supplies required wagons and they remained in short supply throughout the Confederacy. Locomotives and rail cars were even harder to come by. When trains could eventually be diverted from other uses, the non standard rail lines throughout the South proved a major hindrance. Soldiers had to be held back to off-load supplies at the terminus of one line only to reload onto overworked wagon teams moving it to the next rail line, often miles away. This required considerable time-sensitive coordination and telegraphs were nonexistent in many areas or were targeted by the enemy. The only alternative was sending riders back and forth. With communication and transportation both slow, Magruder did his best to continue the grand ruse, knowing there was a limit to the number of performances before McClellan's army, got wise.

Recalling General Lee's specific instructions, *"maneuver as to deceive and thwart"* the enemy, Prince John implored his subordinate commanders to redouble their efforts. "Set grand bonfires up and down the line. Keep marching troops and bands as noisily as possible. Our continuing shortages must be overcome with what we have, through slight-of-hand. Gentlemen, I thought we'd surely have promised reinforcements by now, but hazard to guess it'll be weeks before we see 'em. In the meantime, enemy strength continues to grow. We must continue with ever greater vigilance to affect McClellan's estimate of the situation. I remind you, it's not actual strength, but what McClellan believes us to have, that is critical. As we've heard and seen, he has a great tendency to overestimate and I intend we continue providing him such a show, he remains crippled by self-doubt, his Army unable to move."

Through repeated demonstrations of one form or another, up and down the line, Magruder's men continued effectively fabricating the illusion of a larger force. While a few initially balked at the idea of deliberately making noise, they now understood the importance of immobilizing the enemy and relished their almost comical yet deadly serious duty to deceive the enemy and eagerly tried to top their prior performances. For instance, as soon as supper was concluded, all the pots, pans, and cups –anything and everything with a handle as gathered up. As soon as no longer needed for cooking, these were tied to ropes strung around the necks of mules walked back and forth to make as much banging as possible. Similarly, other crews kept bonfires burning bright whether the night was chill or mild. They understood Richmond itself was at stake, and as the nightly demonstrations wore on, they continued to evoke the desired effect in the mind of the ever-cautious Union commander.

Besides Magruder's orchestrated parades, concerts, and marches by day and night, McClellan was misinformed about the size of the Confederate defenders by his own intelligence sources. Mr. Alan Pinkerton, former head of a Chicago detective agency, was McClellan's chief of intelligence, and while he had a gift for solving crimes, that was hardly the same as military intelligence analysis. The few reports reaching McClellan simply mentioned, 'large and growing enemy forces,' when in fact, reinforcing Confederate troops remained far off in the rolling piedmont of northern Virginia and Shenandoah Valley.

All along the Yorktown line, Confederate buglers sounded from first one spot then another. Combined with bad or minimal intelligence, the 'evidence' of Confederate activities, re-affirmed in McClellan's mind what he wanted to believe. He felt, "his skill in combating these reputedly vast enemy hordes elevated him in his own estimation and in the eyes of his army. Inflated estimates of enemy strength excused his delays and glorified his successes," and in McClellan's boastful psyche, he was certain his opposition numbered many times his own strength. This invoked a near incapacitating dread of losing men. In fact, if truth be known, had McClellan made a move, he would have found Confederate positions so thinly manned he could have swept the line. Fortunately for Magruder, McClellan seemed more focused on the status and disposition of his own forces than those of the enemy.

From shortly after arriving, McClellan had received reports on the buildup of his forces– over one hundred twenty thousand men, nearly fifteen thousand animals, over twelve hundred wagons, forty-four artillery batteries and over one hundred massive siege guns delivered via an armada of some four hundred steamers, tugs, and even private watercraft pressed into service. McClellan was quite familiar with all of this for he'd spent the last six months overseeing the massive build up. He was now glad to finally be in the field with his beloved army where he was free from "that stink of inequity," Washington. After receiving reports on his own strength, McClellan was briefed by his staff.

"Sir, I recommend we move against Norfolk," John G. Barnard, McClellan's Engineer advised. "The port facilities, with connecting rail lines are critical to prosecuting the war from here to Charleston."

"Gentlemen, let me be perfectly clear. As Commanding General, I prepared for President Lincoln a memorandum setting forth my view for the proper and timely suppression of this late rebellion. The overarching strategy is to simultaneously strike at the two centers of rebellion, in the East and West, namely Richmond and Nashville, in order to take this fight to the heart of secession. We will also and simultaneously engage the enemy through expeditionary means all along the coast and the length of the Mississippi. I mean to bring war all along the line.

Now, as to the matter of my current command, my grand Army of the Potomac, the most important of the several armies in rebel terriroty, we aim for Richmond and will not trouble ourselves for Norfolk or any other point that would delay our main objective. No, we move against Magruder first, trapping him in Yorktown, just like Washington and Lafayette bagged Cornwallis to win the Revolution." *And I'll forever be the 'hero' of this war of secession,* thought McClellan. "We've got a report from Pinkerton, their right flank remains unanchored and, see here, these maps show an unimpeded approach to the west from below, blocking Magruder's escape. We send a gauntlet forward that way, while fixing him in place and just like that he's trapped. Then, controlling Yorktown and Gloucester Point we'll have unhindered navigation of the York and can off-load the rest of the Army at West Point. From there it's rail and roads directly to Richmond. Gentlemen it should be quick victory here on the Peninsula and then, On to Richmond!" This soon became his rallying cry.

Figure 30. General McClellan organized the largest assemblage of military firepower in the history of the U.S. (at that time) in order to lay siege to Confederate forces from Federal positions near Yorktown, Va. Courtesy of the Library of Congress, Washington, D.C.

"Third Corps will lead the assault," McClellan pronounced, Brigadier General Samuel Heintzelman, commanding, nodding agreement. "Brigadier General Sumner will take Second Corps through Big Bethel towards Yorktown to cause Magruder to hold, while Brigadier General Keyes marches Fourth Corps up Warwick Road to Half Way House, just northwest of Yorktown, sealing any chance of his escape." I hope, "by rapid movements to drive before me or capture the enemy on the Peninsula, open the James River, and push on to Richmond before he should be materially reinforced from other portions of his territory."[54]

While McClellan was describing to his Corps commanders what he thought was a clear plan, in Washington, it was neither understood, nor its many requirements appreciated. It assumed for example the Navy would bombard enemy guns on the high river bluffs at Yorktown -essential to protecting Union water transport upriver to West Point. However, "the Navy was clearly ignorant of the scope and intent of that plan; was not a party to it; had not promised to join in a combined attack upon Yorktown, and moreover, could probably have affected nothing in such an attempt."[55] When the assumed, but uncoordinated assistance from the Navy was not forthcoming, McClellan had little choice but to again modify his plans. If the Navy wasn't cooperating, McClellan would rely completely on his army. The main advance would remain as detailed, a two pronged attack up the Peninsula, but now, McDowell's First Corps was to land on the northern bank of the York and from there move west to Gloucester Point, then to West Point in order to countermarch back down the Peninsula on the southern bank of the York to attack. This would supposedly allow the main attack up the Peninsula unimpeded.

Although General McClellan continued imagining phantom enemy troops, he finally set his modified plans in motion April 4, 1862 when III Corps on the right was directed to march on Yorktown, while the column on the left, composed of elements of Keyes' IV Corps augmented by the Fifth Regular Cavalry, were ordered to advance towards Warwick Court House. Both columns marched some ten to twelve miles before encamping, at Young's Mills on Warwick Road on the left and at Howard's bridge on the right. The reserve forces, including Stoneman's cavalry, encamped at Big Bethel, a location now infamous as the site of the Confederate rout of Union forces the previous June.

The following morning, April 5th, troops resumed the march by 6:00 a.m. with Brigadier General Samuel Heintzelman receiving orders to advance III Corps to a point within two and three quarter miles of Yorktown. The quick-tempered Heintzelman was neither slow nor

---

54 Webb, pg. 36.

55 op. cit. 41.

infrequent in his criticism of McClellan, noting, "I do not see how any man could leave so much to others, and be so confident that everything would go just right." [56] On the left Keyes was to continue by way of Warwick Court House to an old landmark equidistant between Yorktown and Williamsburg, known appropriately as 'Half-Way House.' Here he was to "hold the narrow ridge… so as to prevent the escape of the garrison at Yorktown by land and prevent reinforcements being thrown in."[57]

But even while just getting underway, Keyes sent discouraging word back to McClellan that he faced a large enemy force at Lee's Mill six miles to his front, "we shall encounter very serious resistance; if so, we shall not be able to reach the Half-Way House…today. Our wagons did not arrive last night, and we shall be obliged to halt at Warwick Court House for the infantry reserve ammunition to come up… It is a heavy march to the Half-Way House, even without opposition."[58] An hour and a half later he added, "roads are very bad ahead. Shall I push on to Half-Way House if artillery cannot get on fast enough? I supposed not, of course."[59]

Keyes reports were not the only bad news McClellan received that morning. The very moment the formidable obstructions at Warwick Court House were discovered, a curt telegram denying use of McDowell's forces arrived. McClellan was furious. His plan for a multi-pronged attack already underway had McDowell in an integral role. Now, his operation had been interfered with radically. "Those damn politicians!" McClellan cursed, "Will they stop at nothing to force my resignation, including scuttling battle plans?" Staring at the maps, he steeled his resolve. "I'll not give them the satisfaction," and he determined to rise to the occasion, win a great victory, drive the Rebels to Richmond, cripple the Confederacy, and win the war; thereby establishing himself as eternal hero of the nation, despite meddling politicians.

"General, we must press the attack along the Warwick while there is still time!" his staff urged. Although McClellan considered their arguments, he remained cautious and had other reports that General Johnston had relocated his forces in his front. While McClellan actually faced some fifteen thousand at most, he imagined the opposing force many times larger. President Lincoln also urged breaking the line at Warwick, yet McClellan remained in place, continuing to argue for the

56 Hastings, Earl C. Jr., and David Hastings, 1997, A Pitiless Rain, the Battle of Williamsburg, 1862. White Mane Publishing Co. pg. 6.
57 Webb, pg. 44.
58 op. cit. pg. 45.
59 op. cit.

use of McDowell's troops. "Under the circumstances that have developed since we arrived, I feel fully impressed with the conviction, that here is to be fought the great battle that will decide the existing contest. I shall of course, commence the attack as soon as I can get up my siege-train, and shall do all in my power to carry the enemy's works; but, to do this with a reasonable degree of certainty requires, in my judgment, that I should, if possible, have at least the whole of the First Army Corps (McDowell's) to land upon York River and attack Gloucester in the rear. My present strength will not admit of a detachment sufficient for this purpose without materially impairing the efficiency of the column."[60]

In truth, even the advance units of Johnston's army, under General D. H. Hill, hadn't arrived and would not, until much later, on the 10th and General Johnston did not come up until the 14th. Thus, for nearly a week, McClellan far outnumbered his opposition but sat, bogged down in front of Warwick Court House, not dealing with the enemy immediately before him.

Instead, he persisted in trying to convince Washington to release the troops called for in his original plans, "Give me Franklin's and McCall's divisions (of McDowell's corps)… and I will at once undertake it. If circumstances, of which I am not aware, make it impossible for you to send me two divisions to carry out this final plan of campaign, I will run the risk, and hold myself responsible for the results, if you will give me Franklin's division. If you still confide in my judgment, I entreat you grant this request. The fate of our cause depends on it. Although willing, under the pressure of necessity, to carry this through with Franklin alone, I wish it to be distinctly understood that I think two divisions necessary. Franklin and his divisions are indispensable to me," McClellan wrote the President.[61]

In response, Lincoln ordered Franklin to report forthwith, but it wasn't until the 20th when the troop ships finally docked below Yorktown and even then, two full weeks elapsed as they planned their de-embarkation.

Fuming over first one delay then another, McClellan busied himself overseeing the siege he'd favored from the outset. Frustrated he couldn't surround Yorktown in the manner after Washington and Lafayette, he continued to overestimate enemy strength when, in reality, he enjoyed a six to one advantage in manpower and similarly disproportionate firepower. While he could have scouts watching for enemy activities or weaknesses, he remained inwardly focused on his army and siege plans not what the enemy

---

60 op. cit. pg. 60.
61 op. cit.

was doing. Even if the requisite intelligence gathering on enemy disposition had been mobilized, the information still had to pass through Pinkerton and his hand-picked staff who basked in the self-assurance that they, and only they, knew exactly what McClellan needed to know. The fact that the enemy had a say in what those plans might be did not seem to register.

By the middle of the afternoon, McClellan penned another note, "I am stopped by the enemy's works at Lee's Mills which offer a severe resistance; the road through the woods for nearly a mile having become absolutely impassable for artillery, I am cutting a new road through. One battery is replying to the enemy and another is nearly or quite through."[62] Heavy rains all day seriously hindered movement and resupply and in the face of the enemy's strong defensive works, Union forces encamped for the night, still east of Lee's Mills.

On the right Heintzelman's force fared no better, coming under fire near the point where McClellan ordered their halt. General Porter noting, "Looming up in the mist and rains were extensive defenses of the enemy from which we are immediately saluted with the fire of artillery."[63] His artillery returned fire from two thousand yards, keeping it up all afternoon, as his division encamped for the night. Intimidated by the strength of enemy works running the length of Warwick River, McClellan was quick to settle for a siege. Earlier pronouncements about 'striking swiftly' were rejected, much to official Washington's displeasure. Instead, the focus shifted to the Herculean and time-consuming tasks of building wharves, roads, and rail lines to emplace a large array of heavy siege guns. Despite opening promises of 'bold action,' the end of the day found McClellan's forces bogged down, left and right, encamped before strong enemy positions only a few miles from where they'd started. This unanticipated outcome didn't seem to trouble McClellan terribly as he still fancied himself the glorious victor and determined to lay siege. He failed to order an attack anywhere along the line. Had he done so, weak points would have been found and could have been exploited to advantage.

While the siege and its myriad planning requirements fulfilled McClellan's love of logistics, no one on his staff grasped that a siege situation did not really exist. The enemy was not surrounded and could withdraw in good order at a time of their choosing. Nevertheless, siege plans continued; McClellan blind to any perspective but his own. Meanwhile, his staff endeavored to provide everything he asked for, but only that which confirmed what he already knew. Caught up in details of positioning the largest assembly of heavy artillery in

---

62 op. cit.
63 op. cit. pg. 46.

the history of siege warfare, and organizing the massive supply trains required, Union forces failed to mount a credible threat at either Yorktown or Warwick, despite their reconnaissance showing good possibilities.

***

April 16th McClellan tasked General Baldy Smith to gain control of Dam number 1 on the Warwick River to, "force the enemy to discontinue his work in strengthening his batteries, to silence his fire, and gain control of the dam existing at this point."[64] Smith ordered Brigadier General W.T. H. Brook's Vermont Brigade forward, supported by the 3rd New York Battery. Augmented by a battery each from the 5th U.S. Artillery and 1st New York Artillery, they kept up a three hour bombardment which eventually silenced the lone Confederate cannon. Realizing the enemy's weakness, Federals organized an assault by four companies of Vermont's 3rd Regiment. If these one hundred ninety-two hand-picked men were successful in taking Rebel rifle pits on the opposite shore, they were to signal for reinforcements, secure the lodgment, and thus break the Confederate line. Among them was Captain Alonzo Hutchinson who was given Brigadier General Brooks' handkerchief to wave as a signal they needed reinforcements.[65]

Approximately equidistant between Lee's and Wynn's mills on the Warwick, Dam number 1, was guarded by 15th North Carolina, under command of Lieutenant Colonel William McKinney. They'd just occupied the still uncompleted earthworks that very day.[66] Viewing the strong reconnaissance of the McKinney's Carolinians by his Vermont Brigade, General Smith remarked, "... scarcely anybody showed above the parapet, the Vermont skirmishers doing good execution."[67]

While Union leaders were deciding what to do about this new information, young Lieutenant E. M. Noyes, 3rd Vermont, aid to General Brooks, took matters into his own hands. Wading in below the dam, whether foolhardy or brave, Lt. Noyes carefully maneuvered across the river to within a short distance of enemy fortifications. Undetected and finding the water no more than waist deep, he reversed course, making it back without being detected. He promptly reported directly to General McClellan just arriving on scene from his headquarters.

---

64 op. cit. pg. 63.
65 Quarstein, pg. 103.
66 op. cit. pg. 104.
67 Webb, pg. 64.

Figure 31. General McClellan's headquarters, near Yorktown, Va. Courtesy of the Library of Congress, Washington, D.C.

"General, Sir, The river can be crossed! You see by my britches the depth all the way to far shore."

"Good work, Lieutenant," McClellan replied, turning immediately to General Smith, "Sir, bring up your entire division immediately."

"Yes, Sir, and while they're getting up, request your consent to "advance a strong party across to ascertain if the works had been sufficiently denuded to enable a column to effect a lodgment."[68]

Momentarily, the aforementioned one hundred ninety-two men under Captain F.C. Harrington, Third Vermont waded in where Lt. Noyes had just crossed, shortly gaining the opposite shore. With enemy now in their midst, defenders were thrown into frenzy, dropping their shovels and running for their rifles. Many more likely would have been gunned down but for the attacker's damp powder. Despite having carried muskets and cartridge boxes high overhead while wading across, much of their ammunition was now useless. Spotting the delay, Lieutenant Colonel McKinney, commanding the Carolinians, led a gallant attempt to regain their positions but fell mortally wounded, a single shot to his forehead. The Vermonters held for the better part of a half hour, but dry powder ran dangerously low, and the defenders, rallied by Cobb's Legion, under their namesake, Brigadier General Howell Cobb, were forcing attackers back to the waters' edge.

Union Generals peering into the distant fight could no longer see their men down in the enemy's rifle pits. Mists off the water, lingering smoke from the cannonade and rising rifle fire obscured the view and no one saw the handkerchief signaling for reinforcements for Captain Hutchinson lay mortally wounded. No one else knew of the prearranged signal.

---

68 op. cit.

Instead of the expected reinforcement of their hard won toe-hold, Vermonters now faced the incomprehensible. With Captain Hutchinson mortally wounded, leadership fell to Captain Samuel Pingree who was already wounded. His thumb shot completely off and bleeding profusely from another wound in his hip, Captain Pingree had no choice under the heavy pressure now being mounted by the Rebels and their own dwindling powder but to order, "Withdraw."

"What the hell!" one of his Sergeants screamed above the din, "We fight all the way here, occupy enemy positions and now we're supposed to go back? What is going on?"

"I don't know. With no reinforcements and running out of ammunition, what choice is there?" "Can't the Generals back on our shore see what's happening? Little Mac himself is yonder."

"They must know something we don't. Have the men withdraw as ordered," Captain Pingree repeated, still puzzled by the failure to capitalize on the situation. Soon, Vermonters were again waist deep in water, this time headed back from whence they'd come. The Rebels, regaining their rifle pits, laid down a murderous fire making the water "boil with their bullets."[69] Unable to return fire while trying to escape in treacherous water filled with trees felled as obstacles, Vermonters suffered most of their casualties trying to leave. By the time they got back they were seventy-five fewer. Others witnessing the failed effort, also understood it'd been a senseless waste of lives, many more needlessly wounded.

"Sir, I really do not understand! We held the opposite shore, while the enemy had time to bring up reinforcements. Where were ours?! Had we pressed the attack, we could have taken the whole place, Sir."

"We never saw the signal calling for reinforcements. We weren't ready for a full attack Captain. That will be all." Logic and initiative were summarily dismissed. Even as blame and recriminations continued, the men did what they could to help one another. Crossing the river at least twice, Julian Scott a sixteen year old Vermont musician is credited with saving "no less than nine of his comrades."[70] One of the wounded he tried to save but couldn't, was Private William Scott who earlier as a young recruit had inadvertently fallen asleep while on guard duty. This grievous offense in war time earned sleepy Private Scott a court martial and death sentence by firing squad. President Lincoln granted a pardon, prompting

---

69 Quarstein, pg. 105.
70 op. cit. pg. 106. Private Julian Scott and Captain Samuel Pingree were both awarded the Medal of Honor, February 1865 for gallantry at the skirmish at Dam number 1.

Scott to remark, "I will show President Lincoln that I am not afraid to die for my country," – a pledge he fulfilled during the disastrous Union attempt to take Dam number 1.[71]

By four that afternoon, Union forces were ready to try again. Despite senseless losses earlier, the costly failure had demonstrated a possibility the enemy line could be broken. This time, four companies from 6th Vermont under Colonel Lord, came up to the same position as the previous attempt. By now, Rebels were fully reinforced and well aware of what the enemy planned. Despite the steady covering fire from the Union's twenty guns, return Confederate fire was heavier and highly accurate, causing General Smith to order another withdrawal. "The moment I found resistance serious, and the numbers opposed great, I acted in obedience to the warning instruction of the General-in-Chief, and withdrew the small number of troops exposed...."[72] Thus, a second Union effort failed even before getting underway. With good opportunity to penetrate the Warwick line expired, no further attempts were made anywhere along the line and plans to lay siege continued with all deliberation.

***

---

71 op. cit. pg. 107.
72 Webb, pg. 66.

Figure 32. The Confederate White House, Richmond, Va. Courtesy of The Museum of the Confederacy, Richmond, Va.

The Confederate White House, Richmond

The well-groomed butler was particularly busy the afternoon of April 16th. President Davis had called a meeting of his senior military leaders to discuss their plans, or more accurately, to inform them of his strategy for countering the Yankee threat on the Peninsula. Ushering them into the oval foyer, the butler quickly assisted General Johnston, then Major Generals James Longstreet and Gustavus W. Smith, in cleaning the worst of the red Virginia clay from their riding boots. All three had just ridden directly from their commands in the field. They were soon shown into the adjacent state dining room where General Lee and Secretary of War George Wythe Randolph, formerly Magruder's commander of artillery, waited.

Conspicuously absent was the one man directly responsible for the defense of the Peninsula, Major General John Bankhead Magruder. He'd not been invited. Even if he had, it was doubtful he'd leave his command with Yankees threatening. Besides, Prince John reported to General Johnston who'd recently inspected the defenses. Thus, even if Magruder were present and happened to disagree, he was bound by General Johnston's decision.

Civil War Comes Home

With its high ceiling and tall windows on three sides extending nearly to the floor capturing the southern exposure, the state dining room was the brightest in the mansion, and favored by President Davis. The Generals took places around the long, gleaming rosewood table and while waiting for Davis, caught up on news, heartily enjoying the excellent coffee for it was becoming increasingly scarce anywhere but the White House. Placing his leather riding gloves aside, General Johnston drained his cup as soon as he was served for he'd been up long before dawn.

While waiting they were under the watchful eyes of the larger than life portrait of George Washington, who President Davis worshipped. He imagined himself leading a second revolution, becoming the 'founding father' of the Confederate States of America.

Figure 33. General Joseph E. Johnston. Courtesy of The Museum of the Confederacy,

Jake McKenzie

Richmond, Va.

Waiting for Davis to begin the meeting, Johnston and Lee were anxious. Each knew the other's position as well as their own and both were prepared to argue counterpoints as long as necessary for this was not their first discussion on strategy. As they'd been unable to either compromise, or arrive at an alternative, President Davis intervened, calling this meeting for the strategy had to be resolved, and soonest.

"Gentlemen, welcome. I trust you've been well," Davis remarked, genuinely concerned for their health; Johnston his most senior General, Lee his hand-picked military advisor. Davis' own health was always of concern and lately the stress of leading the fledgling Confederacy was taking its toll. His wife, Varina wondered if he was physically up to the task. An earlier eye infection had left him blind on the left side and facial neuralgia, rheumatism, nervous dyspepsia, and pneumonia all impacted Davis' health as did the shrapnel from old war wounds. Despite his nearly 6 foot frame, he weighed but one hundred thirty-five pounds. Although the stress was extreme and unrelenting, Davis was tough as nails and refused to allow anything, even chronic poor health, to interfere.

"Yes, well, Mr. President thank you," Lee replied, having taken care to sit appropriately as Davis was partially deaf. Lee, ever careful, would take no chance that Davis might not hear him.

"Likewise," Johnston quickly added, "though truth be known, our camps are not conducive to health, not for me, nor any man in our entire army and that Sir, is no exaggeration. And, I find myself exhausted by all the time spent in the saddle these days." Johnston spoke frankly among old friends, Longstreet nodding agreement.

"Indeed Sir, none of us are young men any more, like Mexico," Davis observed. "The responsibilities of this office wear me down, even as lovely Varina insists I limit appointments -as if that, were somehow possible. Nevertheless, we shall, God-willing, establish in this Confederacy, a new democracy that returns to the principles our founding fathers established," motioning to the portrait.

Connecting Davis' reference to Washington, Lee took the initiative, "Precisely my point, Mr. President. I'm convinced we'll be victorious by allowing Magruder to engage McClellan where they now stand. I've inspected defense works on several occasions and they have subsequently been further strengthened. General Magruder assures me he can hold despite McClellan's superior numbers. By holding 'em in place, we seize the opportunity to win the war right here on the Peninsula. If we could cut off or even reduce their resupply, with their large numbers they'd run out of food right quick. Why there's not enough grass on the entire Peninsula for more than a few days with the herds they got. Mr. President, their very largeness makes them vulnerable. We can and must exploit that," Lee offered.

He knew the danger in taking this contrarian view. The Union was celebrating a string of fresh victories in the far West, Tennessee, and along the Carolina coasts. Riding this crest and with over one hundred thousand troops on the Peninsula, the northern press, citizens, and even President Lincoln took up the call, 'On to Richmond!'

"Beggin' your pardon, General Lee," Johnston interrupted, "but our strategy cannot be 'wait 'em out in place.' That's exactly what Little Mac would have us do. His siege guns would blow this army to pieces. Instead, we must withdraw all our assets from certain destruction and use them to defend Richmond. Our capitol is their objective. Better we should prepare now, in strength in front of Richmond rather than endure his siege. If Mac chases us, he could be here so quick we'd have no time to prepare. Despite his cautious nature, he'd be on our doorstep before we could react."

"What about all our work over the past year, preparing and strengthening good defenses?" Lee countered, knowing full well this had no bearing on the pending decision. "Magruder's men are spoilin' for a fight. If we withdraw, they've wasted the better part of the past year diggin' and morale will suffer."

"I could care less if they're disappointed, Lee, but I do care if they're alive to fight," Johnston countered. "You've seen the siege guns. If we stay much longer, we won't have an army left!"

Lee was trying to read Davis' body language. He knew the President usually allowed facts to be argued without trying to sway the presentation, before making his decision.

"I wish Magruder were here," Lee blurted, taking a different tack, almost in desperation. Although he was confident in his knowledge of the defense, enemy threat, terrain, and every other conceivable aspect of the situation, Lee couldn't help but think, *it's wrong to be debating strategy without the one officer actually responsible.*

"Well, General Magruder is not here, and even if there was time to wait for him, I doubt he'd leave his men," President Davis intoned.

"Yes, of course, Mr. President. I meant no disrespect, Sir, however, Magruder has continued to strengthen his position. He showed his prowess under fire at Big Bethel, and is anxious to again defeat the enemy. I think we give him that chance. If we could defeat Mac now, the war would be over! Even if we just keep Mac bottled up and he does nothing, all that firepower and manpower remains inactive when it would have been brought against us elsewhere. We've taken away the North's alternatives. Short term or long, we win!"

"Yes, the war could be won" Johnston agreed, "but I just have to make sure the Yanks aren't the ones winning! How do we assure the safety of Richmond? Mac's got huge numbers. We can never match him even if we continue to strip forces everywhere and send them all to Magruder. With the flotilla Mac used, he could re-board a large contingent, sail up the York to West Point, offload at the rail head and roll right into Richmond," Johnston countered. It was one of several worst case scenarios he'd war-gamed, pointing out on the map the straight sail up the York to West Point then the comparatively short rail line direct to Richmond.

Seeing Davis' bushy eyebrows raised at this vulnerability, Lee understood his case was fast becoming hopeless, but he was not ready to concede. "I agree there is some risk, but this is war, and we cannot "guarantee" Richmond's or any other city's safety even with twice the force. Anyone thinks there can be such guarantee in war, they're dreaming." Little did Lee know that McClellan had used the same argument with his Secretary of War and the President regarding the defense of Washington. The Generals knew it was impossible to conduct operations while at the same time supposedly 'guaranteeing' the respective Capitols' safety. "Gentleman, we must be bold," Lee continued, "Magruder showed what he can do at Bethel, as he did years ago in Mexico. I say we augment him to the full extent possible and stop the Yankees here and now on the Peninsula as far from Richmond as possible. It is eminently possible to bring this war to an early end. We'd save countless lives and we cannot win a prolonged war. The North, with greater population, an endless supply of immigrant recruits, natural resources and an industrial base, has war-making capabilities we simply don't. They will eventually attrite us down to nothing." Lee argued his case strongly as he could, trying to judge by Davis' reaction what his decision might be.

"General Lee, I appreciate your position, and frankness. I only wish we had the troops to send to Magruder to accomplish what you propose. But even if we strip the Valley and everywhere of troops, we'd only place other towns at risk, as you know. We still have the problem of Mac breaking through or bypassing us with an amphibious operation via the York or to a lesser degree, James, threatening Richmond immediately. He could be here in as little as a day, two, at most," Davis noted. "I have to also think of the thousands of new citizens who've flocked to Richmond. Then there is the iron works. Tredegar is a critical part of our limited industrial capacity as General Lee has noted. I'm left with no option but to take prudent measures to ensure the defense of our capitol."

Lee hung his head, "can we not have more time? Let Magruder hold in place a while longer, maintain surveillance of Mac thus providing valuable intelligence," he suggested.

Davis paused before replying, "Very well, thirty days additional at most, then Magruder must withdraw, not a day longer. During this time he must, even if it means sending a rider daily, keep us fully informed on what Mac is up to. We'll need every hour to evacuate civilians if Mac decides to move."

The Generals nodded acknowledgement, everyone understanding the President's decision. General Lee, an advisor not a commander, would continue studying maps and intelligence reports, looking to exploit opportunities, while Generals Johnston, Smith, and Longstreet returned to their units to execute to the best of their abilities. Johnston left in such a hurry he forgot his riding gloves. President Davis rose rubbing his temples for it was past midnight and he was exhausted. Glancing at the portrait of Washington one last time, Davis hoped he'd made the right decision.

Weeks later Johnston wrote Lee, "We are engaged in a species of warfare at which we can never win. It is plain that McClellan will… depend for success upon artillery and engineering. We can compete with neither." Johnston held Magruder in place at Yorktown for as long as he dared as they'd agreed, but finally, May 1st came the announcement to abandon Yorktown, withdrawing toward Richmond. It remained the prudent decision for Federal siege batteries now included more heavy artillery than had ever been assembled in the history of warfare.[73]

***

A missed opportunity…

Months earlier, flamboyant Professor Thaddeus Sobieski Coulincourt Lowe, aeronaut, beat stiff competition and was invited to bring his considerable equipment, baggage and entourage from his native Cincinnati to Washington. From the White House lawn, he launched his tethered

---

[73] Wheat, Thomas Adrian, 1997, A guide to Civil War Yorktown, Bohemian Brigade Bookshop & Publishers, Knoxville, TN. pg. 8.

hot air balloon, *'Enterprise,'* nearly a thousand feet over the Smithsonian. President Lincoln, with a fondness for inventions, was intrigued by what this new technology might mean for the military. After this successful demonstration flight and considerable self-promotion, Professor Lowe was to establish the Army's Balloon Corps. With Lincoln's urging, Professor Lowe loaded his entire fleet; *'Enterprise,' 'Constitution,'* and *'Intrepid,'* aboard the tugboat, *Coeur de Leon,* headed to Fort Monroe.

Setting up the largely untested equipment proved time consuming, as did repairs to the delicate silk fabric of the balloons. Unfavorable weather, fickle coastal wind, and perhaps the most difficult of all, reluctance by a skeptical Army, were eventually overcome. The monstrous balloons were a source of puzzlement and derision from Generals down to the privates now tasked with additional support requirements for which the supply system was not prepared.

Finally, Professor Lowe managed several sorties over the Peninsula including one in which he found himself far west, running out of hot air. A forced descent in enemy territory was barely avoided as he hurriedly increased the flame, and a favorable gust at the last moment allowed escape. Then there was the flight by an unaccompanied Union General when tethering lines became unfastened. Fortunately, he had the presence of mind to reduce ballast and descended in what amounted to a controlled crash, amongst the pines, luckily on the Union side.

Gradually, Professor Lowe became more experienced navigating the strong coast winds and was eventually able to hold a position to make observations of interest to his patrons, the Union generals. Buffeted back and forth across enemy lines he was a high value target and the Confederacy had offered a rich bounty for anyone who could bring down one of the fool contraptions. The Professor's slow ascents, descents and drifting gradually along front lines presented such an inviting target that even his own forces didn't take kindly to balloon operations anywhere in their sector. When the Professor was aloft, supporting ground forces were immediately subject to collateral damage from Rebel rounds expended in trying for the bounty. Besides the rain of bullets, horses were spooked and dogs howled or gave chase. Quite simply, no one wanted to be near the balloons. Nevertheless, Professor Lowe persevered, earning the undisputed title, 'the most shot at man of the Civil War.'

Despite Army hesitancy to fully embrace a Balloon Corps, Professor Lowe's daring eventually paid off. One day everything was finally right; balloon silks repaired, equipment running properly, and favorable wind

Civil War Comes Home

and weather. The Professor was accompanied by young Captain George Armstrong Custer, making his first ascent. Once they rose to the designated altitude, Captain Custer broke out his field glasses. They remained tethered and despite considerable wind aloft, Custer took out paper to sketch the Confederate works, but stretching for as far as he could see, the lines were completely unmanned!

Figure 34. Launch of Union hot air balloon to observe enemy lines. Courtesy of the Library of Congress, Washington, D.C.

"Quick, bring this damned thing down," Custer demanded.

"I beg your pardon, Sir we only just got up. We got time for a long flight."

"No we don't! You don't understand, look at the lines! Not a soldier anywhere. Get us down so I can report. They've abandoned their lines!"

"Oh, I see what you mean." Though Professor Lowe was disappointed the flight would be cut short, it had revealed critical information which after all, was his point about the utility of a Balloon Corps. "Well, at least you're not afraid of heights," the Professor joked, venting hot air to descend as rapidly as prudent. The basket hadn't even touched before Custer jumped out, yelling thanks back to Professor Lowe. Nearby, the Comte de Paris, one of the two brother French liaison officers attached to General McClellan's staff had been observing the balloon launch and seeing its hasty descent and Custer's excited state, came over to see what was transpiring.

"Sir, the lines are empty, we just saw it from the balloon. The Rebels have withdrawn," Custer shouted hurriedly, running off to find his commanding officer.

Comte de Paris, immediately grasping the importance Custer's observation, immediately turned his mount and headed back to headquarters at a gallop.

Figure 35. Comte de Paris, one of two French liaison officers attached to the Union Army and deployed as a member of General McClellan's staff brings word of the balloon sightings to headquarters. Courtesy of the Library of Congress, Washington, D.C.

As Comte de Paris rode off, Custer continued running. He could care less if the Frenchman brought word first for he was focused solely on finding his boss. "Sir, important information,' Custer stammered, out of breath from running the considerable distance to headquarters, where he finally found General Edwin Sumner. "Sir, I was just up in the balloon and saw Confederate forces have withdrawn. Sir, their lines are empty!"

"Good God! What in heaven's name are you talking about? I was at headquarters not more than a few hours ago and everyone knows Magruder and most of the Confederate army lies in wait behind some mighty impressive fortifications. That Captain is why McClellan brought up siege guns."

"I understand Sir, but you're not hearing what I am saying. Sir, while the Rebels may have been there, they've now pulled out! We could take the entire line without firing a shot! Comte de Paris rode off to tell headquarters. Sir, don't you think we should report this there?"

"Captain, how can that be? Maybe you couldn't see 'em or something. General McClellan and his staff all know the massive force we face and you come rushing in claiming it's not true! What am I supposed to believe, that Pinkerton and his intelligence sources are wrong?"

"I know Sir, it goes against what they think they know, but I'm certain what I saw. My God, what an opportunity! Sir, report this and they can verify, or ask Professor Lowe. We're up there a few minutes ago. He'll verify what we saw. There's no Rebs anywhere along the line."

"All right Captain, I hear you. We'll report it, but we're both going. You tell them yourself what you saw or didn't see. And, be prepared to answer a lot of questions. This directly challenges their information and assumptions. Everything!"

"Yes, Sir, I can't believe Rebs have withdrawn and nobody knows anything!"

"That's just it. It's too far-fetched to believe. Pray they do, and act accordingly. Come on, let's go."

Pinkerton didn't appreciate the interruption but with General Sumner's presence, he had to give audience and hearing Custer out, Pinkerton and staff flatly denied his extraordinary claim.

"I am not sure where you were lookin' Captain, nor what this is all about, but you are clearly mistaken! Perhaps the good Professor was floating over the wrong lines somewhere, but the majority of the Confederate Army sits yonder, been in place for weeks. This General McClellan knows, and is the basis for his planning a brilliant siege campaign. We'll destroy them by heavy bombardment rather than waste precious lives in an onslaught against prepared works. Is that what you would have instead Captain? Lead your men to needless death against a dug-in, superior force? Is that what they taught at West Point?"

"Sir, I am only trying to report actionable intelligence that I just saw with my own eyes," Custer replied, trying to maintain his composure.

"Thank you Captain, noted. We'll attempt to verify this, but I remind you, we are General's McClellan's intelligence advisors and he does not take information from anyone who drops in, thinking they know how the war should be prosecuted. Now Sirs, please excuse me we have a siege to plan," and with that Pinkerton dismissed the visitors, signaling his staff to get back to work.

As General Sumner and Captain Custer exited, the former was not surprised at the cold reception or the manner in which new information was summarily rejected. "Good work Captain, but as you saw, the so-called 'experts' know what they know. Anything that smacks of a fly in the ointment is dismissed. Otherwise their tenure and reliability is brought into question."

"Yes, Sir, but I never thought…" Custer's thought trailing off. He knew his urgent information could change the course of a pending battle, if not the war. Because his observations contradicted accepted 'fact,' he was treated like the rawest recruit, incapable of reporting what he'd seen with his own eyes. *What kind of command is this that won't listen to its officers?*

His thoughts were interrupted by General Sumner, "I expect we'll hear soon enough about the 'official' assessment of the enemy disposition," … *or then again maybe we won't.* Like Custer, he had his doubts about how information was conveyed and utilized by McClellan's headquarters.

***

MAY, 1862.
WITHDRAWAL, PURSUIT, & THE BATTLE IS JOINED

On May 1st Union Battery number 1, on the banks of the York just below Moore House, opened fire on Yorktown and her docks "with great effect." McClellan's plans, straight from texts on siege warfare, called for "remaining guns joining until all pressed with vigor until the final assault should be deemed practicable."[74]

"But the enemy was too shrewd to await our onslaught with guns and storming columns. They had remained long enough at the Yorktown line for their purposes. A month's time had been gained in keeping McClellan in place, and early the morning of the 4th as Custer had tried to report, following an unusual cannonade of our lines the previous night, they abandoned Yorktown and the Warwick line…"[75]

Meanwhile, throughout the Union camp, siege preparations continued. Franklin's long-delayed troops noting, "All these preparations, were about completed, and we were engaged in making scaling-ladders, thinking we might be called upon to assault the works at Gloucester Point, when suddenly the news spread throughout the fleet that the enemy had evacuated Yorktown."[76] As Rebel initiative overtook McClellan's plans, Franklin's delayed troops were now effectively denied any active role.

74 Webb, pg. 67.
75 op. cit. pg. 68.
76 op. cit. pg. 62.

"The evacuation of Yorktown took the Union army by surprise…the movement was not anticipated at head-quarters."[77] "The troops had settled down to siege preparations and a fixed camp life for at least a time longer. Hence, when orders came to break camp and push after the rebels, several hours were consumed in packing and getting the commands provisioned for the march. The (enemy) evacuation was reported at dawn, and the report confirmed soon after; it was not until noon that the cavalry and infantry were fairly off"[78]

"The enemy, on their part, abandoned the place deliberately. If their retreat was a measure of safety, and so far forced upon them, it was still in accordance with a settled plan. They proposed to remain at the Warwick line only so long as prudence dictated, and for the single purpose of delaying McClellan. This they succeeded in doing for an entire month."

General Johnston was abundantly clear on this point, as he'd been in the strategy meetings with Generals Lee and Longstreet and President Davis, "…there were but two objectives in remaining on the Peninsula. The possibility of an advance upon us by the enemy, and gaining time in which armies might be readied and troops organized. I determined therefore, to hold the positions as long as it could be done without exposing our troops to the fire of the powerful artillery, which I doubted not, would be brought to bear upon them. I believed that after silencing our batteries on the York River, the enemy would attempt to turn us by moving up to West Point, by water…Circumstances indicating that the enemy batteries were nearly ready, I directed the troops to move toward Williamsburg on the night of the 3rd."[79] In marked contrast to his adversary, General Johnston had a very accurate understanding of enemy disposition and intent, and thus, by noon May 4th his Rebel troops were passing through Williamsburg enroute to Richmond.

"The Union forces, once finally upon the road, hurried after the retreating enemy. Stoneman, with the cavalry, received orders to harass their rear, and, if possible, cut off that portion… which must have taken the longer route by the Lee's Mill road. The rebels now had some twelve hours head start….

Despite the pursuit, General McClellan remained at his headquarters in Yorktown supervising what he deemed more important –the advance of

---

77 op. cit. pg. 69.
78 op. cit.
79 op. cit.

Franklin's troops up the York. In his place McClellan instructed Sumner, "take command of the troops ordered in pursuit of the enemy."

Straightforward as the order was, it became a source of confusion because General McClellan also ordered General Heintzelman, "take control of the entire movement"[80] In the fog of war, two Union generals thus understood they were in charge of the pursuit. "With the entire army upon its feet again… the eyes of the country (were) intent upon its progress."[81]

Hooker's division was on the march first and was expected to support Stoneman's waiting cavalry. Meanwhile, another division (Smith's), marching the parallel road on the left made more rapid progress until reaching Skiff's Creek where they were temporarily halted by the bridge having been burned out. In order to continue, he was ordered to turn right onto the road by which Hooker's forces marched. Reaching Half-Way House ahead of Hooker's troops who'd arrived shortly thereafter, the latter had to halt three hours waiting for the road to clear.

Two divisions had come at approximately the same time to the single intersection on the only two roads on the Peninsula running east-west. The net effects were the loss of critical hours and the creation of confusion as two entire divisions tried to change places on intersecting roads. The delay and confusion were costly as by now, Confederates were passing through Williamsburg.

After the delay, it was 5:30 p.m. before Smith's division finally came up. Despite the lateness, Sumner stressed, "the importance of pressing the pursuit as fast as possible," and Smith ordered his men into three successive lines for attack. However, another hour elapsed before they were lined up and then they found movement "utterly impracticable" due to thick undergrowth and growing darkness. They settled in place, bivouacking the night while Hooker marched on until 11:00 p.m. before finally halting short of the enemy. The day ending far differently than it had begun as a Union solider recorded.

"Who of those present will forget the morning, (May 4th) so bright – and beautiful – and calm. How full of enthusiasm, how confident that the end of the rebellion was in sight!" [82] observed twenty-three year old Pvt. Robert M. Boody, 40th New York Volunteers. His words capturing the sentiment among ranks as they finally embarked on a battle they thought would soon end secession.

"We had been at the front constantly; built roads, rifle pits, and

---

80 op. cit. pg. 72.
81 op. cit.
82 Carter,

redoubts, and had been under fire more or less constantly by day and by night. This was our first actual battle, although we had been among the first troops to arrive in Yorktown," Pvt. Boody wrote.[83]

Dawn brought a downpour that never let up, turning roads into mud bogs. "How gladly we tramped down that road through the woods. The mud actually up to our knees at times always over our shoes." [84]

Figure 36. Union troops in pursuit of withdrawing Rebels in the pitiless rain. Courtesy of the Library of Congress, Washington, D.C.

Figure 37. Battle of Williamsburg as depicted in a post war Currier & Ives print. Courtesy of the Library of Congress, Washington, D.C.

83 op. cit.
84 op. cit.

Civil War Comes Home

As his Mozart Regiment, as the 40th was known, advanced into an area in which the pines had been felled, "We found cover behind stumps, fallen trees...anything that served as shelter from bullets and shot. Just as we were nearly over [a fallen tree] a bullet struck the poor fellow and he fell to the ground. I was untouched. Never will I forget the look he gave me." [85]

Like many of his comrades, Pvt. Boody was on an emotional roller coaster that day, excited at finally being on the move, to a sickening realization the man he'd shared breakfast with that morning was shot dead. After seeking cover Pvt. Boody and the rest were recalled to camp by the bugle at dusk. As he was far forward, he was one of the last to leave the battlefield. Crawling carefully among stumps, and logs, he heard a weak voice calling, "Help me please help me."

As Boody turned he saw pale and weak Josiah Pike propped against a stump, his right arm shattered by a bullet now lodged in his side. Weak from blood loss, he was unable to move.

"Here let me help you." Boody cut the sleeve off Pike's jacket and used his handkerchief as a combination tourniquet and dressing. No sooner had blood flow from Pike's shattered arm been stopped, when Boody spotted another member of his unit, George Carr, unwounded but struggling to make his way rearward over broken ground and fallen trees.

Crack! A shot rang out hitting Carr, severing his spine, collapsing him to the ground. As it was nearly nightfall they'd thought darkness afforded protection, but a Rebel sharpshooter could see enough for a near fatal shot.

"Oh my God, what am I to do," cried Boody. "Lord please help me." He feared for his own safety seeing Carr shot right next to him. *I can't haul two casualties at once and there's no one else out here.* Besides praying, Boody did some quick thinking, *Pike is no longer bleeding, but he's white as a ghost from blood loss, and now poor Carr is down, probably crippled. I can only take one, who do I save?*

He decided Carr's wound was more than likely fatal but Pike's need not necessarily prove so. He'd correctly determined that Pike would bleed to death if untreated.

"Come on Josiah, we got to get you to the field hospital," at the same time calling out, "Carr, don't worry I'll be back or send someone to get the

---

85 Carter, Rusty, May 4, 2011, Medal of Honor led to Second thoughts. The Virginia Gazette. pgs. 12-13A.

stretcher." But there was no one else. Boody was alone with two wounded friends, both near death, on a day that began with such promise.

With considerable exertion Boody finally managed to deliver Pike to the field hospital. It was little more than a dilapidated tent and footlocker, supposedly for medicine but ransacked, probably for the alcohol, and now lying useless in the mud.

Boody insisted Pike be treated; otherwise he feared he'd be left to bleed to death within sight of the overworked aid station. Once assured his friend would receive care as soon as possible, Boody headed back out. His conscience would never let him to leave a fellow soldier, especially as he'd been the last to see Carr. Boody tried to retrace his path, but twilight had faded and rain still fell in sheets, as he was heading in the wrong direction. *I can't leave him out here to die alone*, Boody kept telling himself, at the same time realizing he could be hit by a sniper just as Carr had earlier. The longer he wandered the more likely his own death.

"Help me Lord! I done run out of daylight," tripping over tree branches and slipping in the mud, Boody finally spotted Carr.

"Thank God, I didn't think you was coming back," Carr said. He could still talk, though weakly, and move his arms, but was paralyzed from the wound down, still lying where he'd been shot.

"Of course I came back, what do you take me for? You think I'd leave a wounded friend out here? Look, Carr, what if it was the other way 'round? You'd come back for me wouldn't you? Now, come on let's get you up."

While Carr wanted to out of there immediately and tried to move, he couldn't even feel his legs, let alone move them. If he was going anywhere, it was up to Boody. He got his right arm around Carr's back and reaching under his arm, had his patient in a crude carry where they could begin to move. Going was slow as Boody literally drug Carr up and down ravines, slippery with mud. Downed trees had to be bypassed, the slightest detour seeming to take forever. Though exhausted, Boody never faltered and refused to give up, determined no soldier would be left on the battlefield. With nightfall the temperature dropped and Carr started shivering uncontrollably. He was critically wounded and having spent the entire day exposed, was going into shock.

Boody redoubled his efforts dragging him to aid, just as he'd delivered Pike. Finally spotting a dim lantern in the distance, he recognized the terrain, and the draw leading to the aid station. Somehow, he'd managed to save his second casualty that evening.

***

The day before, Saturday, May 3rd when General Johnston had ordered withdrawal from the Warwick- Yorktown line, his troops had done so without delay for the move had been rumored for days. They understood their leaving was only a question of when and under cover of steady cannonade, they'd their begun to move to New Kent Court House via Williamsburg. After slogging through deep mud, it was midmorning before the lead troops were passing close by Fort Magruder on Williamsburg's defensive line. As they'd not been involved in constructing the works, they had no specific knowledge of its features, extent, or even the number or location of redoubts. As ordered, they were simply passing through on the way to Richmond. But a short distance away, on pastures recently occupied by the College's flocks of chickens and ducks, dairy herd, swine, and the faculty's and students' horses, 32nd Virginia Infantry was now encamped. Overlooking the mill dam forming Lake Matoka, the recruits settled into camp life.

Although Sergeant Major kept them busy drilling and improving marksmanship, especially the speed with which they could reload, lads found time for a wide range of diversions. Some kept journals and wrote letters home, those that couldn't write dictating to others, often for a return favor such as taking their place standing guard. Newspapers, though far out of date, were passed around until practically deteriorating. Besides mail and news, pamphlets circulated, some prepared by the government, others by religious organizations imploring, 'repent before it was too late,' –hardly comforting to those facing battle. Popular tracts included, "Are you prepared to die?' and the official, 'The Prayers of the Confederate States, Soldier's Pocket Manual of Devotions.' Many carried miniature bibles at all times and stories often repeated told of a musket ball stopped by the many pages of the Bible -clear 'proof' of divine intervention.

Besides reading and writing, music and games of chance were popular -a deck of cards a prized possession, good for countless hours of entertainment. Much of their time, not to mention meager pay, was spent gambling, despite distribution of tracts, 'Ruinous consequences of gambling.' Music frequently accompanied gaming, their instruments ranging from banjos and fiddles, to hand-carved flutes -all carried willingly, for music was integral to camp life. *Shout, Shout the Battle Cry of Freedom,* was popular in both northern and southern versions, as was, *'The Girl I Left Behind Me.'*

The officers did not like it when the men struck up, '*There's No Place Like Home*,' as the desertion rates would invariably increase.

Nothing accompanied music or gambling better than tobacco and drink. Both smoked and chewed, tobacco partially sated their hunger, while alcohol deadened perceptions of hardship and danger.

While the majority entertained themselves with such diversions as could be found; if they were to eat, someone had to cook. While a few eventually became accomplished, it was, 'woman's work' and of little interest to most. This and chronic shortages in the quality, quantity, and variety of foods, made for bland meals. The men resigned themselves to it for no one, it seemed, could solve the chronic shortages, as they existed on what amounted to a starvation diet. Dark smoke curling from cook fires often carried the smell of burnt sugar when dinner was boiled rice with sugar sauce. It was simple, the men liked the sweet taste, and considered it a step up from 'skillygalee,' –stale hard bread soaked in cold stream water then deep fried brown in pork fat. Both armies grumbled about their chow, often with good cause but to no effect. "I must say that Uncle Sam don't feed his soldiers as he ought, hard crackers and salt junk is not a thing for a man to fight on," one disgruntled soldier wrote.[86]

Whether meals were adequate or appreciated, many existed in a state of perpetual hunger. Privates Boody, Pike, and Carr and the rest of their Mozart Regiment for example were off in pursuit with no time for breakfast. By nightfall they'd had nothing but stale water from their canteens as they tried to fight their way out of what would become known as the Bloody Ravine in front of the Williamsburg line. Similarly, Rebels were called to the defense, grabbing whatever scrap of stale bread might be found.

***

The pre dawn quiet of camp was suddenly broken by Sergeant Major's booming, "Break camp!" Now, instead of fanning and stoking embers and filling coffee pots, what was left of campfires were doused and pots secured.

"Damn, moving out in the middle of the night." Thomas' slave muttered. *I sure don't know about this solderin' life.* Everyone wondered

---

[86] Letter dated July 12, 1861, Roxbury City Gazette, July 18, 1861, Letters of the Civil War website.

what was happening as they'd expected to continue in the camaraderie of camp life for the foreseeable future.

"Fall in, Damn it, and be quick about it!" Sergeant Major Joseph Bidgood was in no mood to be questioned, especially by any still wet-behind-the-ears recruit. His temper must have showed for none dared question.

"Captain says we got orders forward, now break camp, quick as you can. We're moving out. Sergeants I don't want to see a bunch a lally-gaggers," Sergeant Major ordered. Their brief encampment at the college's farm was at a sudden end. The scene was now chaos. Many lads were still figuring how to wear or carry all their new gear, and now, practically in the middle of the night, they were supposed to gather it all up and go somewhere else, probably to fight. Most scurried about doing best they could, trying to hide their apprehension in a flurry of activity. Thomas shook off the damp chill, rolling his blanket and gathering his weapon and gear. He was one of the first to report which did not go unnoticed as Captain Cook happened past at the moment.

"Go help the others," the Sergeant said, knowing no one was leaving 'til everyone was ready. Thomas headed over to the slaves' encampment.

"There you is Marsa," his slave invoked, shivering in his boots with no socks, but mostly from fear.

"We're ordered to move out, now gather up your stuff." In helping him pack, Thomas was surprised to find his slave's burden considerably greater than his own. "Yes Marsa, we carries the kitchen supplies for the whole unit," putting two large frying pans affixed by rope over his shoulder, one in front, one aft like some kind of prehistoric tortoise, the heavy pans slamming his body with each step. Thomas noticed for the first time all the slaves were variously encumbered, *"it's a wonder they can keep up."*

"Forward march!" Sergeant Major ordered in his loudest voice. The officers riding up and down the formation, the unit expanding and compressing accordion-like, as men fell into step. From deep in the woods, a horned owl called, its night hunt interrupted by the ruckus. Williamsburg's Junior Guard was on the move, suddenly heading east. *Yes, they were manned, and equipped, but were they ready?* Captain Cook wondered. *No time to fret 'bout that, now!* Messages through the night had an increasingly strident tone, the latest for them to come on the double quick east of town.

They'd gone but a short distance before winds picked up bringing another squall, fat drops then steady downpour. Pulling hats down and collars up, the men struggled, their wet gear heavier and slippery. In steady rain and dropping temperature, dawn barely managed an appearance -an ominous sign.

"Close up, keep up the ranks," Sergeants shouted. The roads, not great even in fair weather, were marched into muck. It was hard to take a step without slipping and even the horses had a hard time. Sergeants eventually gave up attempts to keep ranks closed up, settling instead for just keeping the mass moving. Rain continued and winds whipped hats, coat tails and anything loose, hands numb against cold steel, their feet numb inside soaked boots. Mired down, first ankle deep then to the knee, they tried to keep up but stragglers increased despite wholesale jettisoning of gear to lighten loads. The more they marched, the deeper the mud, now pulling off boots. Leaders cursed them onward but in the down pour and with steam rising from exertion of man and beast, it was virtually impossible to see ahead. When a man or mule got stuck those following careened into a growing pile of tangled limbs and equipment. Forward progress became impossible and many gave up valiant but fruitless effort. The men would have been only too glad to get out of there but it became physically impossible to move. Many could do nothing but collapse where they were. Some used bayonets to slash tree branches, extending to comrades to pull them out, or laying branches so they might step without sinking. Word passed through ranks, a mule sank in muck, drowning before its handlers could extract the poor frightened beast. As preposterous as it sounded, no one disputed the claim. Men and beast alternated between exhaustion and hypothermia, struggling to extricate each other and equipment from clutching mud. An artillery piece had to be abandoned when a team of no fewer than a hundred horses failed to extract it.

Seeing something had to be done, Captain Cook somehow gained the relative shelter of a copse of pines on a slight raise --one of the few places from which water was draining. The massive trunks, the making of ship's masts, provided a slight break. First, he had to figure out where they were, then how to reach their objective. Then the first booms added to the confusion.

Struggling under the weight of frying pans and other gear, Thomas' slave thought, *'Oh no, thunder on top of rain.* He'd always been afraid of lightning, but this was man's fury, rolling cannon fire. Thomas' slave scrambled to the tree line, hands and feet slipping, his terror was real.

Pvt. Barlow and others saw Captain Cook heading into the trees and the idea became contagious. Soon most of the outfit was seeking cover

Civil War Comes Home

there, thin as it was. Rivulets of cold rain running down his back, Thomas peered out trying to get his bearings and saw his Captain struggling to unfold a map - impossible in wind driven rain. The Captain's horse was rearing and skitterish at the sounds of artillery and howling winds. Thomas rushed forward, leaving what little shelter he'd found,

"Sir, can I help you?"

"What's you name son?" the commanding officer asked, surprised by Thomas' appearance out of the storm.

"Sir, Private Barlow, Thomas Barlow at your service Sir."

"Okay, Private Barlow, you're from 'round here ain't you? I mean do you know this area? We got to figure out where we are and quick. From the sound of artillery we ain't got much time before shells will be dropping on your mates back there."

"Yes Sir, grew up around here and been a student at the college. Reckon I know it well as any."

"Good, then go see if you can recognize where we are and come back and show me on the map in relation to the road. Keep a sharp eye out. From the sound of it, enemy ain't far. Be quick about it, we ain't got all day. Report back to me here just quick as you can."

"Yes Sir, reconnoiter and report, got it Sir."

Good luck Private, Captain Cook thought before turning to Sergeant Major, inquiring after their disposition, strung out up and down the woods apparently near the western edge of a ravine.

What have I gotten myself into? Thomas wondered, launching into the gale. The rumble of artillery growing louder, or was the wind carrying the noise? *I've got to figure this out. We ain't marched that long and the rain slowed us considerable,* Thomas peering trying to recognize some landmark, anything familiar. Now alone, the Captain's caution about being captured flashed in his mind, but he managed to calm himself rationalizing *he was only one fool enough to be out at the height of the storm. Okay, there's the main road. This is the stretch just past Ft. Magruder just east of town. That's it we're almost to the ravine just off the road, east of the fort.* And with his critical observation, he turned to head back. Only retracing his steps in the storm was no simple matter. *Things didn't look the same*, even though he'd just passed, *which way did I come?* In his hurry to find out where they were, he hadn't paid attention to where he'd been. It was a rookie's mistake but in war it could prove deadly. Rain never let up a moment, Thomas stumbling about.

"Halt who goes there?" he heard and the fateful click of a weapon cocking, clear as ever, even with the wind and shelling. A sound one never forgets.

"It's me, Private Barlow, Thomas Barlow, hold your fire, Captain sent me out to reconnoiter."

"Barlow ya say, anybody know a Barlow? 'Thomas Barlow,' the guard called out, straining over the wind. The 32nd had so recently formed all the men didn't necessarily yet know every other member. They would learn in time, but it just hadn't happened yet.

"Hold it right there."

"Okay, don't shoot. Why do you think I'd be out in a storm such as this, 'cept Captain Cook sent me?"

"Well, you could be a Yank, hard to tell, this storm and all."

"Hell, I ain't no Yank, damn it. My slave's in the unit. Go ask for Thomas Barlow's slave. You'll see I'm one of y'all."

The call went back. Was there a slave belongin' to Master Thomas Barlow?" and sure enough, shortly the word came back up, "A slave with two fryin' pans wants to know what you got yourself into Barlow?"

And with that the man relaxed his deadly aim, Barlow breathing relief. But he didn't have time to rest. "Quick, which way to Captain Cook. I gotta report."

"Over yonder, bit of high ground, he's trying to get this gaggle organized. Meanwhile, we're forming a line, not so much a blade a grass for shelter," but Thomas was already out of ear shot.

"Sir, Private Barlow reporting as ordered."

Captain Cook spun around, surprised to see his mud-covered soldier returned, "Well, what ya got Barlow?"

"Sir, we're just off the road, east of Ft. Magruder, approaching a large ravine, a natural low area that drains to Tutters pond south of here."

"You certain, Barlow?"

"Yes, Sir, been 'round these parts all my life and I recognize the stretch of road, been down it many times. Sir, we are just off the main approach to Williamsburg, I'm certain."

"Okay, good work Private. Stay close, case I need you again."

Thomas was shaking. He didn't know if it was the cold or the close encounter with the sentry, but the danger in what he'd just done hit him. Victoria's image came to mind as he tried to huddle behind a tree, colder than ever before. While Thomas tried to get control of his thoughts and his shaking, word was passed, make ready to move forward to the edge of the ravine and hold there at all cost.

Sergeant Major had the men dig in along a line southwesterly from the road. They prepared hasty firing positions and felled every tree ahead of the line. Though cold rain continued, their bodies were steaming as they dug and chopped at a frantic pace. Tree cutting left their position clear, branches forming a tangle that'd prove deadly for enemy attempting to climb through making them an easy target. Despite the storm, the work continued past exhaustion. Every man knew his life and the lives of those around him depended on it. They just hoped they had time. As they toiled, sounds of fighting continued, but they were unsure if it was advancing, retreating, or just swirling winds playing tricks. Regardless, the steady booming was strong motivation and they soon had the better part of the slope cleared. Killing fields were set up complete with aiming stakes so squads didn't overlap fire and waste ammunition. Others frantically dug trenches for firing positions, some little more than depressions, others hastily reinforced with the felled trunks reducing exposure to enemy fire. Captain Cook and Sergeant Major quickly inspected the works and although not entirely according to textbook, it was good enough. It had to be for they were out of time.

"Private Barlow," Captain Cook called.

"Yes Sir right here Sir,"

"Take my horse and ride back to Ft. Magruder and tell 'em our position. Draw a map if you need to, but make sure they know where we are. We'll need supplies and reinforcements and I sure as hell don't want them firing on us. Be quick about it and get any information you can about the rest of the line. Do not write it down, in case you are captured. But don't forget any detail either. Supposed to be redoubts below the Fort and more north but we don't know where, or if they're manned. Be nice to know who's on our flanks."

"Yes Sir, got it. Report our position and strength to Ft. Magruder, and find out about the rest of the defense. Yes Sir."

"Good. Now go!"

Turning to Sergeant Major after Thomas left, "Well, I'll be damned if that one ain't usin' his noggin' for something more than a hat rack. Pray he can keep his wits about him and his head down when the lead starts flying."

"Yes Sir we'll all be duckin' soon enough from the sound of it."

While Captain Cook and other commanders struggled to move their men east as quickly as possible, many of their compatriots still headed west, through Williamsburg. Thus, the army was going in opposite directions at the same time and in the same place. It made for jammed roads and great confusion, passing soldiers joking with each other about, *'going the wrong way.'* While the counter movements were both confusing and amusing to the troops, the few residents remaining had no idea of what to make of the chaos. Everyone sensed a great battle was imminent, only when and where remained uncertain.

As the afternoon wore on, remaining townspeople, mostly women, a few elderly and some children, turned out to greet passing troops despite the continuing downpour, hoping to see husbands, sons or fathers, or at least learn of their whereabouts. The residents thinly lining muddy Main Street meant a lot to the men and presently a halt was ordered, giving them their first rest since the night before. Hot coffee and sandwiches appeared from somewhere which the famished troops devoured. Lately, they'd seen nothing but shortages, and rarely, if ever, an act of kindness. To a man they took advantage of genuine hospitality while the hostesses ensured no soldier was omitted. Understandably, no one wanted to leave. Units arriving from the east and joined by others from the west to reinforce as ever greater numbers jammed in to the point where movement in any direction was nearly impossible. An unexpected consequence of Southern hospitality was even more confusion.

Noise of the crowds was deafening. Wagon drivers cracked bull whips trying to drive teams forward, despite hopeless congestion. A cacophony of bugle calls signaled different units to either stop and assemble or resume marching. Townspeople cheered, soldiers shouted; everyone anxious to learn what was going on, but the distant cannon fire was not diminishing and seemed to be growing louder.

Although some units, seeing the congestion, attempted to by-pass the bottle neck, all roads ran through town not around it. Besides, no soldier long in the field under miserable conditions was willing to forego a chance at a warm welcome, hot coffee, a morsel to eat, or whatever comforts citizens of the town might offer, especially women. By afternoon the following day the better part of the whole of Johnston's Peninsula Command, approaching some fifty thousand, seemed jammed in, around, or attempting to pass through Williamsburg.

Over the turmoil, sounds of both rifle and cannon fire continued from the east. Federal pursuers, despite a late start and initially slow pursuit, now moved threateningly close. There was increasing risk Johnston's entire army might be surrounded and captured in Williamsburg.

Figure 38. General Hancock's Division presses the pursuit. Courtesy of the Library of Congress, Washington, D.C.

Somehow, a mud-spattered messenger managed to force his way through jammed streets to find Johnston in his Vest house headquarters. The staff could hardly distinguish man from mount, so thoroughly covered in mud they appeared as one, as if dipped in it. After 20 days rain in April,[87] and the latest down pour lasting twenty-eight hours non-stop, mud was everywhere. Listening carefully to the breathless rider, Johnston quickly spun around to his staff, ordering immediate action.

"Quick, the Yanks are close by. Wheel about and defend, or risk capture!" Johnston running outside, literally commandeered the nearest passing brigade, that of Brigadier General Paul Semmes. Leading the force to Fort Magruder himself, Johnston also ordered, Brigadier General Lafayette McLaws to bring up Brigadier General Joseph Kearshaw's South Carolina brigade and two batteries of artillery,[88] placing General Longstreet in charge of rearguard action, allowing Kershaw's and Semmes' brigades to continue their withdrawal.

With Longstreet's men, Major General D.H. Hill's soldiers defended on the eastern flank while Brigadier General Jubal Early's brigade was held in reserve, ready and waiting on the grounds of the College of William & Mary.[89] Cavalry men were also in town where their leader, General J.E.B. Stuart was enjoying dining, easily recognized in tall black boots, yellow silk sash with tassel, and ostrich-plumed broad-brimmed hat. But there was no more time for hospitality, Stuart ordering immediate assembly of his men.

At first, surprised troops didn't understand the sudden orders to retrace ground they'd just covered, but they grasped the situation, on

---

87 Wheat, pg. 8.
88 Dougherty and Moore, pg. 86.
89 op. cit. pg. 89.

hearing increased firing in the distance. Seeing the urgent movement of troops, townspeople also scurried - mostly in the opposite direction. Soon it was mass hysteria. One moment they'd been hailing heroes, offering refreshment and well wishes, and the next, there was danger the entire lot would be swept up, possibly caught up in cross fire.

Fully grasping the extreme urgency, Johnston led the reversal, clamoring back to Fort Magruder. At full gallop, he shouted last minute instructions, grabbing another brigade enroute. Without warning, or plan, it now seemed there'd be a fight for Williamsburg, though certainly not on terms either side wanted. Johnston knew, *If I have to defend, I'll not find better ground than here. The Peninsula narrows to seven miles and is further reduced by Queens and College Creeks, so less than half the distance is left to defend and all that, studded with redoubts, courtesy of Magruder and Ewell. Thank God!*

Barely making it inside Fort Magruder ahead of the enemy, Johnston had his men lay down as heavy fire possible, temporarily driving attackers to seek shelter in nearby woods. In unrelenting rain, both sides were exhausted, and darkness brought a temporary end to the immediate threat. A heated skirmish thus ended a long day's march and both sides seemed satisfied to temporarily concentrate on repelling nature's fury instead of each other's. An eerie cease fire began, but not on anyone's orders. They simply had nothing left to give, both armies collapsing in place. Johnston knew, however, it would begin anew at dawn and by then, more Union forces would oppose.

Indeed, little comfort could be found that miserable night, foreshortened by renewed Federal bombardment before sunrise. Johnston spent the night in his headquarters, warm and dry but certainly not sleeping. Working his staff through the night, he was desperate to organize the defense and possibly counter attack in the midst of the overall withdrawal. He ordered additional units to Fort Magruder and elsewhere on the Williamsburg line relieving beleaguered defenders. Although moving out smartly, some units still had no idea exactly where they were supposed to be going. None of the officers or men had any more information on the defense line than they had when they'd crossed it the day before. They searched for redoubts in dim light, fog, smoke, and rain; the Federal bombardment continuing unabated. Under constant shelling, the troops didn't need Johnston to tell them something had to be done. J.E.B. Stuart's cavalry would go on the offensive.

Civil War Comes Home

Cavalrymen gathered to attack the center of the Union line. If they could break through they could try to disrupt the murderous cannonade. In a tight formation, sabers drawn, hurtling forth in a flying column, they managed to punch through at the edge of the woods. Once past defenders, they turned left and right, chasing men down. It was murderous, the mounted cavalry running down beleaguered infantrymen, artillery still firing from a distance. Despite their initial success, the bold attack was not adequately supported and could not be sustained against the superior Union strength. Returning to their own lines, Stuart's men were bitterly discouraged. They'd been under fire the entire time and despite their valiant effort, their additional losses had been for naught.

These kinds of heated skirmishes went on all day May 5th, hard fought but not decisive. By late afternoon as light was failing, firing began tapering off. In addition to reduced visibility, utter exhaustion was again a factor. After fighting all day the men had nothing more to give.

Into this uneasy lull General McClellan finally arrived -too late to make a difference. Later he described the situation in a letter to his wife, "I found everybody discouraged, officers and men, our troops in wrong positions, on the wrong side of the woods, no system, no cooperation, no orders given, roads blocked up." Despite this bleak picture, "as soon as I came upon the field the men cheered like fiends, and I saw at once that I could save the day." No one else held such a rosy view.

Longstreet, having accomplished his task to delay Federal pursuit, quietly withdrew under cover of darkness and although the day had not gone as planned, Johnston was not entirely displeased. The outcome was consistent with his overall approach, trading space for time to preserve his army to fight another day. Despite their losses, J.E.B. Stuart's hard fought cavalry remained ready as a screening force covering the continuing withdrawal, but as Longstreet reported, "The pursuit was not active, hardly annoying." [90] McClellan's grand plan, massing unprecedented firepower, and army of well over one hundred thousand had come to naught. With no pursuit of the enemy, any prospect for the war's early end was lost.

***

As the Confederate withdrawal continued, despair swept remaining residents. They'd taken some small comfort, despite day long firing, in being surrounded by their beloved troops, figuring there was safety in numbers.

90 op. cit. pg. 91.

Fearing abandonment before the Yankee onslaught, many resurrected Ewell's argument that Williamsburg should not be left defenseless for the sake of preserving distant Richmond. Many felt they should have continued to fight it out right there, but it was too late and the massive exit of men and materiel could not be stemmed.

Among those passing through town was First Lieutenant Dezzie Barziza, former William & Mary student friend of Thomas Barlow. 1LT Barziza's parent unit, Robertson's Five Shooters, 4th Texas Infantry, had been summoned all the way from west Texas to Virginia and he'd dutifully led Company C for twenty-seven days continuous travel; by rail, steamer and on foot. Although they had not arrived in time for the battle, they joined the exodus heading west, marching his men up Main Street past the very house in which he'd been born. Unfortunately, there was no time to stop and visit much as he wanted to for the Army was on the move.

Dog-tired in the saddle, 1LT Barziza daydreamed of his childhood, then years at William & Mary until startled by commotion ahead. There to everyone's surprise was General Johnston. Dezzie, standing in his stirrups to see, spotted a young woman, *Pretty thing*, at the corner of Main St. and Colonial handing out ham biscuits to passing troops. She reminded the soldiers of the wives and girlfriends they'd left behind. She was none other than twenty-seven year old Miss Victoria King, girl friend of Thomas Barlow. Above the commotion, General Johnston shouted, "That's what we're fightin' for boys!" and a hearty cheer rose from hundreds of cold, wet, tired men. Later that evening Miss King wrote in her diary, "an officer stopped his horse before me and handing me his sword, requested that I clean it and save it until he returned. I cleaned the sword - it was a beautiful weapon, but its owner never came back to claim it."

The following day, Victoria was helping the wounded, carrying buttermilk to patients in the Baptist church which had been converted to a hospital. Making her way inside with the heavy jug she turned a corner and there, "one of the most horrible sights I have ever seen met my eyes: in a corner in the basement room was a pile of human arms and legs." [91] She swooned, almost spilling the precious milk, but managed to keep from fainting. She'd never before seen such a sickening sight. She purposely made no mention in her diary, yet could never forget that horrible image the rest of her life.

---

91 Dubbs, Carol Kettenburg, 2002, Defend this Old Town, Louisiana State University Press. pg. 241.

Figure 39. First Lieutenant Decimus Barziza, former William & Mary student ordered with his Texas unit back to defend Williamsburg. Photograph taken later in life, date unknown. Courtesy, Special Collections, Special Collections Research Center, Swem Library, College of William and Mary, Williamsburg, Va.

Amputations at the Baptist church continued for quite some time as another young townswoman, Delia Bucktrout had a similar experience. Passing by on her way to her post at Bruton Parish, Delia stumbled across, "a pile of arms, legs, and other parts of the human body, the pile higher than a man's head." [92] Just sixteen but appearing even younger, the diminutive Delia nevertheless made her way to Bruton, single-mindedly devoted to the Southern cause. There, she encountered a 'Yankee patient' in considerable discomfort, begging for a drink of water. As Delia's father Richard recounted, his daughter dealt with this dilemma of helping a hated enemy in her own spirited manner, telling the lad, not much older than she, "Remember, this is our land. We did not ask you to come here and fight. I give you the water, but if you were well I would gladly kill you." [93]

***

Meanwhile, what was left of roads turned to quagmires, with men, animals, artillery pieces, and supply wagons impossibly stuck. The jam of soldiers from many different units hopelessly intermingled, was now joined by a belated frantic effort by much of Williamsburg's remaining populous. Hundreds, mostly women and children, fueled by fear and wild rumors of what evil the Yankees brought, were trying to evacuate. No one wanted to remain in the enemy-occupied town.

Everyone who could leave was trying to doing so, though none very successfully, as impatience turned to panic. Only wounded, their infirmness keeping them immobile, were left. Even if ambulance wagons had been available, most patients were too frail to go even a few blocks let alone nearly fifty miles to Richmond. Also remaining behind were a handful of dedicated women and several Confederate surgeons who refused to leave patients' bedsides. The latter were repeatedly reminded in no uncertain terms their decision meant imprisonment, yet all were resolute in their conviction.

---

92 op. cit.
93 op. cit. pg. 242.

Civil War Comes Home

Figure 40. Ambulance wagon loading wounded. Courtesy of the Library of Congress, Washington, D.C.

Figure 41. Ambulance wagon of the Union's newly-organized Sanitary Commission. Courtesy of the Library of Congress, Washington, D.C.

Figure 42. Wounded soldiers recovering. Courtesy of the Library of Congress, Washington, D.C.

In the mass exodus, hundreds of wounded were simply left on the College grounds. Passing units deposited injured comrades no longer able to keep up. Civilians still gathering fallen from the fields and woods, continued bringing them to the College. There was another location however, the city courthouse was now a combination hospital and morgue which undoubtedly provided little comfort to wounded in having the morgue close at hand. It was during this use that the beautiful interior woodwork of one of the oldest courts in the land was torn out for kindling. Later, the building was missing all of its doors and windows. Although General McClellan issued strict orders that private property was not to be vandalized, they apparently did not apply to public buildings. Nor did such rules apparently apply to abandoned property, at least not in the eyes of rampaging soldiers. "Adjacent to the city hotel stood the barbershop owned by a free mulatto, Leroy Randolph. Unfortunately barber Randolph had sought safety elsewhere and his shop was literally pulled down board by board," a readymade source of firewood for occupiers.

Everywhere, people tried to make their way through the congestion. An entire army was on the move and along with them many of the remaining townspeople. "Out of the way," soldiers gruffly ordered

Civil War Comes Home

the compassionate souls trying to ease the suffering of the wounded. Among those rendering aid was Mrs. Mary Peachy, who opened her home to nurse a severely wounded Confederate Major.

***

Figure 43. Major William Payne, 4th Virginia Cavalry. Courtesy of The Museum of the Confederacy, Richmond, Va.

June – July, 1862
Long Journey:
Saga of Major William H. Payne,
4th Virginia Cavalry & Mrs. Mary Payne

Williamsburg,

The toll was horrendous, fifteen hundred dead and wounded Confederates, and even greater Yankee casualties. Initially, exact losses were not really known owing to the chaos of battle and its aftermath, but Colonel Charles S. Tripler, Medical Director, Army of the Potomac, undertook to tally the carnage. He suspected the numbers mentioned were probably underestimates, but by how much no one knew. He was determined to report accurately for there'd already been too much speculation in the northern press, and refused to allow his office to be drug into the political fight.

Although it was a huge undertaking, taking days to complete, Dr. Tripler directed both a body count and door-to-door census of wounded. He knew some wounded were with their units, others in private residences, or even, God-forbid, still lying where they'd been hit, even well after the battle. By actual head count, he learned of seven hundred Federal troops in make shift hospitals in town and an additional three hundred thirty-three wounded Confederate prisoners, not counting one hundred more in crude field depots awaiting wagon transport to docks on the James and York Rivers for pick up by the Union's newly commissioned Sanitary Corps' steamers. In all, more than a thousand required care - a tremendous

Civil War Comes Home

medical workload for which he was not staffed. Even utilizing any local physicians and Confederate doctors who'd stayed behind, it was unclear how medical care for over one thousand seriously wounded would be provided.

McClellan was advised of the situation shortly after occupying the recently vacated Vest house as his own headquarters and dispatched a courier under a flag of truce to catch up with the Rebels. He was requesting that Confederate surgeons return and assist with the care of the wounded.[94] Several turned about immediately and upon reaching Williamsburg were granted freedom to practice medicine wherever patients needed them. In coming days, they worked side by side with Union physicians caring for wounded of both sides.[95]

Fortunately, Colonel Tripler had not been the only one recognizing the urgent need for medical care. Mrs. Letitia Tyler immediately fully mobilized her Ladies Auxiliary and soon filled the former Female Academy which they'd previously converted to a hospital. Then they busily converted every other remaining public building, shop, and many private homes to care for wounded. Nearly everyone remaining in town worked tending wounded as best they could.

A week after the battle, some sixty wounded Confederates remained in town -too badly wounded to be moved. Among these was Major William H. Payne, of Waynesboro and Virginia's 4th Cavalry, horribly wounded by musket shot to his jaw.

Several of his men saw him hit and immediately ran to his aid, repositioning what was left of his missing face and instructing him to press firmly while they carried him to the rear. Seeing their leader fall must have given a boost of adrenalin for they ran the stretcher to an aid station. Major Payne steeled himself to remain conscious during the ordeal, somehow finding presence of mind to keep pressure on his wound.

They carried him to the head of the long line at the aid station. Others would wait as their beloved Major went immediately onto the operating table. At first the doctors were puzzled for his wound wasn't readily apparent as the Major's hands, still clad in leather riding gloves, were tight against his face. As soon as the surgeon relaxed his hands however, the horror of his wound was apparent. They triaged him as not expected to live, and starting removing him from the operating table making ready for the next patient. But the men who'd bore him there had not left their

---

94 Hastings & Hastings, pg. 119.
95 op. cit.

Major's side and gruffly insisted the surgeon save him, regardless. The surgeon consented and beginning debridement, advising them, "only God could save someone with his jaw shot off," and if they hadn't already, "all of 'em better start praying."

Field medical care was like Dante's hell on earth. If lucky enough to be evacuated, most patients were heaved like a sack of potatoes, onto an open wagon, their wounds re-opened and bleeding on the bone jarring ride in solid-axle wagons. The Richmond Ambulance Committee managed to field thirty-nine wagons that fateful day -not nearly enough. Once wounded reached the field hospital, their terror continued. Regimental surgeons, of varying degrees of competency and sometimes sobriety, struggled to stay on the feet after endless hours of surgery. Wounded, dying, and dead were intermingled, the latter heaped in a growing pile, victims on the bottom sinking into muck. Among the still conscious, some slipped in and out of reality, and more than a few expired while awaiting care. Regardless of how fast or long surgeons work, the line of casualties waiting seemed never-ending. Many faced additional trauma in now having limbs amputated, typically without benefit of aesthesia or hygiene. Malnourished, hypothermic survivors were distinguished from their expired compatriots only in still possessing all their limbs.

How Major Payne managed to survive his wound and the surgery was hard to imagine. Perhaps it was due to his innate toughness, his unwavering faith in God, or keeping his loving wife, Mary's image in his mind. Through waves of pain he held the small locket containing her portrait she'd given him when they parted. It and remained around his neck through the ordeals of battle and surgery.

Nearly the size of his precious locket was the oddly deformed Minnie ball removed from against his jawbone. Major Payne was lucky in a perverse kind of way, due to the angle at which the ball struck, it hadn't shattered bone as was usually the case and invariably fatal. While muscle, nerve, and tendon were severed, soft tissue could be stitched and would hopefully heal. Still, there was serious risk of infection.

A medical assistant coming from evacuating other wounded from the field, tried to see in the dim light of a lone candle burning down to a nub across the room in the field hospital. Grabbing a clean rag and pail of fresh water, he repeatedly cleansed and flushed the Major's wound as instructed by the surgeon. Subsequent patients were less fortunate as the same rag was used and water ran low. These other wounds, less well cleansed, were certain to become infected, the onset of gangrene in a matter of days signaling a horrific, slow death.

His wound treated to the standard of the day, without benefit of anesthesia except cheap government whiskey, Major Payne still had the presence of mind to ask after his men and would someone please inform his wife. Then he passed out. Between shock and exhaustion from his wound and surgery, he didn't stir for twelve hours and while he slept, his stretcher was moved to a private home. His luck was holding.

He awoke delirious with pain, parched, and asking after Mary, his wife.

"Well, how you feeling?" asked Mrs. Peachy, quickly realizing her mistake -her patient could not talk to answer. Like nearly everyone left in town, she'd immediately answered the call to care for wounded, never imagining she'd receive a patient requiring such demands. Recalling her earlier meetings with Letitia and others, it had all seemed hypothetical but now it was quite real and none of them ever imagined so many, and with such dreadful wounds. Patients filled every school, store and many homes and still, a few lads remained outside, on porches and landings. Everywhere one went was overflowing with death and suffering.

Nevertheless, Mrs. Peachy, like all the caregivers, did best they could. Though many despised the Union troops for what was perceived as trying to dictate how Southerners should live, rarely did such animosity extend to a patient. Only in isolated cases was there any distinction between those wearing blue versus gray. Every one of these sad cases was someone's husband or son and the patients knew they were the lucky ones. They appreciated being better cared for now than any previous time in their hard military service.

"Can you drink, Sir?"

Major Payne tried to nod though not sure he could swallow. Even slight movement was painful, motioning with his hand as if writing.

"Of course, let me fetch some paper," hurrying downstairs to her writing desk. Already, paper was becoming scarce, but it was the only way her patient could communicate.

"Doctor said you need lots of water to replace blood loss," she announced on returning.

'Water? Not much accustomed,' Payne scribbled.

"Yes Sir, quite safe, been drinking from this well all my life, quite healthful. And I'll bring you some soup, something with nutrition. You need energy and looks as if you could put on a few pounds." Fetching a tray with bowl of chicken broth, no matter how carefully she tried feeding him she was spilling more than her patient swallowed. "I'm sorry. I've got to figure another way."

He managed to swallow, feeling some relief and relished taste and warmth. *I can't recall when I last ate, or drank, for that matter*, he thought, then scratched out a note.

'Thank you. Get word to my wife Mary. Worried. Can pay, telegram. Expecting baby,' he scribbled.

"Oh my, I understand Sir. Well a telegram is out. We ain't got such here, even 'fore the war."

Next he wrote, 'letter?'

"Well, honey," Mrs. Peachy continued.

No one's called me "honey" in years, he recalled.

"Mail ain't none too regular 'round these parts and after the battle, I 'spect it's hard to say whether they'll be deliverin' at all. Why, you'll likely be walking home, fully healed, 'fore a letter gets delivered. Where is she anyway?"

'Danville,' he wrote. *Our family home is near Waynesboro. When I joined up, she went to stay with her family outside Danville, near the Carolina border. We figured it's safer down there, nothing of military importance, lest the Yanks take over the mills. Her family would help her, at least that was the plan,* Major Payne recalled, but could not write long explanations. 'How do I get word to her?'

"Well Sir, I don't rightly know. But I'll ask my husband, William, maybe he can get some answers. Now take some more chicken broth. It'll do you good."

He nodded ever so slightly, still trying to think how he'd get word to her. *I don't have any idea where my men are, or where my unit is*, his mind shifting from one concern to another.

The following morning William Peachy made a point of speaking to Major Payne. The two hadn't met for he'd not wanted to disturb the patient, and Payne was often asleep under the sedative effect of laudanum. Also, William was squeamish about seeing the wound.

"Good day, Sir, you seem to be improving Major."

'Yes,' he wrote, 'feeling somewhat better. Thank you for taking me, and your wife tending me,' he scribbled. *Doubt I would have made it otherwise,* he thought.

Reading his note William replied, "Sir, you are most welcome, of course, but it is we who are indebted to you, for your service and sacrifice. My wife tells me you need to get in touch with your wife in Danville?"

Payne nodded carefully, and it didn't seem to hurt quite as much now, then wrote, 'She's expecting. I must let her know I'm okay.'

"Of course, but postal service wasn't reliable before, and who will run it now?" Peachy continued, "They going to exchange mail across lines? How'd U.S. mail from occupied Williamsburg get to Confederate Danville?"

Though Major Payne was already dozing, Peachy continued, "Yes Sir, mostly one has to send a messenger –time consuming as it is. I expect that may still be the case." Unbeknownst to Peachy, Payne was now asleep.

"Can I bring you anything?" the returning Mrs. Peachy inquired, immediately noticing her patient asleep. "William, get out of here," she whispered, "let the poor Major rest. Lord knows he needs it. What's with you talking on and on?"

"I was just trying to help like you asked." *I wonder where's his 4th Cavalry is now? Could we impose on one of his men to deliver the news?* Mary was opening the window for some fresh air, ensuring Major Payne was adequately blanketed. *God, I hope that is not the awful smell of infection.*

Returning downstairs to the parlor, William thought, *doubt I can find where 4th Cavalry ended up. Men must be spread out on the roads and in woods and fields from here to Richmond - every one of 'em ready to turn around and fight soon as Generals get this gaggle straightened out.*

What if one of his soldiers is here in town? It'd be a whole lot easier and quicker - 'stead of going out who knows where.

"That's it!" Peachy exclaimed, his wife shushing him from the other room, "lest Major Payne be disturbed," she reminded sternly.

"We got to find a 4th Cavalry soldier that's still here, wounded but not too serious. Then when he's healed, he can go to Danville," -thinking out loud to hear how the newly hatched plan sounded. He needed to find a recovering 4th Cavalry soldier. The quickest way was to spread the word among the town's care providers.

Later that afternoon he explained to the Major, "Sir, we don't know where your lads ended up. If one of 'em was wounded lightly and now healed, maybe he could…." Interrupting himself Peachy explained, "but he's a Yankee prisoner." Payne managed an affirmative nod, processing Peachy's plan even as it unfolded. *Yes, occupied territory*, Major Payne understood, trying to listen but dozing off.

"A messenger," Peachy added, "if a man can be found, he'd have to pass from occupied territory through Confederate lines," *assuming of course Yanks don't take Danville, and then return, hopefully with Mrs. Payne and in time. But it's a fool's mission. Who would return to continue as a prisoner? Furthermore, what Yank commander is going to let a prisoner go back to enemy territory on a promise to voluntarily return to incarceration? Any Yank commander would surely not allow anyone to divulge the disposition of his forces. They'd counterattack.* The more he thought, the more he realized the plan was infeasible. *Who'd give up prisoner, allow them to return home, trusting him to come back to rot in prison? What about prisoner exchange?* By now Peachy was grasping at straws, trying to find a way to make it work. *Then the Provost Marshall would get back a blue belly for giving up a prisoner. No, by the time an exchange could be arranged Major Payne would either have expired, or back home under his own power, good Lord willing.* Peachy's ramblings left him discouraged. Although the Major seemed somewhat better, a wound like his took a long time to heal and Peachy wasn't at all sure what to do.

"Honey, I'm going to the tinsmith," Mrs. Peachy said. "I want him to make a funnel so the Major can have soup," but her husband was deep in thought. *I'll figure something out.*

***

Danville

Town folks who'd met the newcomer, Mary Payne, said she was the very definition of determination. She was running the family farm several months now since her husband left and was quite adamant things would be done proper and the farming and livestock show profit, despite inflated operating costs due to war.

Now, Mary grew concerned seeing a lone rider approaching. Not much more than skin and bones, wearing rags it looked. He tethered his thin horse to the dilapidated picket fence though needn't have bothered for the emaciated steed didn't have the strength for any unnecessary steps.

Mary raised the revolver under her apron knowing a woman could not be too careful these days. She wasn't expecting anyone and did not recognize him as from around these parts. Tipping his sweat-stained hat and trying unsuccessfully to brush dust and dirt from his faded uniform, the gaunt rider slowly climbed the front porch steps as Mary came to the front door, revolver at the ready.

"State your business," she called out tensely, pitching her voice lower trying to sound threatening.

"Mrs. Payne? Mrs. Payne?" he called out.

Nodding her head affirmatively, she was trying to ascertain his age. His youth was masked by the stress of battle, wounds and exhaustion, not to mention accumulated dirt. His beard and hair were matted as it had been weeks, more likely, months since he'd seen soap, let alone bathed.

"Yes, I am Mrs. Payne. And who might you be," the fetus in her womb kicking at the sound of her voice.

"Private Jones at your service Mam," removing what was left of his kepi hat. "Mam, would you mind if I set on your porch here? I'm right tired and come a long ways."

"Please be seated."

"Thank you Mam." Noting her pregnancy and the revolver barely hidden by her apron, he sought to calm her fear. "Mam, please take a seat," nodding towards her porch rocking chair. "Please don't be concerned, I'm Private Jones from 4th Cavalry, your husband's unit. I bring news from the front. Won't you be seated Mam? Mam, I rode here from Williamsburg, fast as that starved nag could go and I'm truly very sorry to have to bring you bad news, but your husband was wounded. Right bad I'm afraid, but he's been well cared for in a fine home. They're taking good care of him just like all of us wounded. The husband of the lady that's caring for him sent me to tell you."

Mrs. Payne gasped, trying to catch her breath. She'd long-feared her husband could be wounded or worse, but they'd never spoken of it. "When did this happen? How?" she demanded already replacing the shock with earnest pursuit of additional facts.

"Mam, I am sorry but I have no additional information. We was fighting the Yankees in the rain, cold as winter though it was 5th of May. There was so much confusion. When the Major was hit we hurried him to the field hospital. Later, I was wounded myself but not that bad and soon as I could I got up and they sent me here. They said he's right worried about you with the baby due and all."

"How's he doin' now?"

"Can't rightly say Mam, I left out pretty near a week ago, been on the road ever since." Private Jones knew enough not to speculate lest he create false hope or risk plunging her into deep despair unnecessarily.

"I'm sure they're doing everything for him. Thank you." *My husband is worried about me, and he's the one wounded*, she thought.

Jake McKenzie

"I must go tend his wounds. Thank you for bringing the message. Won't you water and graze your horse? And drink some spring water yourself. I'll have the cook fix you something."

"Why Mam that is mighty kindly but don't go to no trouble."

While he tended his horse, Mrs. Payne went inside to fetch some of her husband's old clothes from the trunk in the attic so the young man who'd traveled so far might leave wearing something other than worn out rags. She instructed the cook to prepare something but all she had were a few recently-gathered eggs and left over biscuits.

"Is there no ham or bacon? Our guest looks to be little more than skin and bones," Mary observed.

"No Mam, sorry" her cook replied, "we down to the last sack of flour and we got just enough ground corn and fat back to fry us some cornbread."

Returning from watering his horse and washing best he could, he tipped his hat to Mrs. Payne, again offering, "Mam, I am truly sorry to be the one to have brought you bad news. More than likely during the time I was on the road here, most likely your husband's feelin' better."

"Don't worry Private, I appreciate you making the long trip here, otherwise how'd I ever know what happened?"

"Now, come on in and rest a spell, the cooks frying you some fresh eggs and biscuits. Sorry there ain't nothin' else but we just barely keeping together what with the men off fighting. If we don't get some supplies soon, I reckon I'll have to let remaining slaves go," Mrs. Payne offered, thinking out loud. "Is the train still runnin'?"

"Why yes Mam, it is and theys loading provisions when I came through Danville, only theys trying to find more rail cars. They got to get supplies and troops to Richmond, only ain't enough cars to load it all."

"I got to see my husband," Mrs. Payne pronounced. While the starved lad was called to enjoy his first home cooked meal in as long as he could remember, she went to pack, regardless of what he'd just explained about the trains.

He'd almost forgotten what it was like to eat sitting in a chair with plate, knife and fork. Lately he sat on the ground or stood around the fire, spooning beans or soup from a cup, grabbing hard tack from the frying pan.

Mrs. Payne called for her old slave. "Gabriel, hitch the wagon, I got to git to Williamsburg to see my husband."

"Yes Mam," came his dutiful reply though he had no idea what this was about.

Packing took no time for all she brought was one change of clothes, hair brush, and family Bible in large canvas bag, along with the revolver, of course. She had no idea how long she'd be gone but she only owned one other dress -the others already cut up to make bandages.

Calling to the cook, "Gather everyone around," she wanted to explain her imminent departure and provide last minute instructions. Although she trusted her slaves to accomplish usual chores, she wanted everything in good order.

Remaining house slaves and field hands gathered on the worn lawn in front of the once grand double-door entrance. Stepping to the head of the porch stairs, Mary cleared her throat, "Well, I reckon y'all seen the messenger a short time ago, come all this way from Williamsburg. Major Payne done got wounded in battle. Thank God he's alive, but he's hurt right bad and I got to go to him."

A hush fell over the gathering, then weeping for he was loved and respected for he'd treated all fairly, even kindly. Though the slaves worked hard, Major ensured they were well fed, appropriately clothed, and had warm homes. If anyone was ill beyond what the slaves or Mrs. Payne could care for, Marsa Payne sent for the doctor –an expense unheard of on many plantations. Marsa never entrusted his slaves to an overseer, preferring to manage things himself, and had never broken up a slave family as was common elsewhere.

They were also saddened by the prospect of Mrs. Payne traveling alone. For any woman, especially with child, to travel alone was unheard of, and these days highways weren't safe. A woman alone in war was not acceptable, but Mrs. Payne would not be put off.

"Beggin' you pardon Mam," old Gabriel voiced their fears, "ain't safe especially that far, let me accompany you"

"Thank you kindly Gabriel, I appreciate your offer, but you're needed here. Someone's got to keep this place operatin.' We can't be lettin' Major Payne see it in sorry condition when he comes home can we?"

"Well no Mam, whatever you say, but you got to be safe," Gabriel replied, trying to fathom what it meant to be left in charge as that'd never crossed his mind. He'd been with the Payne's his entire life and hearing her say she needed him to run the place made him proud. He was genuinely needed at a time of crisis. In that realization his life's work no longer seemed like drudgery but found meaning.

As she bid farewell the cook brought out a satchel of what food could be found. The slaves didn't move, instead, holding an informal meeting. They'd grown accustomed to pretty much running their own day-to-day affairs and only approached Mrs. Payne when they encountered something they couldn't resolve. The patriarch Gabriel spoke first. "It just ain't right I tell you, we cannot let Mrs. Payne go on her own. Marsa would not approve."

"I know," others agreed. "You are right, Gabriel, but you heard, she ain't listening to her own good sense, least ways to us."

"We know you right Gabriel, but what can we do?"

After considerable discussion the only course of action they came up with was for Gabriel to speak with her again about accompanying her.

"Excuse me Mrs. Payne, Mam," Gabriel spoke softly.

"Yes, what is it?"

"Mrs. Payne, Mam, I just gots to say how very sad we all is to hear Marsa Payne done been wounded, and we's all prayin' for him. But Mam you really can't be traveling all that way in your state of motherhood, if you pardon my saying so."

"Gabriel, we already discussed this, and you know I must go. If I didn't, you know I'd worry myself sick sittin' here wonderin' how he's getting' on, and was he recovering, and in someone else's home."

"Yes Mam, well at least let me accompany you."

"Thank you Gabriel that had not occurred to me with so much work needin' doin' here and you being the one I trust most to see it gets done. But, maybe we could get there quicker travelin' together?"

Gabriel stretched taller, waiting patiently, allowing her continued thinking. Finally she resolved she would in fact appreciate his company. The others would just have to do as best they could.

"Very well Gabriel, get the wagon. We'll drive to the station soon as we can. I don't want to miss the train and the messenger said it's crowded."

"Yes Mam, right away Mam," Gabriel replied, pleased. He hadn't thought she'd change her mind and hurried off to see to hitching the mule. He didn't need to pack. He owned nothing but the clothes on his back.

By the time his helper, young Moses, had the mule hitched, and they'd hidden Marsa's shotgun under the seat, Mrs. Payne issued final instructions. Mostly the slaves knew what to do, but there was verification in hearing it from the Marsa's wife that reassured the familiar order.

Arriving at the Danville station, Mrs. Payne immediately encountered the first of what would prove many challenges.

"No Mam, I am sorry this is a military train. No civilians allowed," the station master insisted.

"But Sir, my husband, Major Payne, 4th Virginia Cavalry lies wounded and I must get to him."

"Mrs. Payne I am sorry, I didn't recognize you at first. It's been a while since I seen you or the Major in town. Mam, this is a military train as I said, and we no longer have regular passenger service."

"When is the next passenger train?"

"Actually, Mam, we don't rightly know. The regular schedule is no more. With the war we don't know when or even if we run passenger service."

"Sir, I can't sit here waitin' on a train that might never come. I must get on board, whilst he's still alive. I beg you." She'd refused to think he might not survive or whether she'd get there in time.

Seeing she'd not be dissuaded, and having many other urgent tasks to accomplish, he relented. "Mam, I must warn you, the train could be subject to enemy attack. If they try to blow up the tracks, a bridge, or destroy the train you could be hurt or killed." Neither she nor Gabriel, standing close by listening, had thought of this. "Has there been any attack on trains around here?" Mrs. Payne inquired, "on the Danville-Richmond line we'd be traveling?"

"No Mam, none yet, thank the Lord."

"Then we'll take our chances."

"Our?" the station master repeated. "What do you mean Mam?"

"Gabriel's travelin' with me, to help should I run into any difficulties along the way."

"No Mam, no slave is ridin' this train," the station master exclaimed. "It's bad enough lettin' a woman ride a military train. There's no way a slave can ride. Sorry Mam that's the way it is. No exceptions no matter who, or what the reason," then adding for good measure, "and Mam I must advise the train is no place for a woman traveling alone, especially with child."

Mrs. Payne looked into Gabriel's sad eyes. He'd heard the pronouncement, wondering, *why does it always have to be like this?*

"Take the wagon on home. I'll manage on my own, somehow. Thank you for your help. While you're taking care of things back home, I'll nurse Major Payne back to health and we'll all be back home just like old times. We'll get the old place fixed up and everything will be like it was." Then on second thought, she wondered, *with this war things ain't never going back to the way they were. God, why couldn't those Northerners just leave us be?*

"Yes, Mam," Gabriel replied discouraged, "God-speed and safe travel." Starting to go, he decided to wait 'til the train pulled out.

"Sir, how much is the fare?"

"No Mam, I'll not take a half-dime, knowing Major Payne, off fightin' for us, lies wounded."

Though only recently arrived in Danville, the Payne's were well-respected throughout the community. Both had treated neighbors and town folk well and now reaped return of their kindness. Once word of his wounding became known, others in the community came by the farm house, asking Gabriel what they could do to help. Sometimes it was repair a leaking roof or weed the kitchen garden. Between remaining slaves and occasional volunteers, most of the important chores were accomplished in some fashion.

"Why thank you. I shall surely inform Major Payne of your kind assistance in my time of need."

"You are most welcome Mam, but I regret this train only goes far as Richmond. No trains runnin' to Williamsburg, it's now occupied territory."

"Then how am I to reach my husband?" nearly in tears. Though she hadn't figured on this, her resolve was firm. She'd find a way to Williamsburg, "then I'll go as far as the train runs."

"Yes Mam, may I assist you with your belongings? Help you board? Soon as they unload a final wagonload of supplies we'll be on our way, shouldn't be long."

"Thank you," she replied, carefully climbing rail car stairs one rung at a time.

"Mam, you know I just thought by the time we reach Richmond, maybe Major Payne will be transferred there. I hear they got a big hospital at Chimborazo, on the hills just outside town. It's the largest and best in the entire Confederacy. By time we arrive you might inquire after him there?"

"Thank you, but I think it quite unlikely he'd be there. He was wounded and captured, so unless he was part of a prisoner exchange, I doubt he'll be at Chimborazo."

"Oh I see," the embarrassed station master replied, sorry he'd brought it up.

"I just pray he is under doctor's care somewhere safe. I just don't want to think about all those poor mother's sons left behind, no doctor, no one to take care of 'em. Maybe they had a chance to recover but alone, they die from exposure, or blood loss," she lamented, beginning to cry.

"Mam let me see you to your seat, so you can get comfortable. The conductor will make sure you are not disturbed."

"Thank you Sir. You've been most helpful."

With Mrs. Payne settled, the station master hurried to attend to his other tasks. His main concern was they were transporting munitions and he and the rest of the train crew had limited experience shipping explosives. Yes they'd transported small quantities of dynamite for mining in the southwestern part of the state but that was nothing compared to what they now loaded. They placed the gunpowder in the last car, keeping it as far as possible from sparks from the locomotive. Their preferred fuel, hard coal, was no longer available and the hardwood they now burned gave off more sparks. The station master wondered; *pray I've not put Mrs. Payne and her unborn child on a death train.* A stray ember, Yankee attack or derailing from any cause could blow the entire train and everyone on it to Kingdom come.

"All aboard!" but no one was left on the platform anyway. Mrs. Payne, the only civilian passenger, was traveling with soldiers and they were positioned to defend the train. Thick black smoke mixed with hissing white steam as the giant steel wheels slipped on smooth rails trying to gain traction. Before long they were rocking and swaying along. The railroad had ordered replacement rails long before the conflict broke out but they'd recently been informed that despite their long-standing order, Tredegar Iron works would not fill it. The Confederate War Department now set the production tables for their largest foundry where over twenty-five hundred workers were turning iron into canon and armor plating, not rails, three shifts a day, seven days a week. Even with Tredegar's tall brick chimneys belching clouds of coal smoke and soot 'round the clock,[96] it was doubtful rails would be produced any time soon.

Mrs. Payne was glad to finally be underway, thankful for the comfort of the small passenger compartment. In her privacy, she also realized for the first time, her vulnerability. She was alone, and feared she might remain so for the rest of her life should her husband succumb to his wounds. Drying tears, she resolved to not think on that grim outcome, focusing instead on reaching him as soon as possible and nursing him back to health. Also in the privacy of her compartment, she loosened her tightly bound corset, the whale bone inserts confining her torso so tightly her baby fairly leapt

---

96 Dabney, Virginius, 1976, Richmond, the story of a city. Doubleday, New York. pg. 177.

at the new found freedom. She also undid her shoe buttons, finding her ankles swollen having been on her feet so long. If anyone happened to see her immodesty, she cared little for their opinion for she had but one objective –care for her wounded husband. Realizing that to accomplish her objective she needed to conserve her strength and that of her unborn child, she tried to rest. Exhausting herself short of her goal was pointless. Propping her feet on her carpet bag, the swaying soon rocked her to sleep and she dreamt some day, the good Lord willing, she'd rock her child on the their front porch, her husband close by.

Rattling on for hours, the train stopped only to take on water and cordwood. Although the water to resupply was quickly transferred by gravity from rail-side tanks, loading firewood was another matter. Whereas coal had also been quickly dumped from a hopper, several cords of split hardwood had to be hand stacked in the hopper. The process of loading, not to mention cutting and splitting a mountain of fire wood was labor intensive in the extreme, the hard work falling to younger lads who did the best they could. Their stronger older brothers, fathers, and uncles were all off serving in the army. While the boys hustled, Mrs. Payne, though anxious to get to her husband, welcomed the chance to dismount, taking a temporary break from constant jerking, pitching and swaying which made her nauseous. The chance to stretch her legs on solid ground revived her just in time to re-board.

Afternoon stretched into evening, as fields, farms, and woods passed by on the long ride northeasterly. Finally she felt the lurch and jerk as the train switched onto a different track entering Richmond's Main Street station then screeched to a halt. A soldier threw open the door to her small compartment, announcing, "Excuse me Mam, and good evening. We're to Richmond now. Sorry this took so long. You must be tired out; can I help you with your bag?"

"Why yes, thank you. Do you know when the train for Williamsburg departs?"

"Sorry Mam, you'll have to speak to the station master about that. I don't know the schedule and everything is subject to change. These days, a train is made up and departs as equipment and supplies are available. I can tell you though; there's no service to Williamsburg. Yankees is too close to risk capture of a valuable train. Why we don't have near enough locomotives now and they trying to steal or destroy 'em anyways they can. Reports are their cavalry's conducting raids up and down the line tearin' up track, burning bridges and such. We may hold surroundin' lands but it's too risky runnin' trains through on a regular schedule," the soldier explained, moving on to the next car.

"Good Sir, Pray do tell, how am I to get to Williamsburg? My husband lies wounded, gravely I hear, and I must get to him soon as possible," she asked the Richmond station master.

"Beggin' your pardon Mam but it's not safe to be travelin' these parts. Spies are about and most certainly no one in a family way should be going anywhere."

"Well Sir, I heard that before and I'll not be put off! I've come this far without incident and must get to him."

Seeing her determination and certain he didn't want her giving birth at his station, the master relented. "Mam, perhaps you can find a wagon headin' east," but quickly adding, "Most wagons headin' west though, and no tellin' what they'd charge these days. There's every kind of 'highwaymen' out there these days."

Before he'd finished, Mrs. Payne left the station building. He may have meant well but she didn't appreciate his comments. A soldier standing nearby noting her condition carried her carpetbag. *Where the hell she off to,* he wondered?

Mrs. Payne again inquired after an east-bound train, hoping the answer she received earlier might somehow have changed in the interim.

"Can't hardly say Mam. There's nothing scheduled. No east-bound trains for the foreseeable future. Right many citizens are headin' west, away from there at this time."

"What about a wagon or coach? I can pay cash," and with that Mrs. Payne froze. She knew only too well what could happen to anyone, especially a woman traveling alone, spotted carrying cash. She glanced around nervously trying to see who may have overheard her inadvertent remark. She was relieved to see the station empty except for a boy and his dog.

"Mam, when the Army rushed to Magruder on the Peninsula, they commandeered, or I should say, 'borrowed' every wagon, buggy, cart, just about anything with wheels for miles around. The only movement now is coming in this direction, headin' west. Those that ain't wounded are either helpin' them that are, or double-timin' it to get into position to defend Richmond. I'll be dad burned if they know, is they runnin' from the last fight, or to the next one? Roads is chaotic I hear."

This news was indeed disheartening, Mrs. Payne now wondering, *Should I wait here to see if he's transferred to Chimborazo? Waiting means my not doing anything.* She did not abide idleness, not in her slaves, hired hands, and certainly not in herself. *No, I'll keep trying to get to him*, steeling her resolve.

Seeing her eyes well up, the station master interrupted her, "Mam there is a train headin' north to Manassas Junction, big logistics depot, little over an hour. You want on board? It's the only train leaving out of here tonight."

Wiping her cheeks, Mrs. Payne tried to figure what to do. *There's no place to stay here, 'cept the station itself.* "Sir, how does going to Manassas get me to my husband?"

"Yes, I'll grant it's odd, and the long way 'round, north to Manassas Junction by train, then to Alexandria waterfront. Steamers tie up there, travel the Potomac, then Bay down to Fort Monroe," the station master explained.

"That sure is long and I'd have to go into Yankee territory! How am I supposed to do that?" *but what choice do I have?* Looking him in the eye, "Yes, I'll do it!"

"Now Mam, I want you to understand what you're getting' into -makes riding this rickety train seem like a Sunday outing. Getting to Manassas should be no problem, 'cept it's a long ride, but going to Alexandria means crossing enemy lines, as you mentioned. They'll think you're a spy. Then you still got an overnight trip south by water, then a wagon ride over forty miles to Williamsburg and the road is bad. In all, its several more days travel. I'm not trying to worry you truly but there just ain't a good solution to your predicament.

Mrs. Payne considered what he said. *I've committed to going, no point giving up now. Besides it'd be just as hard gettin' back to Danville as continuing.*

"Yes Sir, might as well go to Manassas. No point sittin' here."

"Of course, Mam, as you wish. I'll help you on board when its time. In the meantime, Mam there's an outhouse behind the station, and if you like, I'll draw some water so you can freshen up. Sorry, we ain't got nothin' else here at the station."

"Yes, thank you, that'd be fine," wondering just how dreadful she must look after a long day on the train with dust and smoke settling on everything.

The train took longer than expected as wagon after wagon rolled up to be loaded. From beans to bullets, everything available was shipped. It

Civil War Comes Home

was not necessarily what troops needed, but it was shipped. While hired men and slaves hurried back and forth, straining to move everything as quickly as possible, Mrs. Payne dosed.

She awakened with a start fearful she'd miss the train but needn't have worried. The engineer eventually gave a long blast on the whistle, which at this close proximity seemed loud enough to wake the dead. She was pleased to again get underway as the giant wheels, almost her height, slowly turned, cars jerking into motion. This time there were no passenger seats so she made herself comfortable as possible on sacks of oats. *Wonder if these will go to the 4th* she pondered, recalling her husband's comments about the difficulty of keeping their horses well fed. She convinced the men loading the heavy sacks to leave the boxcar door part way open so she might have some air and a chance to look out.

Hour after hour she stared at passing country side, alternately verdant woods bright with new growth, and lush fields with cattle and occasionally sheep. Conspicuously absent were men working the farms. At one point she spotted a woman struggling behind the plow, her young son who couldn't have been more than five or six years old trying to help. *Looks familiar,* she thought, *No doubt her husband is off to war too. I wonder how he's doing,* thinking of her own husband. *God, help them to heal and come home safe,* she prayed.

Having already traveled many hours, the small satchel of food was empty long ago. She was hungry and thirsty and knew she needed to eat for the baby's sake, but there was nothing she could do about it now. As the train rattled on, she dozed, awakening when it lurched, eventually feeling it slow. *I hope we're to Manassas,* not sure if it was real or wishful thinking until she heard the shrill blasts as the engineer warned of their approach. Screeching to a stop, each car jerked, signaling they'd finally reached their destination. As the boxcar floor was several feet above ground level, she signaled for assistance getting down and the station master brought a baggage cart.

"Hello Mam, why I didn't know there's any passengers aboard," he remarked puzzled. "You got any luggage?"

"Just this" handing over her satchel.

"Mam, had Yankees attacked, you could have killed or captured, God-forbid. Their cavalry patrols been seen along the line trying to do damage."

"Well, thank goodness they must have gone elsewhere today."

"Madam, allow me to help you down. These cars going to be offloaded. I'm quite certain you don't fancy meetin' those ruffians."

"Yes, thank you. I'm on my way to visit my wounded husband."

"Of course Mam, so very sorry to hear that, and pray he makes good recovery. No doubt he will when he sees you. Mam, how you gettin' to Williamsburg? If you don't mind my asking?"

"Not at all, truth is I don't rightly know. In Richmond I was told to take a steamer from Alexandria down to Fort Monroe then come back up the Peninsula by land. Is that correct?"

"Yes Mam, I'm afraid that is the only way to get there anymore."

"Indeed, that is a roundabout way, but with the good Lord guidin' and protectin' I'll make it. Now if you'd be so kind, where can I engage transportation to the port?"

"Yes Mam, of course, out in front of the station is all manner of coaches and wagons. Far as I know there is no regular schedule, each passenger engages their own."

"Very well then, I'll bid good day and thank you for your assistance."

"Glad to help Mam."

"Good day Sir," turning to go, the heavy carpet bag weighing her down. Eyeing her, he thought again about the chaos waiting outside. It was every man for himself; passengers jostling each other for rides, wagon masters trying to cut off competition. Quickly realizing, *this was no place for a woman, especially one in her condition. Besides, every one of them scam artists and scallywags would charge her double and no doubt demand a generous tip besides,* he knew. Realizing he'd never forgive himself if anything happened, he ran after her, "Mam, Mam, wait a minute."

"Yes, what is it?"

"Mam, I just remembered. There's a young man works 'round here most days, couldn't be much more than fourteen years of age. The others, a little older, done gone off to join up. Some lie about their age and make it, but if they're caught, end up as drummer boys. Only this lad has a bad leg, foot actually, horse stepped on it when he was young, never grew right and Army won't take him 'cause he's lame. Say he couldn't keep up. Anyway, Mam, the thing is, bad foot or not, you'll not find a harder worker anywhere. Why I seen him do a man's days work many times, and without cursing, drinking, smoking, or trying to sneak off somewheres when there's work to be done. Anyways, he's got his own wagon and he'd take you right to the pier no doubt, and wouldn't be trying to cheat you like some of these lowly scum. If you want, I'll get a message to him, see if he can meet you tomorrow, and you two can strike a bargain."

"Why thank you again Sir. Yes, please contact him. I'd like to meet this young man. Now, in that case Sir, can you direct me to a reputable boarding house? I am so exhausted I couldn't possibly go any further tonight."

"Yes Mam, there's a couple of rooming houses not far. Most is fine but the best is Mrs. Smith's. Now whether she has room tonight, can't say, but if you like I'll send a runner over to make inquiry and let her know you'll be along shortly.

Collaring one of the boys always hanging around the station, the master instructed, "Go directly to Mrs. Smith's. Ask if she's got a room for tonight. Then come right back and let me know, and be quick about it."

"Yes Sir." He was off, glad to have something to accomplish.

Returning to Mrs. Payne, the station master invited her to take a seat in the station house, "It shouldn't be long Mam. Now if you'll please excuse me I have other business."

"Of course, I'll be fine here," propping her feet on her bag, closing her eyes, worn out from the long day. Shortly, the lad was back from Mrs. Smith's.

"Sir, there's a room at Mrs. Smith's like you said."

"Good work, now let's go tell Mrs. Payne, and you carry her bag for her."

"Yes Sir."

"Mrs. Payne, you have a room tonight at Mrs. Smith's. Johnny will show you the way."

"What?" Awakening with a start, realizing where she was, she attempted to stand, but a bit too quickly and felt faint. "Here Mam let me help you," the station master offered, steadying her while Johnny moved the satchel from underfoot, then guided her down the street.

"Thank you, again," she called back but the master was already overseeing unloading. She was too tired to ask again about the ride to the pier, thankful the boy knew the way to Mrs. Smith's and was carrying her bag. Delivering her to Mrs. Smith's Johnny returned to the station.

"Thank you Sir," he said to the master, "that nice lady gave me half-dime for helping her."

"Lucky you, now I got another errand for you, and don't expect to be paid for every little thing. Do you know James, the lad with the wagon who hires out to do odd jobs? You know, with the bad foot?"

"Yes Sir, I know who he is."

"Well go tell him to come to the station first thing in the morning. Mrs. Payne be needin' a ride to the waterfront and I reckon James be a good one to take her."

"Yes Sir."

"Wait," the station master called, "have James go to Mrs. Smith's. Tell him he's to meet a Mrs. Payne. No sense him coming here, the place will be jammed."

"Yes Sir."

Early next morning James sat atop his wagon in front of Mrs. Smith's. He'd even cleaned it as he understood he was to transport a lady. *Would do no good to show up for a paying fare in a dirty rig,* he figured. Climbing down, he brushed himself off before entering. *Wonder what she looks like, this Mrs. Payne?* Having never been inside the boarding house, James was immediately struck by the fine furnishings, noting particularly the flower pattern wall paper. Having never seen such luxury, James wondered, *what all this cost, must be expensive.* Indeed, imported from London, the wall paper, especially bold floral was in vogue. But James was more impressed by the delicious breakfast aromas; coffee, bacon, ham, hotcakes, and such. Though he'd eaten hours ago, his stomach growled as he recalled his pre-dawn cold biscuit and weak, bitter chicory.

"Wait here," the hostess instructed.

Before he could reply, he overheard, "Begging your pardon did you spent a comfortable night, Mrs. Payne?"

"Oh yes, quite comfortable, I feel good, ready to resume my journey after breakfast of course."

"Of course, Mam, Glad you slept well. Breakfast is served in the main dining room, and Mam, there's a young lad asking after you."

"Really, I'm not expecting anyone. I surely don't even know anyone here." Then she recalled the station master's comment last evening about a lad who would provide transportation. "Oh yes, I remember now. I'll see him."

"Yes Mam, of course," the hostess replied guiding her to the foyer where James waited.

"Hello, I'm Mrs. Payne."

"Pleased to meet you Mam, I'm James Hudson; the station master sent me."

"Well, yes, I need to get to Williamsburg, to my wounded husband actually, but why don't we discuss this over breakfast?"

"Yes Mam," James replied, quickly adding, "but I can't afford this place, Mam."

"Don't worry about that. You're my guest and looks you could stand to but some meat on your bones." Mrs. Payne remarked, kidding but truthful.

"Why thank you Mam, does smell delicious," as the hostess seated them.

Both Mrs. Payne and James ate well, she famished, having eaten comparatively little the day before, and he likewise as a hard working teen. While enjoying Smithfield ham, buttery grits, and plenty of fresh eggs; their plans were made. James would transport her to Alexandria's waterfront where she'd catch a steamer south. She was reassured, James appeared as the station master had represented, honest and trustworthy.

Checking out of her room, she met James waiting at his wagon, pausing momentarily for she could not recall having ever seen an older looking horse, except perhaps the emaciated steed the messenger had ridden to her farm in Danville. Young James, gangly and growing into manhood, *makes an almost comical contrast*, she thought smiling. James loaded her carpet bag, helping her up the tall step into the seat. Heading east, James assured he knew the way and after several hours negotiating roads busy with traffic they approached a military checkpoint, Confederate guards signaling to stop.

"State your business," one gruffly demanded, the other eyeing them suspiciously.

Having experienced this before, he spoke up, "James Hudson out of Manassas Junction under the employ of Mrs. Payne here, wife of Major Payne, 4th Virginia Cavalry."

At this information the guard tipped his hat, "Hello Mam, how may we assist you?"

Explaining her situation, the guard replied. "Once you pass this point Mam you're leaving the Confederacy. Yes, Alexandria was always in the Old Dominion, but now Federals occupy the town and it's not part of Virginia anymore. You'll be passing to the enemy side. Once across, you're on your own. Anything happens we can't do nothin' even if you need help, Mam. So please take all the time you need, but be sure about your decision to leave the South," the guard cautioned.

"Thank you Private, but I've traveled all the way from Danville, and must get to my husband. But why can't I return?"

"Well Mam, orders came down, no returns after visiting the other side. Too much spying."

"What about James here?"

"Same Mam, if he crosses over, he don't come back."

Turning to James, she said goodbye, thanking him for providing safe transit from Manassas this far. I was the better part of the day and they'd enjoyed lively conversation the entire distance.

"Thank you so much James. I really appreciate your help. You're a fine young man and I wish you all the best."

"Thank you Mam, I hope Major Payne is all right and you find him soon. Glad I could be of some help."

As she went to pay him, James backed away, "No Mam, that's okay you don't owe me nothing. It's the least I can do, your husband being wounded and all and you expectin' the baby."

"Now James, I'll not hear such nonsense. We agreed on my fare and you spent all day and now you've got to go all the way back. Why it'll be midnight before you get back to Manassas. I insist," and stuffed the money in his shirt pocket. "You earned it, your horse has got to eat, and so do you. I'll be fine. All I got to do is find the next ship leaving for Fort Monroe. Thank you so much. God bless you."

James remounted his wagon waving goodbye, calling out, "Be careful Mam. I'd come with you if I could, only I got this horse and wagon now, trying to make a living."

"I'll be fine. You ever need a job, come to Danville and look me up."

Turning to the sentries, "All right, I shall leave and not return, least ways not by this point."

"Very well Mam. Pass and God be with you."

"Thank you, and don't let no Yankee spies across," she joked.

A few hundred feet ahead, she saw another guard post, this one manned by Union troops.

"Halt. State your name and business."

"Mrs. Mary Payne from Danville, come to care for my wounded husband."

"Show us your papers."

"Well, I got no papers. I am who I always been, of course."

"Nothing? Mam we got to know you ain't a Rebel trouble maker or spy, otherwise we'll get put us on report if anyone crossed unidentified."

"Young man, do I look like a trouble maker?" pointing out her pregnancy. "Wait, look here," Mrs. Payne offered, reaching for the locket she always wore. Opening it she held it out for the guard to see the miniature tintype of her husband. "Here's his picture -sent word he's wounded in the battle of Williamsburg and I'm trying to hasten to his bedside. Now, may I pass?"

"I see your husband's picture but how do we know you're Mrs. Payne?" "Private, like I said, do I look like a trouble-maker?" Trying to think of how to resolve the situation, she remembered her family bible. She never went anywhere without it. "Just a minute, I'll show you," extracting the thick, worn leather volume from the bottom of her carpet bag, she opened the front cover. There recorded, generation after generation, was her and all her family's names.

"Thank you Mam," the guard finally acquiescing, "I'm sorry to have given you a hard time Mam but we're under orders and I sure as heck don't want to go to jail for lettin' a spy across."

"I understand, now can you direct me to the waterfront? I got to find a steamer to Fort Monroe."

"Just continue down this lane for another couple hundred yards or so, and see where the path divides? Take the right fork and that will eventually take you down the hill to the pier. Just keep followin' to the end. It's quite a ways though."

"Very well good day." Ready to continue her journey, she wondered, *how far is 'quite a ways?' Wish James was still here with his wagon.*

"Um, Mam, wait a minute. Let me send one of the guards with you to carry your bag. Looks mighty heavy and it's still quite a long walk to the piers," the private offered, thinking *this poor lady has enough to deal with being in a family way, her husband wounded, and traveling one end of the state to the other.*

"Why that would be most kind," as she thought, *I was sure I'd never accept anything from a Yankee.* "I surely don't want to go the wrong way and end up walking further than necessary and yes this bag does get heavy after a while."

Calling a compatriot from the guard house, the private instructed him regarding his escort duty and the pair was off. The guard standing watch felt he'd done his duty helping a woman in need, and his companion, escorting her didn't mind either for he was always looking for an excuse to get to town. Duties were boring and he was already imaging where he'd stop for a drink or two. As they walked and walked, the afternoon wore on for it was farther than she'd imagined. Though she was again growing weary and hungry, she dared not suggest stopping, though the soldier would have gladly obliged. She didn't like the company of this stranger and wanted to get where she was going. Finally they reached the waterfront, which was even busier than the roads she'd spent the better part of a long day traversing.

"Well Mam, here you are, safe and sound. Looks like there's several steamers in port so you ought to be able to book passage without delay," and with that he was off to the nearest of several bars they'd passed.

After learning the first two ships were headed to Baltimore and Aquia Harbor, respectively, she wondered if passage to Fort Monroe was harder than she'd assumed. Approaching the next ship, she hailed a crewmember aboard the *Logan*, "I say, are you going to Fort Monroe, Virginia?"

"Good afternoon Mam," tipping his cap, surprised to see a woman alone on the wharf, "Yes Mam, we go to Fort Monroe more or less continuous. Government contract now, haulin' supplies and soldiers south, mail and such, north. Keepin' us right busy lately. They's been building up Fort Monroe fast as they can. You lookin' to go, Mam?"

"Yes Sir, I am." She decided to omit the part about her wounded husband. "When do you sail?"

"Mam, we cast off next high tide, a few more hours yet. But, Mam, there's a problem, we are under contract to the Army and no longer a regular passenger ferry. We only take soldiers and people the Army has authorized. You got government paperwork."

"What? I never heard of such a thing. Government papers? Where do I get these government papers?" Then quickly adding, "I guess maybe you don't understand, I've been traveling for days, from Danville by train to Richmond, then to Manassas, and then by wagon to Alexandria where I left the Commonwealth never to return they told me, crossed into the Union, tryin' to get to Fort Monroe. When I finally get there, I'm to travel some forty more miles to see my poor dear husband lying wounded in Williamsburg." By now, Mrs. Payne was in tears, her body trembling. Between fear, exhaustion, hunger and dehydration, she'd reached her limit.

Seeing her distress, the sailor offered, "Please Mam, come sit down. Get out of the sun and take a load off. Can I get you some water?"

Mrs. Payne boarded as offered, careful to hold the ropes of the gangway with both hands for she was lightheaded. "Yes, some water if you don't mind."

"Yes Mam, right away. You just sit yourself down here in the shade, rest a spell. I'll be right back with water."

"Thank you, I don't think I could take another step."

Once she'd quenched her thirst, which took more than one cup, she explained her situation, the sailor listening attentively. He was sympathetic, allowing how he had a wife and they hoped to have a baby some day. But this war came, and didn't she think the war would be over soon?

"Mam, I must advise the ship's bursar of your situation. I'm just a deck hand I shouldn't even be talking to you. He or the Captain decides what to do."

"Yes, very well, I'll speak with whoever I need to in order to book passage. My husband could be dying and I don't intend to be in Alexandria nor any other Yankee territory any longer than necessary."

While she tried to relax, the sailor found the bursar, explaining the predicament. The bursar had experienced this before, travelers desperate to get somewhere and usually in a hurry. He'd found, almost invariably, people in such predicaments were willing to pay, and often quite well for passage. Given such opportunities, he'd wasted no time figuring out how to supplement his income at the expense of the displaced and desperate. *All's fair in love and war*, he rationalized.

"Afternoon Mam, I understand you want to travel to Fort Monroe?" the bursar announced, approaching the drowsy Mrs. Payne.

"Yes Sir, that is correct. Where do I buy my ticket?"

"Well Mam since the war, we transport war supplies and there are no regular passenger tickets. However, if you are ready to go when we sail I expect we could come to a special 'arrangement' if you are interested."

"What kind of 'arrangement' did you have in mind, Sir?" already suspicious.

"Mam, the fare to Fort Monroe is one hundred dollars, payable to me in cash before we cast off."

"What, that's piracy! How can you charge that much? Why I saw the sign on the dock said passage was two dollars!"

"Yes, Mam, that two dollars WAS the fare for Washington to Potomac Creek, a shorter distance, and I understand you want to go to Fort Monroe, that's much further, and besides, two dollars was before the war. Since war, cost of everything's gone up. Why coal for our boilers has doubled in the last month."

"Well still, the fare should not jump from a few dollars to a hundred," she protested.

"Mam that is what it costs today." He hadn't explained these exorbitant fares for special passengers went into his own pocket, not the company account.

"Well it's shameful. What you're charging it's a fortune. The only reason I've got to get to Fort Monroe is to see my wounded husband," she explained hoping against reason for some compassion.

"I am sorry Mam, what's your husband's unit?"

"4th Virginia Cavalry," she blurted, immediately wishing she could retract it.

"You mean to tell me he's a Rebel?" the bursar demanded. "Hell, I should charge two hundred dollars. This is a Union ship Mam, haulin' war supplies to fight the secessionists, and you expect to ride to see the enemy? Get off my ship, now!" the irate bursar demanded.

"Sir, as you can well see I am in a family way, my husband is gravely wounded, may not survive, and I pray he's not already dead. Dear God, Sir, show some mercy."

"Mercy? You're the ones that enslave people, whip 'em, separate husband from wife, mother from child; don't talk to me about compassion! Besides, you all started this war firing on Ft. Sumter for no reason."

"Sir, I don't want to argue politics. I just need to see my husband while he still lives."

The sailor who'd invited her aboard overheard their heated exchange. He didn't have much use for the bursar and thought even less of his illegal profiteering. *I got to help that poor woman, but how?*

Angry as the bursar was, he was more greedy than principled. *I could kick her off, but then there goes my one hundred dollars.*

"All right, against my will you may travel, but I don't want no more trouble. Now give me the money. I should charge double, like I said, but since I already quoted one hundred dollars that will do."

"Just a minute." Taking out her family Bible, she carefully opened the inside back cover where an envelope had been glued, extracting and counting out Confederate bills, handing them over. She regretted passage was costing far more than anticipated and she'd soon be bankrupt. "And how much is breakfast, Sir?" she asked sarcastically, suspicious it too would be exorbitant.

"What? Don't give me that funny money. It must be U.S. dollars, or gold," the bursar demanded. "Breakfast is fifty cents," he added, "just pay in the kitchen."

"Well, Sir, I do not have gold. This is all I have, go ahead search my bag if you must but in Danville, Virginia I have no access to U.S. dollars and certainly not gold."

"Rats" the bursar exclaimed, realizing his quick profit was now complicated by foreign currency exchange. His previous victims had been Unionists, traveling in the opposite direction. "Okay, I should not accept your worthless money but give it to me."

Handing over what was almost the last of her hard earned cash, she hoped this would prove the last hurdle in an arduous journey.

Adjusting the mooring lines, the helpful sailor continued observing their interaction and seeing the exchange of cash, he knew what was happening. He'd seen it before. *Looks like she be travelin' after all. Maybe I can still help her somehow.*

The transaction concluded, the bursar returned to his office, while Mrs. Payne found herself a place to sit among the supplies covering nearly every square foot of deck.

"Mam, if there's anything I can help with just let me know," the sailor offered.

Before she could answer, "Prepare to cast off," was heard and the smokestacks belched thicker smoke as they made up steam to get underway. The pilot came aboard and lines were slipped. They'd travel a good portion of their route at night with lanterns extinguished. The ship channel ran close to the Potomac's shore in many areas and Southern sympathizers kept a close watch on river traffic. When Rebel observes did spot a vessel they'd signal by lantern down river, giving compatriots time to prepare an attack. While risk of successful attack from shore on a ship traveling with the tide at full steam was low, caution remained the watchword. This was another reason they no longer sailed according to published time tables. Why announce to the enemy ahead of time when a target would appear?

Besides the Rebel threat ashore, other risks to shipping included sand bars and log snags. Eroding from the river's high clay banks was a seeming endless supply of logs and debris and it'd only take one to punch a fatal hole in the hull or destroy paddlewheel or rudder, leaving a crippled ship at the mercy of swirling currents. Thus, the pilot took care reading the river while available crew kept a sharp look out for both Rebels and floating debris.

Fortunately, the *Logan* encountered no bars, flotsam, or attacks, making an uneventful transit into open waters of the Chesapeake. On a steady southerly course through the night, a brisk stern breeze sped her passage. While pilot and captain had been busily avoiding navigation hazards, the deck hand sympathetic to Mrs. Payne managed to pilfer an extra ham biscuit from the galley and brought her more water.

"Here you are Mam. I expect you're hungry. Wish there was more but this is all I could get," the sailor apologized.

"Aren't you kind, Sir. Thank you."

"Mam, we don't got bunks but I can rearrange some of these here satchels and make you a bit more comfortable and bring a blanket against the chill out here at night. Breeze comes off of the Bay right good at times and water's cold this time of year."

"Why yes thank you. I was quite warm, hot actually this afternoon, walking through town to the piers, and now it's cooled off quite a bit."

"We should make Fort Monroe, just after dawn. That is if we don't run into no storms and this wind holds. Now, Mam, I'll be out and about doing my chores throughout the night, you need anything, you just let me know." Traveling alone and prudently wary, she was suspicious of the man's kindness, but she needn't have troubled herself. He was as he appeared a good-hearted fellow, who missed his own wife and home, and was just trying to show Christian charity to a woman in need.

"Thank you Sir. I'll do fine, long as that bursar fella don't return demanding a docking fee or something," she joked.

"Yeah, he's something ain't he?"

Winds remained favorable through the night, seas runnin' strong, and as the first rays of pre-dawn pink broke the watery horizon, the *Logan* was sighted by the Fort Monroe lookout.

"Ship ahoy. North by northwest" came his call and a runner was sent to ensure Engineer wharf was ready. There really wasn't much to do 'til she rounded the jetty turning west into Hampton Roads and when she did, the deck hands both afloat and ashore were ready to exchange lines. She was soon fast to pilings, gangway extended. Despite the excitement, Mrs. Payne slept. The arduous travel had proven exhausting. With the shrill of the steam whistle on docking, she woke with a start, pleasantly surprised they'd finally arrived. *Thank God*, she thought, glad to have finally made it this far and anxious to disembark on dry land for the waves made her nauseous. Gathering her carpet bag she lined up to disembark, already wondering about getting to Williamsburg.

The guard at the head of the wharf was surprised to see a woman. These days, passengers were all in uniform. Occasionally there'd be reporter or politician but mostly it was soldiers, and a woman had not arrived in quite a while.

Civil War Comes Home

"Good morning Mam, welcome to Fort Monroe," the Sergeant offered, curious to hear her story.

"Thank you, Sergeant; I'm Mrs. Payne, wife of Major Payne here to see him. He was wounded at Williamsburg."

"Mam, I don't know about any wounded Major. Is he supposed to be here at Fort Monroe? We don't have many wounded left anymore. Most been transferred to hospitals near home, leavin' on steamers like the one you come in on. Most is gone, least ways the ones' healed enough to travel."

"No, Sergeant not Fort Monroe, he was in Williamsburg, in a private home."

"Oh Williamsburg, I hear there's quite a lotta boys still there."

"And how far is it? to Williamsburg, I mean."

"Mam, every bit of forty miles or better, quite a ways and the road is still terrible. Things should be gettin' better though, been working clearing busted wagons and such, after the dead is buried of course. Oh, Sorry Mam," the sergeant apologized for invoking such grim images.

"How do I get there?"

"Well Mam, the road is a mess, torn up by troops, horses, wagons after heavy rain, but I expect you can hire a horse," then noting her condition quickly added, "or wagon."

"How much do they charge?" Knowing, *I've already given nearly my entire savings to that greedy bursar.*

"I don't really know what theys charging now Mam," the sergeant replied honestly. "After the battle, with the shortage of horses and wagons, I heard prices gone way up. Some say, it's the cost of doin' business, but some just trying to get rich at other folks expense."

"Oh I know all about that! Thank you anyways but I guess I'll just have to walk. I've nothing left after the cost of that steamer," she lamented.

"Mam?" the solider asked. "*Logan's* no longer taking paying customers. What do you mean?"

Explaining her ordeal at the hands of the bursar, she was puzzled at the Sergeant's sudden interest.

"You don't say," the sergeant replied. "Mam, we been watching that fellow. Seems when he's aboard, shipments been coming up short. We inventory everything and cross check what arrives against what the government was billed. We can't rightly say yet what's going on, but for sure government's paying for more than what's being delivered. Now whether the missing supplies was ever aboard, don't rightly know, but we're watching him. Maybe the inventory was shorted when it left the factory. Now Mam, don't you be saying anything to anyone 'bout this just now," the soldier instructed, fearful he'd already divulged too much about an ongoing investigation. "No tellin' who can be trusted these days."

Given her quandary of needing to get to Williamsburg, Mrs. Payne thought about her situation. The only way she'd ever reach her husband was to be completely forthright.

"Sergeant, My husband is Major Payne of the 4th Virginia Cavalry."

"Oh I see. I guess I should have figured as much. I mean if he was Union, we'd be sending him home to you instead of your coming here," he observed matter of fact. "Mam, I'm going to have to ask you to come with me to headquarters. They's the ones approve movements. Folks can't just go wanderin' about these days."

"Very well, Sergeant, and I can ask them about a ride," Mrs. Payne mentioned.

"Right Mam, now they're going to check your possessions right careful for there's no end of spying going on, and we can't have no information being passed, or picked up."

"Well they can check all they want, I got nothing to hide."

"Yes, Mam and they will check; cipher notes, medicines, cash and who knows what all been passed across lines. Hidin' places you'd never imagine. Why they confiscated a child's doll, had the head hollered out for hidin' medicine. Women sew notes inside skirt hems or jacket liners or even woven into the curls of their hair. You not trying any funny business are you Mam?"

"Sergeant you misjudge me. I'm no spy, just tryin' to get to my husband. Besides I ain't crossing back into Confederate lines, he's in Williamsburg, which y'all now occupy."

"Yes Mam that is correct, Army occupied the city while Rebs high-tailed it all the way back to Richmond. Williamsburg is the closest occupied territory to your Capitol and as such, it's fast become a viper's nest of spies and troublemakers. Just beyond the college it's a kinda no man's land of lies and deceit."

"Well, I found that right here aboard the steamer! The only thing that is of any concern to me whatsoever in Williamsburg is my poor husband."

"I know you ain't a spy but I was just warnin' you on what to expect," and they headed from Engineer wharf to the headquarters building.

"Colonel Dimick, Sir, this is Mrs. Payne. Her Confederate Major husband was wounded and she got word he's in Williamsburg. Sir, if you will excuse me, there is one more thing, we need to speak with the bursar aboard *Logan*, seems he charged her exorbitantly for passage down here."

"What? By all means Sergeant, check out the bursar and let me know. Is this the same one involved with inventory shortages? I'll not have war profiteers operating out of Fort Monroe!"

"Yes Sir," the Sergeant replied.

"Excuse me, how do you do Mam," Lieutenant Colonel Dimick offered, motioning for Mrs. Payne to take a seat.

"Thank you Sir. May I inquire about getting to Williamsburg, Sir."

"Yes, of course, Mam. We'll talk about that momentarily, but first please tell me how you came to be here?"

Mrs. Payne explained about the messenger and her travels. Her hardships, one after another, were unlike anything he'd heard. By the time she'd recounted what she'd been through, Lieutenant Colonel Dimick was not only sympathetic but fully understood she was certainly no threat and he'd do what he could to assist.

"Mam, your journey has been fraught with hardship. Please allow me to make the remainder somewhat easier." And with that he called to one of his clerks,

"Send word to the stables, hitch up a carriage and send the driver over here as soon as possible. I have a requirement for transportation to Williamsburg."

A sudden knock on his office door, interrupted Mrs. Payne before she could thank him.

"Beggin' your pardon, Sir," the sergeant opened. "I have Mrs. Payne's one hundred Confederate dollars. The bursar has been charging passengers high fees for passage, makin' considerable profit on the side," the sergeant explained.

"Well at a hundred dollars a passenger I expect he's done quite well for himself, the little bastard," Lieutenant Colonel Dimick exclaimed, quickly adding, "Good work Sergeant. Throw him in the brig. The charge is war profiteering! He can explain to the military counsel how he came to have one hundred Confederate dollars on his person while on a Union army-contracted ship docked at Fort Monroe. That might get him on treason as well." Lieutenant Colonel Dimick smiled, relishing the thought of bringing the haughty, abusive bursar to justice, "and that should serve as an example for anyone else that tries to get rich off the hardships of soldiers, or their wives," Dimick added.

"Mam, I'll give you a receipt for your funds and I promise they will be returned to you. For now, we must hold these as evidence for the trial," Lieutenant Colonel Dimick explained. "Confederate money is no good here anymore anyway Mam."

"Well, it's all I have. And I beg to differ with you. It is not worthless. I'm trying to run our entire farm and household down in Danville on less than that, and on my own."

"Yes Mam, I imagine your farm is run proper and like I said, you'll get it all back after the trial. I guarantee it. Now shall we go see about your carriage?"

"That would be wonderful Sir. Getting to my husband is my only purpose."

Though Lieutenant Colonel Dimick was tempted to stay and wait with Mrs. Payne, he had several officers awaiting him upstairs. "Mam, if you will please excuse me, I have pressing matters. Here is my letter authorizing safe passage and I do wish you Godspeed. Should you encounter any trouble whatsoever do not hesitate to tell one of the soldiers to send word."

"Thank you Colonel, I can never repay your kindness but will certainly inform my husband, you are a gentleman."

"Thank you Mam, My regards to your husband, he is indeed lucky to have such a fine brave woman as his wife," and with that he bounded back up stairs. Returning to his office he thought, *if Confederate soldiers are half as determined as their wives, the war will prove long and costly indeed.*

Resting momentarily in the lobby, Mrs. Payne dosed off. She was both exhausted and relieved. Her journey was about to enter its final leg, *God, I pray he still lives.*

"Mam, the carriage is ready," the private announced, waking her.

"All right, thank you."

"Yes Mam, of course."

Carefully negotiating the steps on the front porch of post headquarters, Mrs. Payne was assisted into the carriage and they were just about to get underway when another private came dashing out of headquarters.

"Wait Mam, we searched the list of wounded and there's a Major Payne in the home of Mr. William Peachy, Esq. We don't have the address but he's a prominent lawyer. Ask after him and I expect anyone can direct you. Your husband was there as of a few days ago when this report was received."

"We'll go there directly. Thank you, young man!"

They were off, horse trotting, dirt flying from the tall wheels. *You know some of these Yankees ain't such bad fellas as most would have us believe,* she thought. It was a fine morning for a ride in the country, and both driver and steed were as glad as Mrs. Payne to be out in the bright sunshine. Tears of relief streamed down her cheeks, but her attention was soon drawn back to reality.

Immediately upon leaving Fort Monroe they passed through the contraband camps where women were doing their wash, tending cook fires, and caring for infants and little ones. She'd never seen slave women so happy, least not as long as she could recall. *There'll be no end to migration once word of these freedom camps reaches the slaves.*

Figure 44. Political satire captures sentiment of the time regarding the status of escaped runaway slaves and the Federal designation as their being 'contrabands of war.' Courtesy of the Library of Congress, Washington, D.C.

No sooner had they left Slabtown, they approached what was left of Hampton -a couple of bare brick walls of historic Saint John's church, a couple of chimneys and everywhere piles of rubble. "My God," was all she could manage.

"Yes Mam and the rebels burnt it themselves. We did not do that," the driver added almost apologetically.

"Goodness, why on earth would they destroy their own homes, businesses, even their church?"

"Mam can't rightly say. I heard they hated Yankees so much, they'd rather destroy what they spent years building than see us set foot in it. Mam, we ain't invaders. Fact is me and all the boys would much rather be home right now."

She stared in silence, passing complete and utter destruction, saddened by the loss. Presently they were again in a rural area where the evidence of the battle was of a different nature; wrecked supply wagons, some with dead horses still hitched, strewn along the road, the stench of death overpowering. Most of the human dead were no longer in evidence, at least not along roadsides. Contraband laborers were digging mass graves. The worst of their disgusting work was recovery of remains, the corpses either in rigor or disintegrating when dragged to burial pits. *No wonder my slaves fear the underworld,* she thought, turning away. Everywhere military gear was strewn about, some destroyed, some in pristine condition apparently never needed, at least not in the heat of battle. Some would be reclaimed by scavengers.

They rode miles seeing nothing but the beauty of flowering red buds and dogwoods; nature's funeral display edging the fields of death. The beauty was short-lived as they came upon what must have been the site of a skirmish --broken cannon and upset wagon still smolderin,' and bodies, bloated in death, lay everywhere, vultures picking at remains.

Unable to view pervasive death any longer, she cast eyes downward. *Awful, just hideous,* she thought reaching into her bag for the comfort of holding her Bible. She said a silent prayer of thanks her husband was not lying out there somewhere, and one of sorrow for the many who were. *Young lives cut short for what, such needless waste.*

Eventually they started seeing cabins and farmhouses again, but the driver had no time to look around, for roads remained in terrible condition. He tried to avoid the worst of the mud and ruts, and everywhere broken wagon parts and other debris littered their path. Finally nearing town they spotted two boys, bamboo poles over their shoulders. Spotting the driver's blue uniform, they took off running, afraid of any encounter with soldiers.

"Stop, Please wait, we mean no harm," Mrs. Payne called out. Hearing a woman's voice, they did as she asked, the cart pulling alongside.

"I say young man can you tell me where to find the home of Mr. William Peachy?"

"Yes, Mam, Peachy's got a fine house," the boy remarked, giving directions.

"Thank you young man and good luck fishin'"

"We hope so Mam, since the war, ain't nothin' to eat so Momma told us go catch dinner."

Presently, the driver pulled up to the Peachy home and helped Mrs. Payne down, her legs stiff from prolonged sitting. She hardly noticed, however, as she was so excited to have arrived, she proceeded directly up the front steps, not waiting for driver or her bag.

Rapping the brass door knocker, *finally* she thought, tears welling.

Til, the cook slowly opened the massive door, wondering who might be calling, for no visitors were expected anymore. Although slaves throughout town were told by Union troops they were free to go, and, no longer slaves, some left while others stayed. Til stayed on in the Peachy home. Having spent her entire life in service to Mrs. Peachy she knew nothing else. Besides, as a practical matter there was nowhere to go anyway. With shelter and food hard to come by now, *better to remain in the employ of a comfortable home with regular meals than face danger and hunger on the highways,* she reasoned.

"Yes Mam?" Til inquired.

"Hello, is this the Peachy residence? I'm Mrs. Payne."

"Oh just a minute Mam," turning to go find Mrs. Peachy.

"Mam, Mam you got company."

"Yes Til, who is it? I'm not expecting anyone." Normally, Til cooked and would not be interrupted by having to answer the door. Now, however, she did both jobs as the former house servant had gone off seeking her freedom. It was hard keeping house these days what with slaves leaving, turmoil, and shortages, not mention taking care of wounded.

"Mam, it's a young lady, a Mrs. Payne."

"Lordy show the poor thing in," she exclaimed, scurrying to the door.

"Mrs. Payne, do come in child, I'm Mary Peachy, welcome dear."

"Pleased to meet you Mam, thank you. A messenger brought word my husband Major Payne was wounded. Is he here?"

"Oh yes, child, he's upstairs. Been treating his wound best I could but 'fraid it's not healin' good as I'd like."

"May I see him?"

"Of course, dear right this way, and taking her hand, led her through the parlor up stairs. Though still stiff after spending the night on deck all the way from Alexandria, followed by a bumpy carriage ride from Fort Monroe, Mrs. Payne ascended the stairs as if neither exhausted nor expecting.

Opening the door, Mrs. Peachy motioned her to enter, where she saw the form of a sleeping man, turned towards the wall, fearfully thin with matted hair and beard. At first she didn't recognize him.

"Honey, it's me, your wife, Mary come to take care of you.

The sleeping form stirred, then rolled towards the sound, his eyes lighting up. "My God, is that you Mary? Am I dreamin'? How did you get here," bolting upright, wincing in pain having moved too fast.

Stepping to his bedside, they embraced as never before, with tears of joy. At the sight of their reunion Mrs. Peachy also cried, excusing herself, "I'll leave you two. I'll be right down stairs if you need anything."

After their long embrace came rapid conversation -she describing every step of her journey, then he, the battle or what he remembered of it, and how he'd woken up groggy in this fine home with seemingly non-stop care by Mrs. Peachy. Next, she recounted everything about their farm including the well-being of various slaves and animals. Their conversation lasted hours but the afternoon together was timeless.

A light tap on the door was Til serving hot tea and small cakes.

"Here you are Major, Mam, Mrs. Peachy thought you might take some refreshment. Supper won't be ready for quite some time yet -'til Marsa Peachy returns from his day's business." Enjoying the snack, the couple continued discussing events since their separation.

"Honey you need to rest, and while you do, I need to speak with Mrs. Peachy. Try to sleep and I'll be right downstairs."

"I don't know if I can rest knowing you're here. I can't hardly believe you made it all the way from Danville?" He was still in a state of disbelief. Taking the tray she bid him a good rest, and promised, as he insisted, she'd be there when he awoke.

"Mrs. Peachy, I cannot thank you enough. How can I ever repay you?"

"Oh hon, don't mention it. You would have done the same. Can I get you anything?"

"No thank you I am fine. He's napping. I'll just go up and sit with him. Even if he's asleep, I want to be with him."

"Go right ahead dear. I'm so glad you're here. He's been asking after you every day, could scarcely talk of anything else. He was so worried about you and the baby, he couldn't heal. My goodness it's so good to finally have you here."

"Thank you Mrs. Peachy. How can I ever repay you?"

"Now please, call me Mary and I don't want to hear another word about repaying. You and your husband have already paid a great price, fighting for Virginia. Taking care of him for a little while is the least we could do. My husband is not serving, claims he's too old, too important, too unwell or some ridiculous nonsense. I just don't know."

"Well thank you Mary. I look forward to meeting him. You can't know how much this means to me, to us. Now, can you recommend a boarding house?"

"Boarding house, whatever for my dear?"

"Well, now that I'm here, we can't continue to impose on you."

"Child, I know you must be tired, but what on earth are you thinking? I'll hear nothing of boarding houses. He can't be moved and you will stay right here with him, with us. Look at this huge house –plenty of room. Besides, with wounded all over town and all those Yankees moved in, there's no room to be had at any price. I'll put your bag in the spare bedroom across the hall. That way you can go to him any time, day or night. Frankly, I'll be glad for some relief. Don't get me wrong, I was more than happy to care for him it's just that no matter what I've tried, I see little improvement. No energy and his wound keeps draining. Now you're here maybe he'll improve."

"I am sure you did everything humanly possible Mary. I will be only too glad to take over his care. I'm sure by now you need a break and you got this big house to take care of."

"Yes and there's many others need help too. It's been such a horrible time I can't believe it. Besides so many of our boys and men killed and wounded, the Yanks settled in and take over everything. Can you imagine they have the nerve to try to tell us what we can and cannot do? Why I never thought I'd live to see the day when our town was occupied by enemy forces. God save us!"

"Yes, how and when will this nightmare end I don't know. All I do is pray to the Lord Almighty, my husband recovers and we can return home, outside Waynesboro."

"I thought you were from Danville?"

"Oh, I traveled from Danville, my family home. My husband set me up there near relatives before he left but our own place is near Waynesboro and I hope we return there someday."

"Your prayers will be answered dear. Now if you will please excuse me I need to check with Til about supper."

"Yes Mam and I'll just freshen up a bit, maybe rest. It's been a long trip."

"As you wish dear," Mrs. Payne concluded, following the delicious aromas wafting through the house from Til's preparations.

As Mrs. Payne settled in the Peachy home, a new routine was soon established Mary Payne took over primary responsibility for her husband's care, allowing Mrs. Peachy's return to running her household. Almost immediately Major Payne began showing signs of improvement. It was not that Mrs. Peachy had been failing to provide needed care, but his wife's loving touch seemed to have special healing powers. Mary Payne quickly learned from Mrs. Peachy how tasks like feeding were best accomplished, and when the doctor called the following day, she had a prepared list of questions. In a matter of weeks, he was gaining weight, surely a good sign. Between army life in the field and the wound, he'd grown quite gaunt. His recovery was also aided by her insistence he get out of bed and walk, even if only for short distance. Every day they went further, she at his elbow supporting as needed, allowing him to set his own pace. Eventually, he was well enough to manage stairs then the grounds at leisure. But regaining mobility also had its drawbacks for his recovery soon drew the attention of the Provost Marshall. Major Payne was, after all, still a prisoner.

A few days later came a loud rap on Peachy's door. Til answered as usual but quickly ran to fetch Mr. Peachy as it was two Union soldiers, Sergeant and private.

"Beggin' your pardon Sir," the Sergeant addressing Mr. Peachy, "but we're here for the Major. Understand he's healed up right good, your wife a nurse?"

"No, not a nurse, she just feeds 'em and cleans 'em best she can, tries to cheer 'em a bit when possible, given the circumstances."

"Indeed Sir, quite remarkable," the Sergeant noted, referring not only to Mrs. Payne, but the entire town which rallied to the care and feeding of wounded, regardless of the color of their uniform. "Anyways, Sir, we got orders. All Confederate wounded in town are prisoners of war and must be surrendered. He needs to be transferred to prison, and can no longer remain in a private residence."

"Damnation!" *I knew this day was coming, but now that it's upon us, what are we going to do?* Thinking quickly, he responded.

"Right Sergeant, only Major Payne is just barely out of his death bed and if he were to leave now we'd risk all. He can't go just yet, it's too soon." Peachy was uncertain he'd convinced anyone to delay the Major's incarceration.

"Well Sir, I don't know. My orders are to pick him up and return him to the temporary prison, awaiting transport north."

"You'll have to come back later Sergeant. He isn't ready to go anywhere just now. His dressings got to be changed," Mr. Peachy countered, adding, "my wife's gone, trying to find more medicine for him and there's hardly any to be had. We need time to make him ready."

"Very well Sir, I shall return in two hours sharp and take possession of the prisoner." While the Sergeant had his orders, he also knew it'd do no good to try to move a prisoner requiring medical attention enroute. They were hard pressed for medical care for their own troops.

"Very well Sergeant, I'll see he's ready," Peachy promised, thankful for even the few hours reprieve.

"And there better not be any tricks, like him gone missin' when I return."

Closing the door on the soldiers he went to find his wife. "Mary, Mary, quick. They've come to take him to prison."

Overhearing Mr. Peachy's comments and the concern in his voice, Mrs. Payne froze, *Oh no, I only just got here and they want to cart him off to prison! What can we do?* Mary Payne ran into her husband's room, throwing her arms around him giving a tight hug she wouldn't release. "I'll not let them take you dear. Quick let's escape!"

"What?" Major Payne asked, awakened suddenly.

By now Mr. Peachy had come up stairs with his wife, "It seems I am the bearer of bad news. The Yankees were here just now asking after the Major, saying he is ordered to prison. I argued against it, of course, but they're returning in two hours. I am so sorry. I couldn't think of anything else."

"Sir, it's not your fault. I knew this would come," Major Payne explained. "In fact, I'm lucky this lasted long as it did."

"No don't say that," his wife protested, "we can still escape," frantic at the thought of having him torn from her.

"Escape?" her husband replied, "to where? There is no where we can go, the Union forces have occupied the town and besides I'll not have them hunting you down like a common criminal. I was captured on the field of battle and am their prisoner. Mary, I must go when they return. There's no choice."

"No!" Mary Payne screamed collapsing on his bed. They'd not spoken of this day. Though he knew it inevitable, she'd not fathomed it, naively assuming when he was healed they'd simply return home and resume their former life. Her psyche was now wounded as deeply as his body.

Major Payne climbed out of bed even as his wife lay half across inconsolable.

"Mam, you got any dressings to spare?" he asked Mrs. Peachy. "I've watched you clean the wound and dress it enough times I can do it myself."

"Yes, Major, I'll make up a satchel and some food too. Speaking of food, how about we all go downstairs and Til will serve us a nice supper." *I hesitate to say 'last meal' though I know it will be the last time the Payne's will be together for quite some time.*

"That would be very nice Mam," Major Payne replied, "been smellin' right good, making me hungry, and *I sure as hell ain't going to be eatin' good where I'm headed.*

"Yes, that'd be nice Mary," Mr. Peachy added, "Anyone for cocktail?" Customarily, he kept his bar under lock, occasionally bringing out the sherry or port in the evening, but this was a special occasion. *They deserve better than this*, he thought, *but how? With the world turned upside down what am I saving the aged Scotch for?*

The Paynes and Peachys weren't the only families having a hard time. In addition to the demands of caring for the severely wounded, typically without benefit of prior training, there remained the distinct possibility that their patients would not survive their wounds despite the untiring efforts of care givers. Union Chaplains were busy going door to door throughout town praying with the wounded and giving last rites. They also tried to comfort the care givers who were often traumatized by the death of their patients.

Then there was the special case of brothers serving together such as Confederate General Richard Anderson and brother, Edward. General Anderson was in the thick of fighting when he'd gotten word Edward had been killed and with the battle raging it was several hours before he had even a moment to break away and seek out his brother's remains. Later, writing to their father, he recorded,

"The fight continued all day. After dark, when the firing ceased, I went to Williamsburg and, at the home of Doctor Garrett, I saw my brother's body. It was there that I, for the first time, fully realized the dreadful fact. The hand of death was laid upon the face of him whose countenance had only a little while before delighted me by its animation, its courage, its intelligence, and its strong affection. It was the most agonizing moment of my life." [97]

General Anderson was not the only soldier to lose a brother in the battle. A Rebel lad lay badly wounded, and despite all the care the homeowners could manage, expired. When chaplains arrived, too late for last rites, they

---

[97] Hasting & Hastings, pg. 116.

Civil War Comes Home

sent for a detail to retrieve the body. Upon entering the home, one of the Union soldiers sent on this grim task discovered the dead soldier was his late brother. He collapsed and wept, joined in tears by the homeowner widow and daughter who'd done their best to care for the deceased.[98]

Major Payne, despite the gravity of his wound, was among the lucky who'd survived and somehow healed without infection that claimed so many. Now, as the Peachys were preparing to enjoy a final meal together, Major Payne began sorting his meager belongings, packing a small satchel, though his wife remained distraught.

Shortly, Til informed Mrs. Peachy supper was ready. She had decided to set her fine china, usually reserved for Christmas, Easter, or very important visitors. Like her husband, she figured, *what's the sense of saving it, when those soldiers can come in and take my patient right out of my house off to jail.*

Supper was soon served and what a spread it was, Til had indeed put together a special meal; the last of the Smithfield ham with baked sweet potatoes glazed with brown sugar, homemade biscuits fresh-baked, and the remaining jars of last season's garden vegetables; okra, beans, tomatoes. And for dessert, a few apples retrieved from a corner of the root cellar made a deep juicy pie complete with the last stick of cinnamon in the house. Mr. Peachy tried to match Til's efforts serving wine with each course including the last of a sweet dessert wine.

By now Mrs. Payne had composed herself, though she'd lost her appetite, refusing to accept her husband's imminent departure. Adding to the difficulties and psychological impact of trying to heal the wounded, was the fact that even when all the hard work, sacrifice, and prayer were successful, and the patient recovered, the outcome was still the same, at least for the Rebels. They were still prisoners of war. They were not sent home to recuperate or back to their units, of course, but instead went to prisons so vile and cruel that even had they not been wounded, survival was not assured in the least.

The Paynes and the Peachys sat around the table, men showing their appreciation of Til's cooking with heaping seconds, while the wives could only push food around their plates, too distraught to eat. Conversation was difficult at best, Major Payne trying to engage his host on the prospects for business in an occupied town. "No doubt some may yet prosper by

---

98 op. cit. pg. 119.

supplying Yankees, but the majority of us face financial ruin, I fear," Mr. Peachy offered.

As they savored the last morsels of pie, Til taking hers in the kitchen as she cleaned up; there was a loud rap at the door.

Checking the mantle clock, "Damnation" Mr. Peachy exclaimed, "Right on schedule."

Major Payne rose from his chair, brushing crumbs from his lap, cleared his throat and turned to Mrs. Peachy, "Mam, I cannot thank you enough for taking me in and nursing me. You have done your Christian duty and saved my life. I thank you from the bottom of my heart." Next he addressed his host. "Good Sir, thank you for your generous hospitality these many weeks. Had it not been for you and your lovely wife I shudder to think I should not be alive. And to my loving wife, despite the good healing by the Peachy's, I despaired and could not mend proper until I again laid eyes on you. My darling Mary, I had no idea you'd travel all this way, and despite the many hardships and dangers you encountered, I am eternally grateful for your devotion and continuing to nurse me back to health. Now I must take my leave but know I will always keep you in my heart and mind, no matter what. I shall return to help raise our child and until then, may God keep you safe," and with that he grasped her in his arms, tears flowing freely in both.

"I love you Mary," extracting himself from her grasp, heading for the front door, grabbing up the small satchel, and exiting, "I'm ready," was all he said as two guards marched him off to the town jail now serving as Yankee brig. The Peachys sat, too stunned to move while Mrs. Payne collapsed.

Suddenly, Mr. Peachy jumped to his feet, threw open the front door, shouted, "Wait! Stop."

The guard detail halted, wondering, what could this interruption mean.

"Take me instead," Mr. Peachy offered, his wife incredulous. "He's wounded. He still requires healing, I'm fine. Let him recover," Peachy offered, completely serious.

"No Sir, I cannot let you do that," Major Payne countered. "You and your wife have already done enough, more than enough really. You don't know what it's like in those prisons, why a man your age, well Sir, frankly, you would not make it," Payne explained bluntly.

"That's my point," Peachy volunteered, "whatever happens, I've had a full life. You on the other hand Major got soldiers counting on you and a little one to raise, maybe more after this first one."

"Shut your yaps," the older of the guards shouted, "stupid Southern code of honor, I never. Look here, our orders are to return with Major Payne. Can't change that, for any reason. Besides old man, you ain't in the military and from the looks of it, never were, so you ain't worth nothin' to my Colonel. On the other hand, a field grade Cavalry officer, well now if'n he be lucky, might git his self sent back in a prisoner exchange assuming 'course that wound heals up good, and we don't starve 'em first." His snarl and menacing look made both women shudder.

As Til reentered the dining room to see if anyone wanted more coffee she was instructed to assist Mrs. Payne to bed and have smelling salts at the ready. Rejected, Mr. Peachy plopped down, sheepishly pouring himself another glass of Scotch, raising it in salute to Major Payne. Staring out the window, he wondered, *where will this all end?*

The next morning Mrs. Peachy had to convince Mrs. Payne to eat something, at least for the baby's sake. "Now dear, you'll be staying here with us 'til that little one is born. We can't have you travelin' and off on your own somewhere. It's not safe. Make this your home until you can be reunited, the latter comment was meant to comfort but only set Mrs. Payne off in another round of uncontrolled sobbing. Mrs. Payne had been too upset to discuss this with her husband but she knew he'd not want to turn Mrs. Payne out, following her husband's incarceration.

Despite many hardships, the Peachys, like most other residents of Williamsburg, managed rare glimpses of happiness during occupation. The healing of a Southern hero thought too badly wounded to bother with surgery, the arduous travels of his loving wife across literally the length and breadth of war-torn Virginia to be at his side, and the dedicated nursing by a stranger who took him in, gave hope during those dark days. Despite the occupation, residents sought and occasionally still found reasons for happiness.

***

August, 1862
Wedding Bells

Also among the hundreds of wounded, lucky, like Major Payne, to be taken to private homes, was Captain John Willis Lea, 5th North Carolina infantry. A cadet in good standing at West Point when war broke out, like many of his classmates from the South, Lea resigned his Federal commission as soon as word of secession arrived. Taking the next passenger ferry down the Hudson, he cleared New York about as fast as anyone could, headed straight to his beloved Carolina. Once home, he was soon appointed company commander because of his military training. With President Davis' urgent call for reinforcements for Magruder, Lea led his unit north almost as fast as he'd left New York.

The 5th North Carolina Infantry was in the thick of fighting in Williamsburg, Capt. Lea leading from the front as he'd learned. Unfortunately, visible also meant vulnerable and Lea was severely wounded. His men evacuating him as quickly as possible, Captain Lea soon found himself in a large barn, with increasing numbers of wounded, some from his unit, but no surgeons or medical personnel. The barn was simply shelter and in the rush and confusion of battle, sites for field aid stations had not been designated. Units in combat did not necessarily know where their supporting medical personnel were located, nor vice versa.

One of Lea's sergeants remained at his side, and after making his Captain as comfortable as possible, left frantically trying to find a medical unit. Once he'd done so, he tried his best to convince them to divert to the barn to tend the many wounded collecting there. The Sergeant's tenacity paid off, and when surgeons finally arrived, they agreed the barn made for about as good an operating room they'd find anywhere, especially in the midst of storm and battle. It had been purposely-built on a slight rise, so the site drained, allowing livestock to lie on straw instead of in the mud. In present utilization the patients were thus spared lying in their own blood.

Fortunately, Captain Lea was one of the first treated and remained conscious. After the surgeon and attendants did what they could, he was moved to the far corner to recover on his own, as they went on to the next of many cases. It was here his friend, Captain George Armstrong Custer found him after several hours searching. They'd become good friends during their Academy days.

Captain Custer had ample time after the battle to pursue his own priorities –finding friends and former classmates, given the delayed Yankee pursuit and the jammed roads. Custer and other West Point officers knew in which units their friends served even when they were now the enemy. As an officer, Custer freely rode throughout the area, determined to find John Lea and other former classmates who may have been wounded or captured. In the unlikely event he was challenged about what he was up to, Custer quickly put a questioning sentry or Sergeant in their place for daring question his authority. In his bold manner, Custer ventured wherever he had an inkling he might find comrades. Riding between clusters of lagging soldiers, and groups of wounded, he repeatedly inquired, "Anyone heard the whereabouts of 5th North Carolinians? Anyone know Captain John Lea?" Having searched for about as long as he dared, Custer knew he must soon report back to his own command, whether he'd found his friend or not. Then, finally someone mentioned, "Sir, have you checked at the field hospital, in the barn on the hill?"

Galloping there, Custer barged in, drawing the ire of surgeon and staff in the middle of another amputation. Working all afternoon, they would continue long into the night as wounded kept being brought in. The longer wounded lay on the battlefield before treatment, the lesser their chance of surviving, so the surgeon was working feverishly against the law of diminishing returns. He did not appreciate Custer's interruption.

"Uh, sorry Doc. Excuse me," Custer offered meekly then quickly asked, "Sir, have you treated a Captain John Lea?"

"Damn, Captain we've amputated dozens of limbs," pointing to the grim pile heaped to the side. "We hardly have time to get their names, and certainly don't recall specific patients. We been at this for I don't know how many hours now, and they keep bringing 'em in."

"Of course Sir," Custer apologized, starting to look among comatose patients now nearly filling the barn, when one of the Surgeon's assistants directed him to the far corner. There against all odds, lay his wounded friend.

"Thank God! John wake up, it's me George. John can you hear me?"

Captain Lea stirred, still in pain, drowsy from the remaining effects of chloroform, and a shot of cheap government whiskey. "What, who is it?" he mumbled.

"John, its George Custer come to get you out of here. Remember, from the Academy. I've come to bring you where we can get you taken care of. *Lying here in dirty straw, having no one tending him ain't doing him no good,* Custer knew.

"What," Lea stirred, "just leave me be."

Custer persisted, carefully reaching under Lea's armpits trying to sit him up, but seeing him wince in pain, thought better of it. "Medic, bring a stretcher. We've got to get this man out of here." Failing to elicit any response, Custer persisted.

"Sir, we got patients lined-up waiting, some of 'em already laid out on the battlefield for the better part of a day. Your man there already had surgery. Nothin' more we can do for him. If we don't tend to these others, they'll not make it. We did best we could for him, Sir."

"Well, then give me a stretcher damn it! He's my friend and I'll not have him laying here unattended. I'm moving him to where he can be cared for."

"Sir, with all due respect, patients may not be moved. If you move a patient how can we possibly care for him elsewhere?"

"Well, I certainly can see he'd not be cared for here when he's left unattended. Some where's else at least he be tended to," Custer snapped. Regaining his composure, he tried again, "because you're understaffed for the large number of patients, I'll take this patient elsewhere. Reduce your workload," Custer offered.

"Sir, patients may not be removed," the Sergeant repeated firmly. "If you do so, against our instructions, when he dies, which he will from having been moved when he needs to lie still, his death will be on your hands," the sergeant explained, his surgeon looking over from the operating table, nodding agreement.

"Understood, and that's my point, you have more patients than you can handle now, as you state, and they're still arriving. I'm just going to ease your workload by one patient, and agree to take full responsibility."

"Sir, we're in the middle of surgery. This is not the time to discuss disposition of a recovering patient. I've got to assist the surgeon, holding down the patient during amputation 'cause we're out of chloroform and whiskey. You want to help, get us more medical personnel, and supplies and equipment. You want a stretcher wait 'til the next patient is off loaded," the Sergeant now impatient with the continuing interruption.

"Very well," Custer agreed, retrieving a litter as soon as it was vacated. It was already blood-soaked and he hesitated using it, but then saw they were all like that. All the stretchers had already carried an endless stream of severely wounded. His patient John was too out of it to notice anyway. Custer again reached under Lea's armpits and half lifted, half drug him onto the wet stretcher best he could. By then the medic had a moment after disposing of a limb, and got on the other end of the litter and helped Custer carry Lea out of the barn where an ambulance wagon had just finished off-loading other patients.

"Hold up there private," Custer instructed. "We got this patient to load."

Surprised, the driver did as instructed, "Yes, Sir, where to Sir?"

Uncertain where he was headed, Custer simply instructed, "Back into town. We got to find someone to take care of him."

Tying his horse to the wagon, Custer climbed in back alongside his friend. Once the driver saw they were situated, he turned, heading to town.

Although the ride was not far, it seemed to Custer to take forever. He didn't really know where to take his friend and was becoming increasingly worried about his getting paler by the minute, recalling the medical sergeant's comment about care now being his responsibility, telling the driver, "Hurry, man."

As the turned onto Main Street, Custer saw the yellow hospital flag flying on the former Female Academy. Thanks to organizing by Mrs. Letitia Tyler Semple, it now served as one of the larger hospitals in town. As the driver pulled up in front, Custer jumped down and bolting inside, heard, "I'm sorry Sir but we are full." Despite his protests, he heard the refrain, "I am sorry Sir. We couldn't possibly accept even one more patient. There's no soap, bandages, medicine, equipment, or help left –not enough of anything. However, I will refer you an excellent private home on Francis Street, one of our many volunteers providing care.

"Yes, Mam thank you. That would be most kind."

Redirecting the driver, Custer again ran to the door and pounding heavily, was met by the gracious Mrs. Durfey, wife of Colonel Goodrich Durfey, who like the Peachy family and many others, opened their hearts and homes to the wounded.[99]

"Thank you Mam. I fear he's not well. He's paler now than when I first set eyes on him in the barn they're using for a hospital."

"Yes, I see he's had a hard time of it," Mrs. Durfey noted, explaining she'd cared for other patients successfully and would be assisted by daughter Margaret. "Now Captain, don't fret about your friend. I assure you he's in good hands. You did the right thing bringing him. He'll have two of us round the clock. Had you left him there, I doubt anyone would even bring water once a day."

Just as she'd put Custer at ease, he did likewise for her. She was anxious allowing a Yankee officer in her home but seeing his genuine concern, she was calmed. *Maybe he's not so bad after all.*

Though neither mother nor daughter had any formal nursing training, both had applied basic first aid to care for family members and slaves. Mrs. Durfey possessed extensive practical knowledge of medicinal herbs and plants and was now passing this on to Margaret, just as she'd learned it from her mother years prior. Her understanding and use of herbal remedies was important for several reasons. First, as all the physicians were off to war, there was no other source of care to turn to. Although a few medicines could still be had, most were in short supply or unavailable while others could only be obtained by smuggling. Medications were rapidly becoming unavailable, even at grossly inflated prices and were never assured or sufficient, herbal remedies being the only treatment available in some cases.

Since Captain Lea had arrived shortly after surgery, the Durfeys took great care in applying juice of un-ripened persimmons, effective in stopping bleeding. To ease pain, they administered an extract of hemlock leaves, careful not to make the potion too strong and poison him. Opium was no longer to be had and the poppies in kitchen garden were not yet ripe.[100] To prevent diarrhea, common among soldiers, wounded or not, they prepared extracts of blackberry roots, ground up charcoal, and other home remedies of varying effectiveness. However strange the elixirs seemed, they proved

---

99 The Durfey house is now known as Bassett Hall, the residence of John D. Rockefeller, Jr. during the restoration of colonial Williamsburg.
100 Dabney,

beneficial and with home cooking, their patient began gaining weight. Soon, Captain Lea was not only recovering, but falling hopelessly in love with Margaret.

While Lea gained strength, occupying Yankees continued going door-to-door compiling names of wounded and where each was located --trying to create order in the post-battle chaos. Overnight, Williamsburg had become a town of death, dying and wounded. Initially, no one knew who'd survived or perished and there was actually greater order in death than in recovery. Rebels were buried in cemeteries by their state of origin. Wounded were taken to many private homes and virtually all public buildings were converted to hospitals or recovery wards. The wounded ending up wherever space could be made. Under such conditions it took days to compile casualty lists Even when completed, lists soon became inaccurate as patients expired, were discharged, or were moved to a different facility. Thus, official records of losses remained a work in progress and such difficulties were further compounded by the necessity for mass burials to clear thousands of corpses from roads, fields and woods. In time, copies of the patient and casualty lists made their way from surgeon to headquarters where the adjutant, not entirely sure what to do with the new information, posted it outside the headquarters.[101] This proved an expedient solution.

Checking casualty lists soon became a common past time as everyone wanted to know if friend or relative had survived. If so, they'd want to pay a call, bringing a cigar or plug of tobacco to share news of family or friends over whiskey.

Custer continued perusing the lists, but remained most concerned for Captain Lea. He kept intending to visit but demands of duty, namely the now failed campaign to take Richmond, precluded. Soon weeks then months had passed before he was able to return to his friend's bedside. When finally able to do so, Custer saw first-hand how prayer, home cookin', home remedies, plenty of rest, and round-the-clock nursing combined to work miracles. Lea was nearly healed and gaining strength daily. He was anxious to get out of bed and had recently tried walking again, -slowly and not far, but it was a start.

On one such walk, all the way to the Durfey front porch, John spotted Custer coming up the front walk, recognizing him instantly.

"George Custer, how in creation did you get here?"

---

101 Official notification of next of kin of soldiers wounded or killed in action did not yet exist on either side.

"John, how are you?"

"Darling, I'd like to introduce my classmate from the military academy, George Armstrong Custer. George, meet my fiancée, Miss Margaret Durfey."

"We've already met," Custer replied. "You don't remember do you John? I brought you here right after you were wounded. Now engaged! I am happy for you both, to see you on the mend, and now to be married. Did you know each other before?"

"No, I'd never been to Williamsburg 'til our unit was called here to repel the invasion, err, your threat on Richmond. Though I was wounded, this little angel of mercy and her mother nursed me back to health. Why if it hadn't been for Margaret and her mother, I'd most likely not be sitting here today."

"Yes, so I've heard," Custer allowed, giving an all-knowing glance to Margaret.

"Hush, John, now don't you be talking about what might have been," Margaret cautioned. "You know the good Lord isn't finished with you yet. I'll hear no more talk of, 'might not be here.'"

"Yes, dear, of course, sorry," John replied, embarrassed.

George looked away. *I'll never have a woman telling me what to say, think, or do!* Then returning to the moment, asked, "So when is your wedding day?"

"It's coming up quick, August 18th can you attend?"

Margaret was taken aback, *not only was a Yankee in her parents' home but he was now invited to our wedding. What's John thinking*, she wondered. *If he is that good a friend why haven't I heard of him before? Despite living under the same roof for several months, I still have a lot to learn about my future husband.*

George looked at the couple, reading the expression of hope on John's face and quiet shock on Margaret's. "Why certainly, John, I'd love to. Not only will I attend, I'll be your best man!" he boldly declared. "Think about it, you're in an occupied town; your 5th North Carolina comrades are off fightin' and couldn't return even if they wanted. Far as I know I'm not going anywhere. You understand of course, I'll have to get permission."

Figure 45 . Captain John Willis Lea, 5th North Carolina Infantry, wounded in the Battle of Williamsburg. Courtesy of the Museum of the Confederacy, Richmond, Va.

Figure 46. Captain George Armstrong Custer. Courtesy of the Library of Congress, Washington, D.C.

"Great! Good idea," John replied. *My family is in the same fix -even if anyone could travel, no one would come to occupied territory.* "Glad we resolved that aren't you Margaret?" John asked, but she didn't reply.

Wedding preparations were extensive, undertaken in meticulous detail. Everyone, from the Durfeys to their former slaves was glad to have something to talk about besides war, for a 'general want of good spirits,' had settled upon the town. [102] A wedding would be a refreshing, but fleeting interlude in a depressing routine of hardship, shortage, and occupation. Guests eagerly anticipated a grand social event the likes of which had not been seen in quite some time. Even the most ardent secessionists

---
102 Thane, Elizabeth, Yankee Stranger.

Civil War Comes Home

now realized the war hadn't been won at Big Bethel or Manassas, despite the successive routs. They'd reluctantly come to the realization the war would not be short. Thus, any opportunity to celebrate was welcome news, and Colonel and Mrs. Durfey determined to spare no expense for their daughter's wedding.

Like many these days, they saw no point in saving for the future. Besides tragic loss of life, war time inflation steadily devalued the currency on both sides and simultaneously, the cost of everything shot up due shortages, increased demand, and blockades. This understandably led to a 'spend it all, now' mindset for many.

The list of invitees was checked and rechecked. Under occupation, each attendee had to be individually approved by the Provost Marshall. While Margaret took this as a personal affront, any gathering or meeting of Rebels, even social, was prohibited. The fact that a Union officer, Captain George Armstrong Custer, was attending a Rebel function, further heightened concern. Rumors of threatened Confederate raids on the town persisted, and pickets routinely stopped everyone, demanding identification and passes, and increasing tension and animosity between residents and occupiers. So far, guerilla raids had not materialized, nevertheless, rumors of such and the Durfey's plans for a large gathering necessitated a considerable guard force be kept on alert.

Even when attendees were finally approved, they didn't receive the customary invitations, for paper had become far too scarce to be wasted so extravagantly. Instead, guests were personally invited which presented no difficulties as no guests from out of town were allowed. Even the Durfey's extended family members could not attend if residing elsewhere in the Confederacy. The Provost Marshall would abide no border crossings, fearing sympathizers to the Southern cause would gather intelligence during a visit to Williamsburg then once home, promptly report all they'd seen to the nearest Rebel officer. If such were to happen, the rumored guerilla raiders might know exactly where and when to strike.

Despite myriad restrictions and shortages, preparations for a lavish ceremony continued, nothing, not even war, would detract from Margaret's wedding day. Flower arrangements were created from cuttings from the grounds and neighbor's gardens, and wildflowers were gathered from meadows and fallow fields, though this late into summer heat, most were past their peak. Nevertheless, striking bouquets would be displayed throughout the parlor and outdoors.

Although the flowers and other decorations were impressive, the piece d' resistance was the food. The Durfeys would serve the finest refreshments possible, and wanted the occasion to be the talk of town. They could easily afford the costs, and secondly, there'd been so few social occasions of late that anything they pulled off would be widely appreciated in a time of want. Margaret refused to consider the recent "starvation balls," in which guests were served nothing but water, as having any place whatsoever in Southern hospitality.

Despite shortages mounting with every passing day, Mrs. Durfey ordered an ambitious if not demanding menu. Though her kitchen staff, her former slaves, would be working longer hours to accomplish this, it was well within their skills and abilities to create not only palatable but impressively delicious dishes out of the most ordinary ingredients. The cooks were well versed, having learned to make do in preparing their slave meals. Gradually, word of needed ingredients was spread by the kitchen help and portions of carefully managed, if not hoarded, supplies were provided by other area cooks, -whether their masters or their ladies approved, or even knew.

With the town's population doubled by occupying forces, and widespread destruction and looting, nearby farms could scarcely supply sufficient produce, eggs, meat, and milk and local forests were so depleted of game; the cooks had to become creative. While rural areas like the counties surrounding Williamsburg were used to being self sufficient, towns and cities, especially larger ones were experiencing severe food shortages. For example, Richmond had very few stray cats or dogs anymore, as the meat was sold as 'lamb.' As conditions worsened there, dressed rats hung in butcher shops, selling for as much as $2.50 a piece.

Fortunately, conditions hadn't yet gotten that desperate in Williamsburg and the Durfeys would never consider such fare for their grand event. Because of the Federal occupation, the town actually suffered fewer shortages of basic commodities than elsewhere. Federal supply ships continued offloading a veritable bounty to feed McClellan's massive army. Whether by theft or black market dealing, a goodly portion of that Federal larder could be had, - if one approached the right people with ready cash. Of course, it was illegal and risky business, for the Provost Marshall arrested more than a few for war profiteering, but for every one caught, dozens avoided detection. They not only profited but continued to eat well. Hunger and greed were powerful motivation and a kind of 'unofficial appropriation' from Federal warehouses went on most nights and the cooks knew better than to ask where supplies came from.

Still, many items remained unavailable, and the northern commissary stores hardly reflected Southern tastes anyway. When a needed item was lacking, Mrs. Durfey's cooks substituted creatively. For example, given their popularity, both coffee and tea were soon quite dear; the former now up to an extraordinary 30 cents per pound, while the later was reserved almost exclusively for invalids.[103] Despite shortages and price increases, the Durfey's remained unconcerned, or at least her staff did.

"Now don't you worry Mam," Mrs. Durfey's cook assured. "We got okra seeds for coffee. They ain't quite ripe as I like, but browned in a skillet, theys the best for replacing coffee. And if we run out of okra, there's chicory, dandelion root, burnt corn meal, or if it comes to it, even acorns. Soaked then parched to remove the shell, and roasted with bacon grease they make 'coffee.'

"Well I never heard of such," Mrs. Durfey interrupted.

"Yes, Mam, and for tea we gots berries, from the garden or gathered wild, and the leaves and roots of berries to make any flavor tea. Why sit down right here Mam, and let me make you cup a spiceberry tea right now." Adding a small handful of the dried crushed leaves to boiling water, and letting it steep for a few moments, the cook soon poured her a cup.

Sipping tentatively, Mrs. Durfey was pleasantly surprised. "Why it tastes like wintergreen."

"Yes, Mam, and good for you too," she was pleased with her Mistress' confidence in her to pull off a bountiful, and delicious wedding meal in the midst of war.

"But besides coffee or tea, a wedding calls for champagne," Mrs. Durfey ventured, half joking. "I had my husband check and he tells me champagne's nearly impossible to find at any price, anywhere, and even if he should be able to locate any, we cannot obtain quantities sufficient to serve our guests," Mrs. Durfey worried.

"Mam, again, I tell you not to worry, 'cause we gots a solution for that too," her cook chuckled at this chance to show her problem solving skills. "It's an old recipe, we take one part corn mash and three parts spring water and set it in an old molasses barrel. Mixin' it up real good after a couple of days, or better a couple of weeks, depending on how warm it is, and we gots alcohol." Although the substitute champagne lacked effervescence, it would prove a popular if unexpected treat.

While creating alternatives for beverages was comparatively easy,

---

103 op. cit.

baking made for some real challenges, given war time shortages of key ingredients.

"Necessity was indeed the mother of invention," Mrs. Durfey repeated to her cooks. "Margaret simply has to have a traditional wedding cake," she pleaded, laying down a difficult and non-negotiable requirement. "Sugar is already scarce I know," Mrs. Durfey allowed which was surely an understatement.

"Don't you worry Mam," her lead baker replied, "We got molasses, honey, several kinds a fruit sugar, and fig trees growing all around. If we dry 'em in the sun, then grind 'em up, makes a sweet pulp good for fillings. And before wedding day, the melon crop will be in. We take ripe watermelons, quarter 'em, and cook 'em down good in a large vat. This makes sweet syrup which we boil down to a fine white powder -watermelon sugar. And sweet it is!"

"What about flour?"

"Why yes, Mam, the price of wheat has shot up. Both them armies got plenty of bakers, and long as troops ain't on the march, the bake ovens is working seven days a week. If we can't get wheat flour, we can substitute rye flour or corn meal, or we can get rice flour from the deep South. And Mam, while we're at it, butter's gone scarce too. Dairy cows require daily care and that's hard to come by with the men and boys off to war. Besides, most cattle were bought or stolen by the armies.

"Now, as for salt, we's lucky to be near the coast," the cook explained. "Salt has so many uses; for baking, as a preservative for meat, every kind from pork to fish, it's become quite scarce.[104] But if there's no wagon to bring us some salt, we can still git it -from the smoke house. Those salted hams Marsa like so much, when they cure, they drip salt. Over many a year, salt done built up so we take dirt from the smoke house floor and boil it in vats. Now, there's a smell for you! We mostly do this when a strong wind is blowing. We skim off the floating fat, and then transfer to cold water, makes the salt sink and we pours off the waste, leaving clean salt."

"Now for leavening, baking soda can hardly be found. For this we burn corn cobs in a red hot skillet nestled in a bed of coals 'til they become a fine white ash. This we use in place of baking soda."

---

104 Virginia was fortunate in having geologic deposits such at Salt Lick, but transportation from the southwestern region was problematic. Wagons and horses were in great demand everywhere so salt had to compete with other items deemed more pressing or commanding a higher price. On the coast, salt was 'made' by evaporating seawater but it was labor intensive, slow, and wagons were still required to move the product inland.

Armed with these substitutes and many more, the kitchen staff undertook to carefully modify recipes slightly each time until the resulting product was deemed satisfactory. Although it took a lot of work to refine each recipe with the many substituted ingredients, the cooks didn't complain. They liked Margaret and her mother and took the extra baking and cooking as a personal challenge. They fully intended to lay claim to bragging rights for years to come as the best bakers and cooks in town. Their young kitchen helpers didn't mind either for every attempt at modifying recipes resulted in baked goods to be sampled. Some proved tastier than others but all were shared, and there was more than enough for any who cared for seconds. Usually baked goods, other than coarse corn bread, had been reserved for the master's table but with these baking trials, everyone, even young helpers and the cook's children enjoyed their fill of treats. For many, this was one of the few times in their lives, if not the first, they'd eaten cake.

While baking continued despite sultry heat, seamstresses and tailors also toiled. There was not only Margaret's gown, but dresses for her bridesmaids, ring bearer, flower girl, and of course, mother of the bride. Before the first stitch however, fabric had to found and with the war it was no longer a matter of ordering selections. Popular calico was simply no longer available and while cotton may well have been 'King', as many in the South proclaimed, all of it was exported. The South had no cotton mills and the naval blockades all along the Atlantic and Gulf coasts resulted in very little fabric being imported. Shortages began immediately as every woman hoarded, knowing her children would grow and wear out clothes. Unfortunately, the women were now competing directly with buyers for military quartermasters and companies awarded lucrative contracts for uniforms.

It was virtually the same for every raw material used in clothing; wool, leather, and finished goods, from buckles to buttons. Just as the South had no capacity to spin raw fiber into cloth, there was no Southern manufacture of thread, buttons, pins or needles. Sewing needles became so scarce that after a battle, the satchels and knapsacks of victims were searched. Soldiers knew they could trade needles for food, even when the women were themselves near starvation. [105]

105 One reason needles were in such demand was because home spun thread did not have the tensile strength to be used in sewing machines. As a result of the lack of factory-made thread, which the North banned from export as contraband, sewing machines throughout the South mostly sat idle, as their owners were forced to revert to hand-sewing.

Mrs. Durfey's seamstresses and tailor, despite the many shortages, somehow managed to proceed with the work for Margaret's wedding. For the bridal gown, front parlor curtains were taken down and cut up, the damask adding detail and richness to a classic design of simple but elegant lines. The colors for the wedding party were based on the natural dye plants that could be harvested that time of year, indigo rendering a beautiful blue.

But dying the cloth meant considerable labor, as one of the seamstresses explained."First, indigo has to be harvested just as flowering begins, and we have to watch the season close. Then you cut the whole plant close to the ground and gather it up in great quantity. Cut bushes are packed into vats, covered with water and allowed to ferment nine days. Then you stir this stinkin' mess to break up pieces. Next you add big chunks of lye, and the solids eventually settle out to the bottom. After you drain the vats, a paste or "mud" is found in the bottom. Scrape this out and put it into sacks and dry. Later, grind up the dried chunks, mix with water and stir for a long time. It'll take hours of stirring 'til it's fully mixed, but now it's finally time to dye the fabric. Usually we do it by the bolt. If someone didn't take great care in harvesting and preparing the plant and in maintaining the fermentation, the resulting poor or uneven coloring might render all the work for naught, and the bolt ruined," she cautioned. Despite the lengthy multistep process, it was worth the effort for indigo blue was quite popular. Once the vat was set up it could be kept indefinitely with the dye renewed as colors faded. Certain trim pieces in the dress design were dyed a different shade of blue than indigo using a different process involving the bark of the swamp maple. Seamstresses, weavers, and workers in the fabric trades likewise developed special knowledge of natural dye stuffs, from plants to minerals, and the processes by which desired effects could be manipulated.

The newly-dyed indigo fabric was cut and hand sewn into custom-fit dresses, each containing no store bought item; buckle, button or bow. Finally, it was time for fitting, hemming and final adjustments. Just as Mrs. Durfey had initially been anxious that a proper wedding cake could be baked, she'd been concerned the bridal gown or any of the attendant's dresses might be ill-fitting or suffer from the shortages of supplies and fabric. Now for the first time seeing the entire bridal party fitted and gowned, she was well pleased with the outcome, thanking her beaming seamstresses profusely.

After the fittings, Mrs. Durfey was called to the kitchen where the tables, shelves and pie safes were filled to overflowing with a sample of the wedding cake and a wide variety of other delicious goods –all baked with substitutes. It was good the dress fittings were completed for the cooks and bakers insisted they sample the many creations and everything was so delicious they consumed more than polite sample tastings. Again, Mrs. Durfey was impressed with the labors of her cooks, bakers and kitchen helpers. "Thank you so much for all your hard work. These are wonderful. I truly do not know how you manage to do this but my hat is off to you ladies." Most everything at the informal tasting was as good as the original recipe version, causing Mrs. Durfey to remark more than once, "I'm not sure that I don't like this new recipe better." Like their sisters the seamstresses, the cooks and bakers basked in the satisfaction of jobs expertly accomplished, under the most trying conditions.

With everyone having done their best, all that remained was for the wedding party and guests to get ready. Although bathing was still thought to pose considerable risk of illness, exceptions could be made in this special circumstance. The evening before the wedding all but a few holdouts scrubbed and cleansed as best they could. For some, this meant water heated on the stove, carried pot by pot to a tub. For most of the males, if cleansing were accomplished, it was done at a nearby pond, bathers appreciating the coolness after the heat of August.

Most households made their own soap before the war, using lye, produced by pouring water slowly through a vat of fine white hardwood ash, mixed with water and grease. But now that animals were scarce, meat was seldom served and thus, even grease was in short supply. Instead of animal fats, oil pressed from cotton seeds or china berries was added to make soap. Or, native plants such as soaproot or yucca root were harvested and used as substitutes for lye soap.

To complete one's cleansing, toothpowder made from charcoal, or a mixture of charcoal with honey, or the tubers of arrowroot harvested from the many freshwater marshes were used. Those who didn't have toothbrushes used a small twig, often dogwood or licorice root, one end of which was chewed and softened until it was brush-like.

Grooming was not complete until the addition of hair oil made from lard to which rose petals were added. With hairpins as scarce as sewing needles, hair oil became an essential styling aid. For the ladies a final touch was a dusting of rice flour lightly on face and hands. This hid both wrinkles and age spots and lightened any tan skin, lest a lady of means be severely misjudged by her peers as having been outside. Only commoners and laborers suffered sun exposure.

Wedding day dawned clear and cooler after overnight storms brought welcome relief. Right after breakfast, laborers began setting up tables and chairs, many borrowed from neighbors, in the Durfey's back yard under the spreading limbs of massive magnolias, still dripping from the night's precipitation. The Durfey home, though large by the standard of the day, was too small to accommodate the crush of guests. Instead, the house would be used as a staging area for food and refreshments served on the lawn.

While the women were busy with baking and sewing, their husbands and brothers had the grounds well-groomed for the occasion. Colonel Durfey directed preparations for a grand garden party, with the grounds, formal gardens and floral displays completing the beauty of the day. As guests began arriving, boys from the neighborhood, at least ones that could be trusted were engaged to take guest's horses or carriage, leading the animals to vacant lots where they were fed, watered, and secured until needed for the ride home.

Captain George Custer, despite being best man, was one of the last to arrive. "Pressing military matters," he offered. While John Lea merely rolled his eyes, *typical Custer*, he thought, Mrs. Durfey had so hounded her husband about where was the best man the Colonel opened the bar early, even before the ceremony began.

When guests saw a Union officer in dress blue uniform, complete with sword that had drawn Rebel blood, in their midst, a great murmur swept the crowd. Everyone had a comment or remark, "*Well, in all my life, I never…*" before falling embarrassingly silent. During the several months of occupation, Custer was certainly no stranger to such reactions. Frankly, he could care less what they thought or whether they welcomed him or not. He was attending for his good friend, and soon, groom and best man were side by side a dozen yards or so from the rear porch steps.

The Rev Thomas Ambler, Bruton Parish church, was officiating. From the outset he'd tried to convince Colonel Durfey the ceremony should be performed inside the church not outdoors but Durfey women would not hear of it. They were not concerned so much whether space would be sufficient, but knew the good Reverend's proclivity to use his pulpit to launch into political rhetoric against the occupying Federals. No one wanted the wedding turned into yet another diatribe by the short-tempered Reverend Ambler against Custer, McClellan, Lincoln, or any other Federal.

Although miffed at first, for Reverend Ambler was used to having his way in what he claimed was 'his' parish, he finally relented. Nevertheless, indoors or out, he despised any Yankee presence, whether Captain Custer here, or sentries outside Bruton Parish during services and evening vespers. When Colonel Durfey glanced over and saw Captain Custer and Revered Ambler sizing one another up, he was just as glad the ceremony was taking place at his home. That way, Mr. Durfey felt, or at least hoped, he'd have some control over the situation.

Momentarily, the double doors to the rear porch opened, gradually revealing the bridal party one-by-one, from young flower girls in indigo blue to beautiful Margaret in her stunning bridal gown of rich ivory damask. "Excuse me Revered, I've got a daughter to escort," Durfey explained, joining her on the porch as a hush of "Ohhs" and "ahs" rose approvingly. John Lea, in the garden with Custer was speechless. He could not believe Margaret's beauty, that their wedding was really happening or that he'd survived battle, healed and was standing at the altar. *Maybe I did die on the battlefield and this is a dream in heaven,* he thought. Though he'd not speak of it, Custer felt reassured he'd played some role in his friend being alive today.

Margaret entered on her father's arm, all eyes on her, first down the stairs then the gentle slope of the garden to her waiting groom. Inwardly she chuckled with the same delight she had while a little girl running this same garden path. *Those days are long gone*, she thought, quickly adding, *but happier times will return.* Many guests had similar thoughts, *we've see the worst of fighting right outside town and we survived, and we will continue to do so, whatever occupation brings.*

With the exchange of vows, uniting Captain and Mrs. Lea, husband and wife, Colonel and Mrs. Durfey shed tears of joy, receiving the heartfelt congratulations of everyone attending. Like a butterfly going from one blossom to the next, Margaret flitted between guests, while, despite the gaiety of the moment, groom and best man consulted on military matters.

"How much longer you think you're going to be able to stay," Custer asked?

"Well, George, I'm not really sure. I was hoping you might be able to tell me. Your troops run every aspect of this town now," he jested in truth. "I realize my time for recovery is coming to an end but I hope you can put in a word for me to allow me to stay with Margaret a while longer. It'd break her heart if I'm off to prison right after our wedding."

"I'll see what I can do, but can't promise anything. The Provost Marshall has a job to do and certainly can't allow prisoners to remain after they've healed, possibly fomenting discontent. Why, if you and the Durfey's hadn't been laying low, one of them Provost Marshall soldiers looking to make a name for himself would be over here arresting you even on this, your weddin' day."

"I know, I am lucky in many ways, including the day you brought me here, but I was somehow hoping for a prisoner exchange. Can you do anything about that, George?"

"I don't know John, but I will find out. It may sound like a good idea to you but we can't exchange wounded. As long as you're still recuperating, your name doesn't show up on the prisoner roster as eligible for exchange. Once you're in the prison system it's a different matter."

"Well the army ain't changed at bit from West Point. Always rules and procedures, and don't seem to matter if they make no sense. I can be a patient, or I can be a prisoner but I can't be both at the same time? I dare say I am already a prisoner. Certainly, I wouldn't leave the Durfey's home one day and just walk away now could I?"

"Well, don't be so sure. More than a few have tried I suspect," Custer countered. "Some might have got lucky and made it but most just gets themselves shot or at the very least, beat up and thrown in the brig. Anyway, enough of this depressing talk. This is your wedding day John, go enjoy it," Custer instructed, adding, "I will see what I can do about getting you a little more time to recover, but it can't be much. This whole occupation and prisoner exchange business is all still pretty new so there's a lot yet to be worked out. Now go to your wife, and my congratulations to both of you."

"Thanks George, and not a word of this to her or anyone. After all, she'd not understand and why spoil her day?"

"Of course not, I expect I'll be leaving shortly. Though I'm not one to pass up a party, especially yours, the remainder of your guests will enjoy it a whole lot more when a Yankee's no longer in their midst."

"Oh don't think a minute about them. Most of 'em I don't even know, and if they insist on being bull-headed, I don't care to. Thank you for standing up as my best man. You don't know how much that means to me, especially after all these years."

"It has been my pleasure, one I'll always remember," and with that the two officers shook hands, then parted ways. Captain Custer strode purposefully across the yard signaling the lads for his horse, while drawing the stares and whispered comments of guests, while Captain John Willis Lea beamed at his wife's side.

UNTIL APRIL 1865 AND BEYOND[106]
LIFE UNDER OCCUPATION.

Colonel David Campbell, 5th Pennsylvania Cavalry was appointed Williamsburg's first military governor and in attempting to establish control, immediately ordered arrest of several prominent citizens. Dispatched under armed guard to Norfolk and brought before Union district commander General Henry M. Naglee, the citizens finally had the opportunity to state the facts concerning their arrest. They were soon released on a finding of no material charge against peaceful citizens.

While Colonel Campbell seemed to have accomplished little with the arrests, beyond antagonizing residents, the episode was part of establishing 'ground rules' by which Federal forces managed occupied territory.

In a similar vein, Colonel Campbell took over the town press and instead of the Gazette, published the 'Cavalier,' proclaiming, "...Union forever and freedom to all." Needless to say, this was also not popular among townspeople who'd exercised and treasured freedom of the press since British rule.

Responsibility for running a town during wartime was clearly a new mission for the Army. Myriad details had to be worked out about supervising civilians and in time, an uneasy kind of status quo would

---
106 Although General Lee surrendered Confederate forces in Appomattox, Virginia in April 1865, Federal occupation of Williamsburg continued for five more long years until 1870 when Virginia was restored to the Union.

develop. Residents were permitted to remain in town unmolested by troops as long as they caused no difficulties.

While Colonel Campbell devised new governing 'rules,' the occupation itself was repeatedly challenged. Confederate lookouts constantly watched, looking for any sign of weakness, waiting for an opportune moment to free the town, or at least, wreak havoc on hated occupiers. Their reasoning was along the lines of, 'anything that cost Yankees dearly enough, they might decide they didn't really need after all.' So, given enough mischief, headache, and difficulty, maybe the Yanks would reconsider and withdraw. It was more wishful than realistic for Williamsburg was now, and would remain, the closest Federally-occupied territory to Richmond. The heretofore sleepy little backwater had become an important source for intelligence gathering, negotiating prisoner exchanges, and clandestine activities.

Overt attempts to disrupt Union control included partisan-led guerilla warfare and several outright attacks, the first coming after just months after occupation. With town folks chaffing under curfew and Colonel Campbell's various prohibitions, former Virginia Governor Henry Wise led his cavalry into town early Sept 9, 1862. Engaging in a short skirmish on College grounds, they killed six Union soldiers, wounding an additional fifteen before withdrawing. While their bold attack put Federals on notice their situation was more fragile than secure, it accomplished little else. Later that afternoon, in apparent retaliation, drunken members of the 5th Pennsylvania Cavalry set fire to the Wren Building. It was almost totally consumed, and was just as well that President Ewell, William & Mary professors and students were off fighting, thus being spared witness to the senseless destruction.

Partisans continued secretly watching, biding their time through a bleak winter of blockade hardships. By spring they were ready to try again –this time with a force sufficiently large that it might have succeeded in retaking Fort Magruder, but for a series of errors. Late March the following year, three days before Palm Sunday, elements of 59th and 46th Virginia Infantry, just over 100 muskets in all, and a small cavalry force supported by a battery, convened at 2:00 a.m. on Richmond Road several miles west of town. Three companies were detached under Captain G. A. Wallace to circle north and surprise sleeping occupants of Fort Magruder. "Through ploughed fields, over fences, deep and wide ditches, through a swamp that took the men over knee-deep and through some timber with very thick undergrowth,"[107] the guides led Captain Wallace's troops in darkness. After two arduous hours they still had not covered four miles, and by then, dawn was breaking and two of three companies were lost. The remaining company finally emerged from the woods into the open field a mile or two from the fort. Captain Wallace sent back one of the guides to find the lost companies and by the time he returned with them it was so light there were undoubtedly seen. Despite losing the element of surprise, they pushed on to northeast of town. Near Capitol Landing Road at about five o'clock they found three mounted Federal pickets approaching, who upon spotting Wallace's approaching column, "turned tail and took a volley at their back while galloping into Williamsburg." [108] The delayed attackers soon found themselves in a sustained gun battle and were lucky to barely escape for they were surely outnumbered.

A third and final attempt to dislodge or at least disrupt the occupiers was not made until much later, Feb 11, 1865, when eight members of Mosby's raiders, 43rd Virginia Cavalry Battalion, rode into the eastern part of town, overrunning a picket post, killing the guard and wounding four others. At most, this raid caused early morning confusion, amounting to little more than a misguided excursion.

While such outright attacks were sporadic and unsuccessful, townspeople's resistance was immediate and continuous. Though largely inconsequential, cumulatively the petty theft and vandalism wore on the Federal's patience. Even more annoying, however, were the constant insults and snubs invoked at every possible opportunity every day, often by women.

On one occasion, troops erected a large Union flag overhanging the street. Rather than walk under it, ladies diverted to walk around, even when it meant soiling their footwear in the muddy street. Not to be outdone, soldiers hung a larger flag in the form of a banner, full across the street, effectively closing the thoroughfare unless one walked under the nation's ensign. Not only did women still refuse to pass under, but they took considerable care that a "Yankee, whom they despised and hated," might never so much as brush against them. "The ladies compressed their dresses whenever they met an officer or enlisted man, so that the garment

---

107 Dubbs, pg. 287.
108 op. cit.

would not touch the person as they passed. They pulled their hats over their faces to preclude scrutiny."[109]

One of the more belligerent was Julia Thompson Sully, who while engaged in conversation across the neighbors backyard garden was overheard saying, "tell Captain Bolling that he had better be more careful...If he isn't more careful, the Yankees will get him." A passing sentry overhead, duly reporting her remarks and early next morning she found herself before a stern Provost Marshall questioning her about the Confederate Officer she was hiding. Mrs. Sully reluctantly agreed to give him up and grudgingly led a guard of soldiers to her home where they'd arrest this mysterious Captain Bolling. Leading the guard detail into her backyard, Mrs. Sully pointed to her chickens, "That's General Lee. That other is General Magruder," and pointing to a large rooster, "that is Captain Bolling. You can have him if you can catch him." The guards felt more sheepish than amused, having marched across town on a serious mission only to find they'd been duped. At great embarrassment to the Yankees, Mrs. Sully repeatedly relished retelling the tale with great frivolity.

Another trouble maker well known to the Provost Marshall was Sallie Galt, sister of Dr. John Minson Galt II, superintendent of the lunatic asylum. After her brother's passing, Sallie occupied his home at the corner of Francis and Blair.[110] From her porch she had once handed food to passing South Carolina cavalrymen prior to the battle of Williamsburg, but now, under occupation the only thing she passed out were dirty looks and harsh remarks. She continuously taunted the troops who were just going about their assigned duties. Sallie's continuing blatant action did not sit well with the Provost Marshall and he twice had her hauled in, demanding she take the oath of allegiance to the United States. Sallie steadfastly refused, and it was only through the intervention of Dorothea Dix, superintendent of Union nurses and friend of her late physician brother, that Sallie was allowed to remain. As her verbal assaults continued, some pickets chose to march their posts avoiding the intersection to spare themselves her string of epithets.

It was not only women voicing displeasure. Reverend Thomas Ambler was well-known to the Provost Marshall for his fire and brim stone sermons on the Southerner's Christian duty to overthrow the invaders. When hauled before Major Christopher Kleing again in May, 1863, religious services, which had been held continuously at Bruton Parish since even

---

109 op. cit. pg. 242.
110 The Nelson-Galt house

before there was a United States, were summarily suspended. Until such time as Reverend Ambler could control utterances against the Union, his preaching was forbidden.

While residents like Sallie Galt and Reverend Ambler maintained their prolonged defiance, others were only too glad to leave town and Federals willingly obliged, advising recipients 'never return.'[111] By October's end, they'd purged the district of many residents they found obnoxious.[112] Among those departing was the 'little rebel', young Delia Bucktrout who was granted passage to her grandmother's in New Kent County, from whence she made her way to Richmond for the duration of the conflict.[113]

While a succession of Provost Marshalls dealt with Williamsburg's recalcitrant, using arrest and issuing one-way passes to leave, they also had their hands full with maintaining law and order. Picket reserves on College grounds were then under the command of First Lieutenant William W. Disoway, described as a "neat and orderly" nineteen year old, "growing his first slender mustache, on his intelligent, handsome, boyish face." His superior, Colonel West had a brief interview with young Lieutenant Disoway and returned to headquarters, "long enough to write out an order which he folded and addressed to Lieutenant Disoway, dispatching a guard to deliver it,[114] that evening at dress parade, General Orders, No. 47, dated 5 October, "1st Lieutenant W.W. Disoway, 1st New Your Mounted Rifles, is hereby detailed and announced as Acting Provost Marshall of this Command to be stationed in the City of Williamsburg. He will be obeyed and respected accordingly."

Like his predecessor, "...the genteel Disoway quickly became a favorite among the ladies and on the morning of 13 October, only a week after he assumed the office of provost, Disoway, called on Miss Isabella Sully, attempting to resolve her apparent displeasure with life in occupied Williamsburg."

"He told me he had heard I wished to go into the Confederacy," Isabella wrote in her journal, "and that he had called to offer his services to procure a passport for me, as he was that day going to York Town. "He seemed a gentleman," engaging the youthful officer in conversation, asking why he, an only son, left his mother for this war. "He made some foolish reply about the flag –as they all do. Lieutenant Disoway had only been

111 op. cit. pg. 315.
112 op. cit.
113 op. cit.
114 op. cit. pg. 316.

gone about an hour when I heard a pistol shot." A friend, Lucy Tucker rushed in with news he'd been killed by one of his own men."

As the story was retold, "Disoway was seated in the doorway of the Vest House, which was designated for the Provost Marshall, reading a newspaper, when a provost guard, William Boyle[115] was brought up in custody. The previous day Boyle had been sent back to his company camp for being intoxicated at his post, 'an extremely rare offense,' and seeking revenge on Disoway, he'd tried to force his way past the guard east of town. In arresting Boyle the Corporal of the guard had neglected to take away the prisoner's weapon – a revolver worn at the belt.... Looking down from the doorway, Disoway realized Boyle was drunk and ordered him back to camp. At that point, Boyle drew his weapon and rousing it toward Disoway, with a curse, threatened to shoot him. The other guards instantly leveled their guns pushing Boyle's weapon aside and trying to secure it. Failing in this, they aimed their pieces to shoot him down. The Lieutenant sprang up and ordered them not to shoot, saying he would disarm him, himself, and descending the steps advanced toward Boyle who, at that moment, fired, the ball entering Disoway's mouth, killing him instantly. Before he could shoot anyone else, Boyle was disarmed and taken to the guardhouse."[116]

The young Lieutenant had, in the short time since assuming duties as acting Provost Marshall, established himself as quite the ladies man. Despite the contempt with which the town's women held most Yankees, Lieutenant Disoway's funeral was well attended. On the next day, 14 October, at Fort Magruder, a 'most impressive funeral service were held in the presence of the entire command turned out in line formed a square. Isabella Sully and her friend Lucy Tucker, 'got some beautiful flowers which were sent with our cards to be put in his coffin."[117] The tragic death was so senseless people forgot their differences, at least for a brief time. Mourning the loss of one cut down while so full of promise, even in hard times, people were upset and sought solace trying to console one another.

With the facts of the case clear, and many reliable eye witnesses, a speedy trial was widely anticipated. The prosecutor, to his credit, would not allow the case to be railroaded into quick sentencing while emotions ran high, lest someone later claim Boyle hadn't received a fair trial. In fact, Boyle was found guilty, sentenced, and his case sent to Washington,

115 Boyle's rank is variously reported as either Private or Sergeant (Dubbs and Hudson respectively).
116 op. cit. pg. 317.
117 op. cit.

but President Lincoln delayed, for he'd temporarily suspended executions. As a result Private Boyle remained imprisoned at Fort Monroe and while languishing there somehow managed to strike up a jail-house friendship with one of his guards. The smooth-talking Boyle managed to convince the naïve young guard to first to release his handcuffs, then later of the wrongfulness of his conviction. Boyle went on at length about injustices of the military, and how life was better anywhere other than in uniform. Finally, the unhappy guard was apparently sufficiently convinced to look the other way when Boyle made his escape.

By this time Boyle certainly had his fill of Union service and figured his only chance was to change loyalty to the other side. Somehow, Boyle managed to sneak past Union pickets all the way from Fort Monroe to the Confederate lines west of Williamsburg where he cautiously approached Rebel pickets, explaining his escape and asking to be taken to headquarters. He was offering firsthand knowledge of Union forces, their disposition, and Union plans in exchange for safe passage and service in the Confederacy. Already under a death sentence for murder, Boyle apparently had no qualms about adding treason to the list of charges against him.

Meanwhile, the young guard at Fort Monroe who'd allowed Boyle's escape was himself arrested, convicted of allowing a prisoner to escape and summarily executed. The temporary Presidential suspension of capital punishment had been lifted. Thus, the traitor Boyle who'd murdered Lieutenant Disoway, now claimed the life of a second Yankee, one he'd tricked into befriending him while jailed.

***

While townspeople and soldiers continued learning how to deal with one another, slaves were also experiencing completely new roles and relationships. Major General Butler's contraband decision the year prior unleashed a flood of escaping slaves and made their freedom a top national political issue. By now, the Northern press had so politicized the issue, Lincoln found he could no longer maintain the position that the time for freeing slaves was not yet right. He had to act to get in front of increasingly rabid abolitionists and started the New Year, 1863 by making the end of slavery a cause for the war. The Emancipation Proclamation was heralded throughout the North, though few actually read it, and fewer still understood its provisions. Contrary to popular impression, Lincoln's proclamation did not 'free slaves' everywhere. Rather, it only applied to slaves in states in rebellion, i.e. the Confederacy, not the United States. Slaves from areas in rebellion under Federal control were freed, but those in rebellious areas not under Federal control were not freed. Locally, York County was under Federal control, while neighboring James City County was still considered rebellious, not fully under Federal control. With the dividing line between the two counties at Main Street, Williamsburg slaves on one side would be free while those on the other were not, at least according to the letter of the new law.

The Provost Marshall could only shake his head in disbelief, *what could Washington possibly be thinking?* The new proclamation presented an untenable situation for managing the occupied town. His hands were already full with rumors of partisan attacks, and daily taunting by townspeople from ministers to grandmothers, and now this. He wisely decided the Proclamation was unenforceable locally and as a practical matter, slaves on either side of Main Street were free. In so doing, he was technically countermanding his Commander-in-Chief's order, but he had no choice. The City would be unmanageable if Main Street were somehow a legal dividing line between freedom and slavery, as Washington mandated.

***

With the number of slaves attempting to escape areas of rebellion increasing, the Union army's focus was shifting to determine how to use this manpower for something other than day laborers. Eventually determining that freed slaves could in fact serve effectively as soldiers, it must have been the height of irony for the likes of Lucy Tucker, Isabella, Julia Sully, Sallie Galt, and Letitia Tyler when in 1864, the 1st and 6th U.S. Colored Infantry, were quartered just outside town and patrolled Williamsburg.

While political issues played out on the national stage, they also profoundly altered individuals' lives. Miss Eliza Baker, for example, a young slave girl belonging to Mrs. Whiting did not quite know what to make of it all, from occupation, to emancipation. "She was stopped by a man in uniform one day while she was doing her chores in town, and asked what she thought of the Yankees. She replied that she did not know since she had never met one. When the stranger said he was a Yankee, the young girl was surprised to find he was not a devil with horns as Mrs. Whiting had told her. The soldier, more angry than amused by her response, hurried to Mrs. Whiting's house where, to Eliza's utter amazement, he gave the lady a short lecture on the appearance of soldiers in the Army of the Potomac."[118]

"Eliza Baker stayed in town after the battle, working for Mrs. Whiting as before. However, a strange thing happened one day when she applied to the Provost Marshal for a pass to visit her mother in the country. When the officer asked her why she wanted the pass for Sunday in particular, she replied that it was the only day Mrs. Whiting would let her go. The officer told her that she could really go whenever she chose because, as he put it, 'you are as free as she is.'" Eliza was dumbfounded, later recounting, "He gave me a pass for Tuesday. So I went back to the house. The children told their mother about my asking for the pass and what the Marshal had said to me. I went upstairs and got my dress (I only had two), and that night took and went down home, and I ain't never been back to the Whiting's since."[119]

Like original contrabands; James Townsend, Sheppard Mallory, and Frank Baker; Eliza Baker finally took her freedom. Although the battle of Williamsburg was long over, McClellan's 'On to Richmond!' had failed and the war drug on for nearly three more years, causing unbelievable suffering and profound change not only in Williamsburg, but throughout the South, and the United States.

***

---

118 Hastings & Hastings, pg. 120.
119 op. cit. pgs. 121-122.

Postscript

With the passage of 150 years, historical records are incomplete. Yet, some information is available on the fate of some residents and participants in the Peninsula campaign. As the tragic deaths of President Abraham Lincoln and General George Armstrong Custer are well known, they are not repeated here.

Major General John Magruder

"Prince John" performed poorly following Williamsburg; some blaming his heavy drinking, others the unrelenting stress he'd been under, but the fog of war also played a role. At Malvern Hill, for instance, local guides led his men astray, causing considerable delay in his arrival. Orders to attack had been dispatched earlier in the day, but with no time noted by new commander General Robert E. Lee. When they were finally received after Magruder got into position, he mistook them as current. Confusion was compounded when another set of orders from Lee reaffirmed the attack. In response, Magruder led an assault that was uncoordinated, accomplishing little and suffering considerable losses. Afterwards, when Lee asked, "Why did you attack?" Magruder replied, "In obedience to your orders, twice repeated."

In reorganizing his forces after the Seven Days, Lee replaced those he thought ineffective, reassigning Magruder to command the District of Texas, New Mexico and Arizona. On January 1, 1863, Magruder recaptured Galveston and its important port, and he was recognized for "bold, intrepid, and gallant conduct." After the war, Magruder fled to Mexico, entering the service of Emperor Maximilian I as a Major General in the Imperial Mexican Army, but by May 1867 returned to the United States. He settled in Houston where he died in 1871 and was buried in Galveston, scene of his greatest military victory.

GENERAL JOSEPH E. JOHNSTON

Magruder's commander during the Peninsula campaign, General Johnston's effectiveness was undercut by ongoing tension with Confederate President Jefferson Davis, and lack of aggressiveness. Although Johnston considered the battle of Williamsburg a success in that he preserved his forces to fight another day, the opportunity to defeat McClellan and possibly bring the war to an early end were lost. Severely wound at the Battle of Seven Pines, Johnston was replaced by West Point classmate, Robert E. Lee. In 1863 Johnston was transferred to command the Department of the West where he was criticized for the loss of Vicksburg. The following year, he fought against Maj. Gen. William T. Sherman but was relieved of command after withdrawing from northwest Georgia. In the final days of the war, he was returned to command of the small remaining forces in the Carolinas, surrendering to Sherman, April 26, 1865. After the war Johnston served as a railroad executive, in insurance businesses, a term in Congress, and commissioner of railroads under President Grover Cleveland. He died of pneumonia after serving as a pallbearer at the funeral in inclement weather of his former adversary, William T. Sherman

GENERAL ROBERT E. LEE

Replacing Johnston after Seven Days, General Robert E. Lee was later promoted to the commanding officer of all Confederate forces, but would ultimately surrender, April 9, 1865. Lee then rejected a guerrilla campaign against the North and called for reconciliation and reconstruction, and served as President of what is now Washington & Lee University. While opposing giving freed slaves the right to vote, he worked to prevent taking that right from ex-Confederates, urging reintegration of his former soldiers into the nation's political life. The great Southern hero of the War, Lee's efforts at reconstruction made him popular even in the North, especially after his death in 1870.

President Jefferson Davis

President Jefferson Davis remained in Richmond until the last possible moment, barely escaping on the last train leaving at midnight April 2nd, 1865 headed to Danville, trying to continue the fight. Plans for the Davis government to flee to Cuba to regroup were never implemented and he met with his Cabinet for the last time May 5, 1865 in Georgia, to officially dissolve. He was captured five days later attempting to flee wearing his wife's overcoat, which lead to unflattering caricatures of him captured disguised as a woman.

On May 19, 1865, Davis was imprisoned at Fort Monroe and after a year indicted for treason. While imprisoned, he arranged to sell his Mississippi estate, ironically, to one of his former slaves. After two years he was released on bail of $100,000 posted by prominent citizens, Northern and Southern. In December 1868 the court rejected a motion to nullify the indictment, but the prosecution dropped the case in February 1869.

In 1877, he visited England, and over the next several years wrote *The Rise and Fall of the Confederate Government*. Davis' reputation in the South was restored by the book, his touring the region,1886-'87 and a second work the following year, *A Short History of the Confederate States of America*. On a steamboat that fall, he became ill and his wife, Varina met him on the river. Arriving in New Orleans, he was stable for two weeks, though bed-ridden, before taking a turn for the worse in early December. Just when he appeared to be improving, he lost consciousness the evening of the 5th and died at age 81, December 6, 1889. Davis was first entombed at the Army of Northern Virginia cemetery in New Orleans, his funeral one of the largest in the South, but in 1893 Mrs. Davis had his remains exhumed and transported by rail for reburial in Richmond.

Major General Benjamin Butler

Major General Benjamin Butler was transferred to New Orleans, where he was appointed military governor. Although he was able to bring order, he again stirred up controversy and was known to pilfer goods of the Southern households he was supposedly safeguarding –hence his nickname, "Spoons" Butler. His Order #28, stating any lady in New Orleans who showed contempt for Union soldiers would effectively be treated as a prostitute, drew great criticism, North and South, earning him another nickname, "Beast Butler." He was removed from New Orleans

December, 1862 and given command of the Department of Virginia and North Carolina in November of 1863. While commanding this force, he performed poorly during the Bermuda Hundred campaign, and when he failed again at Fort Fisher, North Carolina; was ordered home by General Grant to "await orders." On November 30, 1865, Butler resigned his commission and returning to politics was elected governor of Massachusetts in 1882 after several unsuccessful campaigns, and in 1878, to Congress, and was a presidential candidate during the election of 1884.

GENERAL GEORGE B. MCCLELLAN

After McClellan's Peninsula Campaign ended unsuccessfully and his performance at the Battle of Antietam allowed Lee a precarious tactical draw, McClellan's leadership during battle was questioned by President Abraham Lincoln. McClellan was eventually removed from command, first as general-in-chief, then from the Army of the Potomac. Likewise, General McClellan proved to be perpetually derisive of, and insubordinate to, his commander-in-chief. After being relieved, McClellan became the Democratic Party nominee opposing Lincoln in the 1864 presidential election. His party had an anti-war platform, promising to negotiate with the Confederacy, which McClellan was forced to repudiate, damaging the effectiveness of his campaign. He served as Governor of New Jersey, 1878 to 1881, eventually becoming a writer, defending his actions during the Peninsula Campaign and the Civil War. While many assess McClellan as a poor battlefield general, others maintain he was fully capable, but his reputation suffered unfairly as a scapegoat for Union setbacks. After the war when Ulysses Grant was asked to evaluate McClellan as a general, he replied, "McClellan is to me one of the mysteries of the war."

PRIVATE ROBERT BOODY

Young Union men were equally brave, among them Pvt. Boody, of the 40th New York Volunteers, or Mozart Regiment, who was awarded the Medal of Honor for his actions in the Bloody Ravine during the battle of Williamsburg in saving fellow soldiers, Carr and Pike. Pvt. Boody fought in eight battles in all, was wounded in the battle of Fair Oaks and three more times before being mustered out in 1864 after having been promoted to first sergeant. Pike, the crippled soldier wounded in the spine who was saved by Pvt. Boody, regained the use of his legs but years later, caused Pvt. Boody to second guess his battlefield actions. Years after the war, veteran

Pike had fallen into drinking heavily, and in one of his rages, robbed and murdered a Massachusetts farmer and his wife. When Pvt. Boody learned of this tragic incident he questioned his decision to rescue Pvt. Pike, "Had I but known, it would have been much better for him, better for his friends, better for the two old people he afterwards murdered," to have left him in the ravine."[120]

MAJOR AND MRS. WILLIAM H. PAYNE

Mary Elizabeth Winston Payne, wife of Major William Payne who, while pregnant, traveled from Danville to be at her gravely wounded husband's bedside gave birth and the couple would have nine more children. After Major William H. Payne, 4th Virginia Cavalry recovered from his wounds in the battle of Williamsburg; he was released in a prisoner exchange, and returned to duty as Lieutenant Colonel, 2nd North Carolina Cavalry and fought in the Chancellorsville Campaign. During the subsequent Gettysburg Campaign, he was again captured after being dehorsed and falling into an open vat of tanning liquid. After being imprisoned at Johnson's Island, Ohio, he was eventually freed in a prisoner exchange and promoted to Brigadier General, leading a brigade in Early's Valley Campaigns of 1864. He was wounded and captured a third time in the Battle of Five Forks, the very night of Lincoln's assassination. During the final operations in early 1865 around Richmond, he commanded a cavalry brigade. After the war, Payne returned to his Virginia law practice outside Warrenton, serving as general counsel for the Southern Railway Company and in the state legislature 1879–80. He died in Washington, D.C.

CAPTAIN JOHN WILLIS LEA

Captain John Willis Lea's Company I, Fifth Regiment, North Carolina Infantry was organized at Camp Winslow, Halifax County, June 20, 1861. At just twenty-three, Lea was the company's first captain, and by the following year was promoted to Lieutenant Colonel and transferred to regimental headquarters where he became Colonel in 1864. He was married on 18 August 1862 to Miss Margaret Goodrich Durfey, age 18 and their son, William Meade Lea was born four years later. They had four sons and two daughters in all, one daughter died at five months age. John became a minister and the family moved to St. Albans, Kanawha

120 Carter,

County, West Virginia in 1880. After Margaret died in 1883 (age 39), John remarried Mrs. Kate Wilson, widow, from Shadwell, Virginia, but just eleven days after their marriage, on May 15, 1884, John died of blood poisoning. The new Mrs. Lea made her home in Huntington where she cared for the two younger children, John and Maggie, ages 1 and 3, respectively.

WILLIAM & MARY STUDENTS AND FACULTY.[121]

Of the sixty-three William & Mary students at the time, sixty-one served in the Confederate Army, one became a high-ranking Confederate civil servant, and one joined the Union Army in his native Baltimore. Forty five students enlisted, of these thirty-eight as privates owing to their lack of prior military experience. Seventeen former students became officers with Peyton N. Page rising to Major, the highest rank held by a William & Mary student. Those enlisting included, James V. Bidgood, Sergeant Major of the Williamsburg 'Junior Guard,' 32nd Virginia Infantry, who later earned a battlefield promotion to Lieutenant serving as regimental adjutant at the battle of Five Forks. LT Bidgood was captured, along with nearly one-third of the remaining Confederate forces at the Battle of Saylor's Creek, April 6, 1865.

Quartermaster Sergeant Thomas Joel Barlow was among the four William and Mary students captured. Barlow was captured at Antietam but paroled a few weeks later at Shepardstown, while Sergeant George Fosque, 38th Virginia infantry, was captured twice, first at Roanoke Island in 1862 and again in 1865 and remained imprisoned at Point Lookout, Maryland until the end of the war.

Another William and Mary student, Thomas Mercer enlisted but quickly earned his commission as Lieutenant and served as drillmaster for the 1st Virginia Regiment and later, as an artillery officer, was cited by General A.P. Hill for 'coolness and daring' during the battle of Williamsburg. LT Mercer served for the duration of the war, and, along with former William and Mary students, Privates Robert Armistead and John G. Williams were present at the surrender in Appomattox April 9, 1865. Sadly, LT Mercer died scant months later on Sept, 7 of pneumonia.

---

121 Heuvel, S.

His grandfather, Dr. Waller, grieved his passing, "OH! His death is a sad blow, after his escape from all the great battles he participated in."

Student Thomas S. Beverley Tucker, grandson of St. George Tucker became an aide to General Lafayette McLaws, while fellow student John. G. Williams of Orange County rode as a courier for General Jubal Early. Student Richard A. Wise left the college to return to Richmond, serving as an aid to his father, Virginia Governor and Brigadier General Henry Wise. Richard enlisted but received a commission and served as Captain and Assistant Inspector General. After the war Richard Wise was elected to the U.S. Congress and later returned to William & Mary as a faculty member.

Three William and Mary students were fatally wounded; Private T.R. Argyle, 4th Virginia Cavalry in 1861 near Goochland, Sergeant William Browne, 12th Virginia Infantry, at Malvern Hill, July, and Captain Sterling H. Gee, 1st North Carolina Infantry at Five Forks.

Several William and Mary students succumbed to disease while serving, as was common in both armies. Private James H. Dix died of typhoid fever September, 1861, while his brother Private Henry S. Dix, 32nd Virginia Infantry was discharged due to diseases of the spine in October, 1862. He re-enlisted the following year and was assigned to assist an enrolling officer, recruiting others. Private John N. Williams, 6th Virginia Infantry was discharged after a bout with typhoid fever, spring 1863 but recovered and rejoined the Richmond Howitzers.

First Lieutenant Barziza who arrived as reinforcements from Texas just as Confederates withdrew from Williamsburg was later promoted to captain and led a company into battle at Gettysburg. During the attack on Little Round Top on July 2, 1863, he was wounded and left behind when the Confederate troops were forced to retreat. Although feigning death, he was discovered by Union troops and taken prisoner. After a year in federal hospitals and prison, he was part of a contingent of prisoners sent to Point Lookout, Maryland. Enroute he escaped by diving through the open window of a train and made his way to Canada, where he was one of the first to use a network set up by rebel agents and Canadians to send escaped Confederates back to the South via Nova Scotia and Bermuda. Barziza arrived at Wilmington, North Carolina, April 1864, and was allowed to return to Texas to recover from the hardships of his imprisonment and escape. In February 1865 he published his war memoirs anonymously under the title, *The Adventures of a Prisoner of War, and Life and Scenes in Federal Prisons: Johnson's Island, Fort Delaware, and Point Lookout, by an Escaped Prisoner of Hood's Texas Brigade.* Settling in Houston, he established a law practice and became active in politics. Barziza married Patricia Nicholas of Buckingham County, Virginia, in March 1869. They had no children, but in July 1872 adopted Barziza's orphaned nephew Phillip Dorsey Barziza. Decimus et Ultimus Barziza died after a lingering illness on January 30, 1882.

Like their students, William & Mary professors also served with distinction. First to sign up was Professor Edwin Taliaferro joining the 32nd Virginia Infantry where College President Ewell assisted him in obtaining a commission as First Lieutenant. Taliaferro became a Captain of Ordnance serving in McLaws Division and was later promoted to Major and commanded the Confederate arsenal in Macon, Georgia until the end of the war.

Professor Thomas P. McCandlish, Williamsburg native and W&M graduate class of 1857, enlisted in June in the Peninsula Artillery and a month later was commissioned Captain, serving as the 32nd' Infantry's Regimental Quartermaster. Also serving as Captain in the 32nd Virginia Infantry was W&M History Professor Robert J. Morrison but he tragically died of typhoid fever that fall. Law Professor Charles Morris returned to his native Hanover County, joining "Hanover Troops" and was later attached to the 4th Virginia Infantry, seeing action in the Peninsula campaign as a staff officer to General Lafayette McLaws. Adjunct professor of mathematics, Thomas T.L. Snead, W&M class of 1856, assisted President Ewell in the survey and lay out the Williamsburg defensive live, then joined the Confederate Engineer Corps, earning a commission and serving as engineer under General Stonewall Jackson.

COLONEL BENJAMIN S. EWELL

After the Battle of Williamsburg, Ewell became chief of staff for General Joseph E. Johnston, later serving as adjutant to his younger brother, General Richard S. Ewell, a senior commander under General Stonewall Jackson. Despite Ewell's exemplary record of military service, it pales in comparison to his tireless efforts to restore the College of William and Mary. After the war, the College was in ruins; the local and Virginia economies destitute, but Ewell repeatedly sought reparations, appearing several times before Congress including, the testimony,

> "No institution of learning in the South lost so much by the civil war, by actual destruction of property, and by consequent inability to resume its exercises as soon as peace was declared...The College, if this prayer be granted, will rise with renewed vigor, with improved faculties to repay any beneficence (sic) which Congress may bestow, by giving again back to the Union what money cannot buy, another host of mighty men to guard constitutions and laws, and to love the nation as devotedly as even its liberties."

Ewell mortgaged his nearby family farm which he'd purchased in 1858, and using these personal funds, re-opened the college, losing his farm to foreclosure in the process. Despite Ewell's efforts, the College was forced to close again for financial reasons in 1881 and did not reopen until 1888. During those long seven years, Ewell arose every morning to ring the bell calling students to class, so it could never be said William and Mary abandoned its mission to educate the young men of Virginia. In 1888 the state General Assembly appropriated $10,000 to support the College as a state teacher-training institution, allowing it to reopen. Some additional funding was eventually provided by the U.S. Government, but not until 1893.

Only when he'd finally ensured the College he cherished would survive, did 71-year-old Ewell relinquish the presidency. He remained in Williamsburg as President Emeritus until his death June 19, 1894. Although Ewell had formed and commanded the Williamsburg Junior Guard, as well as designed and oversaw construction of the Williamsburg defenses that figured so prominently in the battle, he is most-remembered for his tireless efforts against overwhelming adversity to rebuild the College of William and Mary in the aftermath of the Civil War.

***

References

Bailey, 1983, Forward to Richmond; McClellan's Peninsular Campaign. Time Life, Alexandria, VA

Britton, Rick. "To War! Big Bethel: The Civil War's First Battle." Command Magazine, 53: 34-43

Carter, Rusty, May 4, 2011, Medal of Honor led to Second thoughts. The Virginia Gazette.

Dabney, Virginius, 1976, Richmond, the story of a city. Doubleday, New York

Dougherty, Kevin, and J. Michael Moore, 2005, The Peninsula Campaign of 1862, a military analysis, University Press of Mississippi.

Dubbs, Carol Kettenburg, 2002, Defend this Old Town, Louisiana State University Press

Foote, Shelby, 1958, The Civil War a narrative, Fort Sumter to Perryville." Random House, New York, NY

Hastings, Earl C. Jr., and David Hastings, 1997, A Pitiless Rain, the Battle of Williamsburg, 1862. White Mane Publishing Co

Hudson, Carson O. Jr. Civil War Williamsburg. Colonial Williamsburg Foundation, Williamsburg, VA, in association with Stackpole Books, Mechanicsburg, PA

Heuvel, Sean Michael. 2006, The Old College Goes to War: The Civil War Experiences of William and Mary Students, Faculty, and Alumni, M.A. thesis, Univ. of Richmond.

http://myloc.gov/Exhibitions/lincoln/presidency/CommanderInChief/BattlingIncompetence/ExhibitObjects/DraftGeneralOrderNo1.aspx

http://thomaslegion.net/roberteleesresignationletter.html

http://www.classicreader.com/book/3766/263/

Markle, Donald E., 1994, Spies and Spymasters of the Civil War, Hippocrene Books, New York, NY.

Quarstein, John V. 1997, The Civil War on the Virginia Peninsula, Arcadia Publishing, Charleston, SC.

Roble, George. C., 2010, God's Almost Chosen People: a Religious History of the American Civil War, The University of North Carolina, Press.

Thane, Elswyth, Yankee Stranger. Buccaneer Books, New York, NY.

Webb, Alexander S., Campaigns of the Civil War: The Peninsula. Blue and Grey Press, New York, NY

West, George Benjamin, edited by Parke Rouse, Jr. 1977, When the Yankees Came, Civil War and Reconstruction on the Virginia Peninsula, Dietz Press, Richmond, VA.

Wheat, Thomas Adrian, 1997, A guide to Civil War Yorktown, Bohemian Brigade Bookshop & Publishers, Knoxville, TN

Educators note

A teacher's guide for using 'Civil War Comes Home' in the classroom, (based on national educational standards for historical thinking and Virginia's standards of learning for the Civil War) is available, and includes sample lesson plans, test questions, and references on the effective use of genres other than textbooks for teaching history. For more information please visit
www.civilwarcomeshome.com or email: jakemckenzieauthor@gmail.com